VEVANG

FAMILY HISTORY

VEVANG

FAMILY HISTORY

By Debra Vevang Menzel

Researched and compiled by
Debra Vevang Menzel, Bonnie Vevang,
Cheryl Watkins Tanaka, and Warren Vevang

FIRST EDITION

ISBN 979-8-218-34451-1

Vevang Family History

Debra Vevang Menzel

Researched and compiled by Debra Vevang Menzel, Bonnie Vevang, Cheryl Watkins Tanaka, and Warren Vevang

Cover design, formatting, and editing by Jenny Menzel **www.jennymenzel.com**

Printed in the United States of America

*This book is dedicated
to the Vevang family.*

*To us,
to those that came before us,
and to those that will come after us.*

TABLE OF CONTENTS

ACKNOWLEDGMENTS

This book was written to preserve historical facts for the descendants of Iver Andrew Vevang and Serina Hustad Vevang and would not have been possible without everyone's contributions. Let's give thanks—

To our ancestors, for their courage to emigrate, and their hopes and hard work to create better lives for themselves and their children.

To Bonita J. Vevang, Cheryl Watkins Tanaka, Warren Vevang, Larry Vevang, Henry Hanson Jr., Douglas Hanson, Johnny Montgomery, Dennis Vevang, James Vevang, Bruce Watkins, James Watkins, and Sonja Danielson Cordray Quillen—your contributions were especially helpful! Bonnie was instrumental in her knowledge of the Vevang family history when she completed the Vevang family tree in 1988 and shared it at the Vevang family reunion.

To my daughter, Jenny, for taking on the tall task of being my editor, book formatter, graphic designer, and publisher.

To my husband, Bill, for fact-checking and cooking while I worked away at my computer.

To all who contributed family information and pictures, and everyone who donated to the fundraiser. This printed hardcover of our family history simply would not have been possible without your generosity!

And to the top contributors, the Vevang children—Julius, Hilda, Elmer, Ingvald, Selmer, Laura, Ella, Alida, Myrtle, and Lawrence. They took such great pictures. Their stories are told in letters written and saved, in transcribed voice recordings and telegrams, and in each photo—many of them in front of the Vevang house and out in the fields, standing sharply dressed next to their cars and loved ones.

This has been such a great experience for me. I am so very appreciative of each and every one of you for contributing the way you did, so that we could bring this book to your family as a keepsake to be enjoyed for generations to come. This was truly a family effort, and I hope we can all stay connected.

INTRODUCTION

The journey to publish this book started from a framed photo that Larry Vevang sent to me many years ago of Iver and Serina Vevang with eight of their children on the Vevang farm. I have always been interested in how life was for them, raising so many children, but that photo was the first catalyst to begin compiling this book. Others that followed were pictures of Norwegian trips shared by my parents, Ingvald and Alberta Vevang, and my cousins— Cheryl Watkins Tanaka, James Vevang, Warren Vevang, and James Watkins.

At age 22, Iver Andrew Vevang, the youngest son of Jakob Vevang, set sail from Vevang, Norway in 1888 for the United States, with high hopes of making a better life for himself. He never saw his home, his father, stepmother, half-brothers, or half-sister again. This book is a timeline of Iver's life before and after coming to America, which extends beyond the length of his life through his children: Julius, Hilda, Elmer, Ingvald, Selmer, Edvin, Laura, Ella, Alida, Jacob, Myrtle, Lawrence—and their children, and their children, and so on. Born between 1897 and 1915, the twelve Vevang children were part of a unique generation that was integral to the development of the United States.

This is me, Debra, at about five years old in front of the Iver Vevang family home in Roslyn. I may have posed just like this at my desk several times while working on this history book, which is richly steeped in family photos, stories, and historical documents.

Born in 1954, I'm the youngest of the 30 Vevang cousins you'll meet while reading, with Spencer (born in 1921) being the eldest. My father, Ingvald, was 52 when I was born—my mother 18 years younger. Dad was a true Norwegian daydreamer. During his last years alive, he spoke of life on the farm, taping it on a cassette player. Ing then asked a classmate of mine who worked with his sister, Laura, at the City Hall, to type out what he recorded. He wanted his grandchildren to listen someday—to understand how things were on the Vevang farm. Growing up, I listened to a lot of my dad's conversations with his brothers and sisters. My dad had a farm, too, north of his parents. Although we did not live on that land, I sensed it was very important to him. Today, both farms are still owned by Vevang descendants.

Organizing and publishing this book was a bigger undertaking than I first imagined it would be. In the last six years I have pondered our ancestors' stories, shed some tears, laughed, and experienced countless goosebumps while learning about where we come from—I feel I have gotten to know each of you, if only a little, along the way.

My daughter, Jenny, was a big part of bringing this book to life. She challenged me in ways I didn't always enjoy! But she taught me a lot about publishing, pushed me to think a bit more outside of the box, and I learned to trust her. At first, I was hesitant to hand over the project when I came to her with publishing questions. I'm happy to report she has made this presentation of our ancestors' lives better than I could have ever done on my own.

At the beginning of each chapter, you'll find vital information on each of the Vevang children of Iver and Serina, with information on careers, spouses, and children threaded throughout. At the end of each chapter, if marriage and kids were involved, you'll find a "FAMILY" section that lists all important dates and locations of vital info (birth, marriage, death, and burial). Please use this book as a starter for your family and make additions in the lined notes section left in the back of the book as time marches on.

Any genealogy book is never complete, and every effort has been made to make this book as accurate as possible. However, there may be errors, both typographical and in content. Do let me know if you find any so we can correct them for future editions.

Those who came before us left a legacy, with each picture whispering of the past. Whether born by blood or chosen for adoption, we are each so important to the Vevang story. This book is more than just names, birth dates, marriage dates, and death dates. It has been an investment in writing it, and it will be an investment in reading it.

So read, listen, learn, imagine, ponder and enjoy the stories of those who came before us.

Debra

Debra Vevang Menzel

CHAPTER I

FROM WHERE WE CAME

THE CONDITIONS IN NORWAY AND CAUSE OF IMMIGRATION

Vevang, Norway

Needed Heirs

During the 19th century, inheritance laws made it necessary to have a child to pass on property to heirs. The heir not only inherited the farm but also the responsibility to keep it in the family to provide security. Usually the oldest son took over the farm, but if no sons were alive, a daughter and her husband were able to fill this role. Whoever inherited would provide a home and pension for the parents while they contributed to the farm work and house chores if they were physically able. Farmers' wives were expected to not only be capable of bearing children and managing a household, but she was also required to do more work on the farm than was commonly expected of women in other parts of Europe. They often tended the fields alongside their husbands.

Limited Opportunities

The tillable land in Norway was sparse and unable to produce enough food for the growing population. There simply was not enough land to go around. Many suffered failed crops and severe economic depression set in. The imposition of heavy taxes left many farmers unable to raise money to buy out their siblings, pay the required pension to their retired parents, or pay their debts. Few opportunities for profitable employment existed for young people, and poor economic prospects in rural Norway made life intolerable for many people.

Economics, Religious, Class Distinctions, Political Rights, and Military Reasons

While it was largely the rapid growth of population during a period of economic hardship that drove most Norwegians from their homeland, others left due to religious reasons, class distinctions, lack of political rights, or to escape military service. These people grew eager to take advantage of the boundless opportunities that lay in settling the American landscape. For many, there was not much to lose by leaving Norway in search of a better life, but they also knew little of the world outside their home community. They lived in relative isolation from the rest of the world, and even from other districts in Norway. But their lack of first-hand knowledge of the world outside did little to deter them. They only heard of vast tracts of fertile soil and cheap land available in the United States, and that was enough to set their sights abroad. Once they departed, many would only communicate with their loved ones through letters and telegrams—never going back to Norway again.

The Great Nordic Migration

Norwegian seamen first came to the United States in the colonial years before 1776, but the Great Nordic Migration began in 1825, when a group of 52 persons in Stavanger, Norway purchased a small sloop named Restaurationen, and sailed it to New York to settle near Rochester. These early immigrants were not poor, as financial resources were required to afford the journey. Most of them were motivated by religious discontent.

By the mid-1830s, most of the immigrants settled in northern Illinois, later in Wisconsin and Minnesota, and eventually in the Dakotas and the Pacific Northwest. Between 1825 and 1925, 850,000 Norwegians immigrated to the United States. Immigration slowed during the Civil War years, 1861-1865, but increased with the post-war prosperity and the passing of the American Homestead Law in 1862—allowing any U.S. citizen, or person intending to become a citizen, to acquire 160 acres of free government land.

By the 1880s, immigration of the poorer classes had increased because of lower travel costs and money sent to Norway by relatives and friends already in America. By this time there was less homestead land and more industrial employment. Many Norwegians still longed for their land in the new country and would work as farm laborers while saving enough money to purchase their acreage. This was likely the circumstance under which Iver Andrew Vevang immigrated to the U.S. from Norway in 1888, at age 22. It was the custom for the first son to inherit the family farm, and with Iver being the last-born, there wasn't much promise for him to inherit land.

Steam Travel and Cost to Travel Across

Steam travel to America gained traction in the 1860s after Britain repealed the Navigation Acts in 1849, which permitted ships of all nations to be able to land in Canadian ports. Norwegian ships first began arriving in Quebec in the mid-1800s, a port where 90% of all Norwegian immigrants entered America. Entering through Quebec was considerably cheaper—an adult could travel for $12.00 to $30.00.

Dignified and Determined

When contemplating the emotions involved in deciding to leave Norway, it's interesting to think about how one pondered such an idea to leave all they knew for unverified promises. Was there an inherited aggressive quality in their character? An innate spirit of adventure? Were they dreamers? If so, were their dreams dampened by a traumatic departure? Regardless of one's pondering, the fact is that many Norwegians decided to leave their homes. How many did so with dignity, desperation, determination, or depression? We can only speculate.

The Lineage of Jakob Jonsen Vevang

Jakob Jonsen Berget Vevang was born in 1820 in Vevang, Norway. Jakob's middle name most likely came from his father's first name, Jon. Jakob's last name (Vevang) came from the town of Vevang, and the land they farmed was called Berget. Their farm names were often part of their full name. It is believed that Jakob's father's name was Jon Toresen, with his last name coming from his father's first name, Tore. It is believed that Tore's last name was Kaspersen, with his father's first name assumed to be Kasper. The history of these names has been found on Ancestry registries and I have not been able to prove or verify this to be factual. Children were generally named after their fathers, with their fathers' first names becoming a part of their last names. For sons, "sen" was added to the father's name. For daughters, "datter" was added.

In 1843, at age 23, Jakob got married for the first time to Ingeborg Anna Nilsdatter Sandoy. They lived on a farm called Berget in Vevang, Norway. They had six children born between 1844 and 1861 before Ingeborg died in 1863. Jakob was left to raise his children Johanne Jakobsdatter (19), Nils Jakobsen (16), Iver Jakobsen (13), Jakob Jakobsen (9), Margrete Gurine Jakobsdatter (5), and Jonas Nikolai Jakobsen (2).

In 1864, about a year after his first wife died and at the age of 43, Jakob married his second wife—32-year-old Sigrid Sivertsdatter Skotten, born in 1832. They had one child whom they named Iver Andreas (Andrew) Vevang in 1865.

I remember my father, Ingvald Vevang, telling me that his father was born the year President Abraham Lincoln was assassinated.

JAKOB J. VEVANG
Photo given to Warren Vevang in 2010

It isn't known why Jakob had two sons named Iver. Perhaps the reason had to do with the name being important to Jakob in some way, and the two Ivers were born to different mothers. When Sigrid's Iver was born, Ingeborg's Iver was already 15 years old—he died in 1870 at age 20. Jakob's daughter, Margrete, also died four years later in 1874 at age 16. Jakob and Sigrid were married for seven years until Sigrid died in 1871. Iver was only six years old when his mother died.

Iver was born in the family home in Vevang, Norway

Jakob raised Iver and his other children by himself for about five years until 1876, when he married for the third time to Ane Marta Langory, born in 1825.

Jakob and Ane didn't have any children together, and 22 years after marrying, Ane died of pneumonia in 1898, at the age of 73.

Jakob Jonsen Vevang died in Norway in 1912 at the age of 92.

JAKOB JONSEN VEVANG

Born
November 5, 1820
Vevang family home
Vevang, More og Romsdal, Norway

Died
December 21, 1912
Vevang, More og Romsdal, Norway
Laid to rest in the Vevang Norway Cemetery

Photo taken by Cheryl Watkins Tanaka in 1981

The Timeline of Jakob Jonsen Vevang

November 5, 1820	Jakob Jonsen Vevang was born
1843	Jakob married Ingeborg Anna Nilsdatter Sandoy
1844	Johanne Jakobsdatter Vevang was born
July 17, 1847	Nils Jakobsen Vevang was born
1850	Iver Jakobsen Vevang was born
February 3, 1854	Jakob Jakobsen Vevang was born
1858	Margrete Gurine Jakobsdatter Vevang was born
1861	Jonas Nikolai Jakobsen Vevang was born
1863	Jakob's first wife Ingeborg Anna Nilsdatter Sandoy died at age 43
1864	Jakob marries for the second time to Sigrid Sivertsdatter Skotten
November 23, 1865	Iver Andrew Jakobsen Vevang was born in Vevang, Norway
1870	Iver Jakobsen Vevang died at age 20
1871	Jakob's second wife Sigrid Sivertsdatter Skotten died at age 39
February 10, 1872	Serina Hansdatter Hustad was born in Hustad, Norway
1874	Margrete Gurine Jakobsdatter Vevang died at the age of 16
1876	Jakob marries for the third time to Ane Marta Jonsdatter Langory
1888	Iver Andrew Jakobsen Vevang immigrated to the U.S. from Vevang, Norway
Fall 1892	Serina Hansdatter Hustad immigrated to U.S. from Hustad, Norway
1898	Jakob's third wife Ane Marta Jonsdatter Langory died at the age 73
1901	Johanne Jakobsdatter died at age 57
1901	Jonas Nikolai Jakobsen Vevang died at age 40
December 17, 1904	Jakob Jakobsen Vevang died at age 50
December 21, 1912	Jakob Jonsen Vevang died at the age of 92
October 9, 1914	Nils Jakobsen Vevang died at age 67

At age 22, Jakob's youngest son, Iver Andrew Vevang, left his homeland and family behind, setting sail in 1888 for the United States with the hope of making a better life for himself.

UNITED STATES OF AMERICA.

STATE OF SOUTH DAKOTA, ss. IN THE _County_ COURT.
COUNTY OF DAY.

Iver J. Vevang personally appeared before the subscriber, the Clerk of the _County_ Court, in and for the County of Day, State of South Dakota, being a Court of Record, and made oath that he was born in _Norway_ on or about the year A. D. Eighteen Hundred and _Sixty five_; that he emigrated to the United States and landed at the port of _New York_ on or about the month of _May_ in the year A. D. Eighteen Hundred and _eighty eight_; that it is his bona fide intention to become a CITIZEN OF THE UNITED STATES, and he renounces forever all allegiance and fidelity to any foreign Prince, Potentate, State or Sovereignty whatsoever, and particularly to _the King of Sweden and Norway_ whereof he is a subject; and that he will support the Constitution and Government of the United States.

Iver J Vevang

Subscribed and sworn to before me, this _15th_ day of _November_ A. D. 1893

William Atchison
Clerk _County_ Court, in and for Day County.

Iver J. Vevang personally appeared before the subscriber, the Clerk of the County Court, in and for the County of Day, State of South Dakota, being a Court of Record and made oath that he was born in Norway on or about the year A.D. Eighteen Hundred and Sixty Five; that he emigrated to the United States and landed the port of New York on or about the month of May in the year A.D. Eighteen Hundred and Eighty Eight; that it is his bona fide intention to become a CITIZEN OF THE UNITED STATES, and he renounces forever all allegiance and fidelity to any foreign Prince, Potentate, State of Sovereignty whatsoever, and particularly to the King of Sweden and Norway whereof he is a subject; and that he will support the Constitution and Government of the United States.

Subscribed and sworn to before me, this 15th day of November A.D. 1893

Iver Andrew Vevang was born in Vevang, Fraenen, Romsdalen, Norway to Jakob J. Vevang and Sigrid Sivertsdatter Skotten. Iver's wife, Serina Hansdatter Hustad was born in Hustad, Fraenen, Romsdalen, Norway to Hans Larsson Hustad and Maline Pedersdatter Smorholm.

MORE OG ROMSDAL (ROMSDALEN) COUNTY, NORWAY

Vevang, Norway is located between Hustad and Kornstad municipalities

KORNSTAD

HUSTAD

FORMER MUNICIPALITIES IN MORE OG ROMSDAL (ROMSDALEN) COUNTY

CHAPTER II

IVER & SERINA

Married June 1, 1896
Grenville Lutheran Church
Day County, South Dakota

The Story of Iver and Serina's Immigration and Life in the United States
Written by Bonita J. Vevang and Debra Vevang Menzel

IVER was a quiet man and never said much about his early years in the United States. But we do know that he eventually found work on the Hendrickson farm a few miles northwest of the present town of Roslyn, South Dakota. Eventually, Iver met Serina Hustad, who had arrived in the United States from Hustad, Norway in the fall of 1892.

Serina's reason for coming to the United States was quite different than Iver's reason. She had family members who had immigrated earlier. Serina's oldest sister, Maren, her husband Lars Stavig, and their three sons left Bergen, Norway in May 1876 to make their home near Morris and Starbuck, Minnesota. In 1877, Lars was hired by a contractor to help cut wood for the soldiers at Fort Sisseton in Marshall County, South Dakota. Lars became familiar with the area since the wood cutting was performed in Marshall, Day, and Roberts Counties, and in 1884 the Lars Stavig family as well as three other families moved to Nutley Township, Day County, about a half mile east of Hazelden Lake.

Maren and her family thus led the way for her parents and many of her brothers and sisters to follow, including her sister, Serina. Serina's sister, Beret, and brother-in-law, Iver Holm, lived across the road from the Hendrickson farm where Iver worked. Iver and Serina soon met and they were married on June 1, 1896.

Mr. Iver Vevang of Nutley Township and Miss Serina H. Hustad of Nutley Township were united in marriage according to the Ordinance of God and the Laws of the State of South Dakota at Grenville Church on the 1st day of June in the year of Our Lord, One Thousand Eight Hundred and Ninety Six.

Witnesses:
M.L. Stavig and Thomas Hustad

John Granstog as Pastor

The Twelfth United States Federal Census taken in 1900
Raritan Township, Day County, South Dakota

TWELFTH CENSUS OF THE UNITED STATES.

SCHEDULE No. 1.—POPULATION.

In the 1900 United States Federal Census, Iver lived in Raritan Township, Day County, South Dakota. He was 34 years old in 1900. Serina, his wife, was 27 years old. Their first years of marriage were spent in a small house approximately one and a half miles south and half mile west of present-day Roslyn. There are no longer any buildings on this site. That is where their first two children were born, Julius Selmer and Hilda Marie. Julius was three years old and Hilda was just one in 1900.

The 1900 census indicates that 17-year-old "Berndt Vevang" also lived with Iver and Serina Vevang. Per previous written and oral information received from Berndt's granddaughter, this young man was Bernhard Oluf Jakobsen Vevang, born July 17, 1882 in Norway. Bernhard was the son of Jakob Jakobsen Vevang (Iver's half-brother) and Elen Dortea Bottolfsdatter Aarsbog, making Bernhard Iver's nephew. Iver was also Bernhard's godfather. It is not known exactly when Bernhard arrived in the United States and how long he stayed, but it is known that he left the United States before World War I, which started in 1914, and he intended to return to the U.S.

The war and the death of his wife, Ronnaug Hansdatter Kongslibakken, changed his plans to return. Ronnaug was born on April 27, 1887, and died on October 21, 1918 from Spanish influenza. They had a daughter named Alminda "Minda" Jacobsen Knutsen, born in 1915, which probably also played a part in his decision to stay in Norway. The census indicates he was a laborer in 1900, but it is known from oral history that he later taught school while in the United States. Bernhard died on July 27, 1928 in Norway.

Iver and Serina's first child was born — Julius Selmer Vevang

Serina gave birth to Julius Selmer in their home in 1897. In the 1900 United States Federal Census they lived at the time in Raritan Township, Day County, South Dakota. He attended country school in Nutley Township and registered for the draft in 1918. In the 1920 census at the age of 23, he was considered a part of the Vevang household. Julius was stationed in Michigan serving in the United States Army. When he was discharged, he moved to Watertown, South Dakota. He married Hazel Gilbertson in 1921. In the 1930 census, their employment was listed as a machinist and a department store saleslady. Julius worked for the Minneapolis and St. Louis Railroad for 49 years. In about 1970, they moved to Webster. Julius died in 1990 at age 93. Hazel died in 1994 at age 92. Julius and Hazel had no children.

Iver and Serina's second child was born — Hilda Marie Vevang

Hilda Marie was the second child born to Iver and Serina. She was born in 1899 on the farm located in Raritan Township and attended country school through the eighth grade in Nutley Township. Hilda was the first child to leave the household when she married Ed Olson in 1919, at the age of 20. In the 1920 census, she was a member of the Sigvart Olson household as a daughter-in-law. In the 1930 census, Sigvart and Minnie lived in one household, while Ed, Hilda, and their children, Spencer and Rosalie, lived in another. Spencer was born in 1921 and Rosalie in 1923. Calvin, Hilda and Ed's third child, was born December 1930 on Iver and Serina's farm. In 1932, their fourth child, Viola, was born. Hilda and Ed decided to leave the country life in 1935, moving to Waubay Township. In the 1940 census, the family of six lived in Waubay Township, Day County, South Dakota. Sigvart lived with them at the time. They could take their horses and cattle with them for a smaller dairy farm living. The United States was getting ready for World War II in 1942, and the Olson family moved to Minneapolis where Ed was employed at a defense plant. Hilda worked a short time at Honeywell. Ed died in 1983, at age 92. Hilda died in 1998, at age 99.

Iver and Serina's first farm was in Raritan Township (also known as Township 123) in Day County. He owned 40 acres in Section 11, and 120 acres in Section 12. It is located 1.5 miles south of Roslyn when taking the township gravel road on the east side of Roslyn. After traveling 1.5 miles turn right onto another gravel road. The land is located a half mile west on the north side of the road. They were on this land until after the 1900 United States Federal Census. Julius and Hilda were born on the farm in Raritan Township. The family of four then moved to Nutley Township sometime after the census was taken and before their third child, Elmer, was born in 1901. Information on legal papers and the title abstract notes that Iver Vevang purchased the farmland and house from Swen A. Hazelden. Swen owned 40 acres close to a lake that would later be named after him. It is spelled differently on some maps.

Raritan and Nutley Townships in Day County, South Dakota

South Dakota Atlas & Gazetteer,
Topo Maps of the Entire State,
First Edition 1997, DeLorme, pg. 21

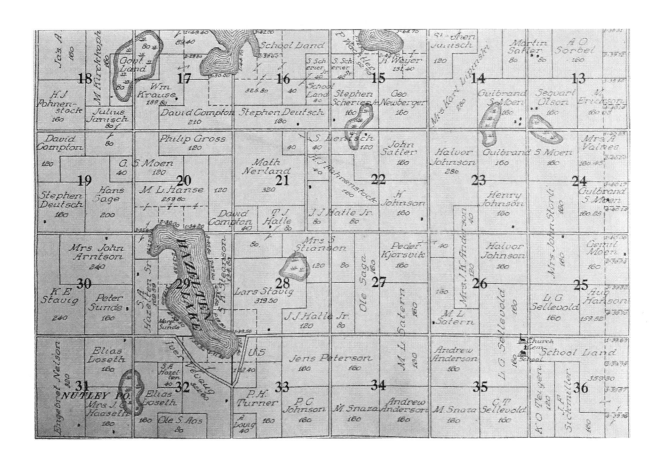

Published in
Day County Museum in Webster, South Dakota,
1909 Plat Map of Nutley Township

Sigvart Olson owns 160 acres in Section 13.
Hilda married Sigvart's son, Edwin Olson.
Iver Vevang's farmland is in Section 32.

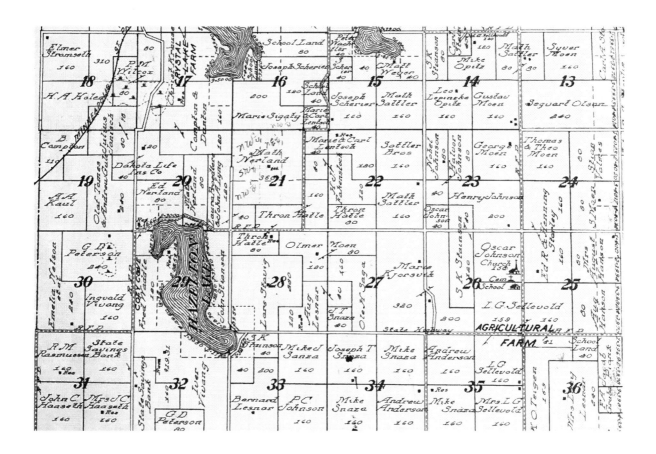

Published in
Day County Museum in Webster, South Dakota
1929 Plat Map of Nutley Township

Sigvart Olson, owns 240 acres in Section 13.
Ingvald Vevang purchased a part of Iver Vevang's land in Section 30.
Iver Vevang's farmland is in Section 32.

1900

Iver and Serina Vevang purchased land on the west side of Hazelden Lake in Nutley Township, Day County, South Dakota. There were no buildings on the property except for a small two-story house on the southeast corner of the pasture.

They did not like the location of the house, so they decided to move it next to a large grove of trees about a half mile away, but still on their land. You can imagine the difficulty this might have been with limited resources to accomplish the task. We have been told through oral history that a wagon was used, and no doubt they used horses. When they were about three quarters to their destination, the house began to slip, or as we were told—"had fallen off the wagon." At this point, they looked around and decided it was a nice spot on top of a knoll, a slight elevation in the landscape. They left the house there, facing south, where it still stands today.

house moving affair
up on stones, beams bars under, lifted house
onto horse-drown trailer, move
across field to shady grove; house
fell off collapsed trailer.
moving around the lake

Written by Myrtle Vevang Watkins

We don't know exactly how long it took them to realize that the house was not big enough for them, especially with an expanding family, but they eventually did add to the east side of the house, doubling the size of the house, with a dining room and new kitchen on the first floor and a large bedroom upstairs. The main floor of the addition consisted of a 15x15 ft. dining room, a very small bedroom, and a small kitchen. Eventually, the wall between the kitchen and the bedroom was removed to make a larger kitchen. The upper east wing was one large bedroom upstairs.

Iver and Serina worked hard to build up their farm. The first buildings they constructed were the barn, granary, and the outhouse, followed by a milk house, chicken coop, pig house, and blacksmith shop. Farming was diversified in those days. They had cattle, pigs, chickens, a few sheep, and workhorses. They harvested oats, flax, and barley. They butchered the farm animals for meat and lard, grew potatoes and other vegetables, milked the cows, and churned their own butter.

They had their grain milled at the Webster elevator to use in baking. Serina sewed, crocheted, and spun yarn. Her piano doily with crocheted edges is still in place today. Before 1914 they had to travel 14 miles to Webster by horse and wagon for their supplies, as Roslyn was not established until 1914 when the railroad line was laid.

Far Left:
Chicken coop

Left:
Julius Vevang made the wind-powered battery charger shown here on top of the granary

The Vevangs
were considered
to be relatively
prosperous for
the time as
successful
farmers in
the area.
They were
able to afford
good farm
equipment
and nice farm
buildings.

Iver Vevang with
a team of horses

Vevang Family Farm

Iver and Serina's third child was born — Elmer Nicolai Vevang

Born in 1901, Elmer was the first child born on the Vevang family farm in Nutley Township. He attended country school there and was confirmed in 1915. It has been said that Elmer was good with horses. At the age of 22 in 1923, he furthered his education by attending barber school in Minneapolis. He barbered in Roslyn, Aberdeen, and Eden before returning to Roslyn in 1925 and purchasing the Roslyn Barber Shop from Melvin Einerson. Elmer married Elna Olson in 1931 and they made their home in Roslyn to raise three children—Darlis, Warren, and Allen. In 1950, the family moved to Moorhead, Minnesota where Darlis attended high school classes to prepare her for nursing school. She graduated in 1951. Warren graduated from Moorhead High in 1952, and after that, the family moved back to Roslyn, where Allen graduated from Roslyn High School in 1954. Elmer barbered in Roslyn until 1989 and Elna was employed at the Day County Hospital in Webster for several years. Elmer and his family lived in a mobile home that was put on the east side of Iver and Serina's Roslyn home in the summer of 1952. When Iver died in January of 1954, Elmer and Elna purchased Iver's house in Roslyn and lived there the rest of their lives. Elmer and Elna died just three months apart—Elmer in August of 1994, and Elna in November. Elmer was 93 and Elna was 83.

Iver and Serina's fourth child was born — Ingvald Vevang

Ingvald was born on the Vevang family farm in December 1902 and attended country school through eighth grade in Nutley Township. He didn't have any other formal education beyond grade school. In the 1920 U.S. Federal Census, Ingvald was 18, and in the 1930 census Ingvald was still living in the Vevang family home at age 28. By 1930, siblings Julius, Hilda, Elmer, and Selmer had left the family home. In the '20s and '30s, he worked many small jobs and wrote about them. He's been a farmer, railroad worker, and road construction worker. He wrote of the cars he had through the years and took photos of their life in rural South Dakota. He was a little bit of a musician, too,

it seemed. He owned a threshing outfit and worked the farms in the area for about ten years. He traveled across the United States in search of other places to settle down to see what else life had to offer. In 1945, he started his own road construction business. Ingvald married later in his life, at age 37 to Alberta Syverson in 1940. They lost their first child at birth, a daughter named Sandra Kae. Linda was born in 1943, Dennis in 1945, Pamela in 1949, and Debra in 1954. Alberta died in 1982 at the age of 61, and Ingvald died in 1985 at 82.

Iver and Serina's fifth child was born — Selmer Edwin Vevang

In August 1904, Selmer was the fifth child born to Iver and Serina. He graduated from Roslyn High School in 1924 and furthered his education by attending Normal State Teachers' College in Aberdeen, SD. He taught for two years. Selmer then attended Augustana College in Sioux Falls, SD, graduating in 1930, and attended the Luther Theological Seminary in St. Paul, MN, graduating in 1933. Selmer married Bernice Marcel Sholl the same year and was installed into the ministry in Elizabeth, NJ, where they remained until 1945. Beverley was born in 1935, and Shirley in 1936. In the 1940 census, it was noted that Myrtle, Selmer's sister, lived with them and was a student. At the time, Myrtle was 25. There was also a roomer living with them. Paul was born in 1942, Timothy in 1943, and James in 1945. In 1945, they moved to Galesville, WI, where they stayed until 1953. They then lived in Seattle, WA until 1960 when they moved to Redwood Falls, MN. Selmer retired from the ministry in 1969. They moved to Seattle, and Sam died in 1972 at age 68. Bea died in 2009 at age 97.

Iver and Serina's sixth child was born — Edvin Vevang

Edvin was born on the Vevang family farm in Nutley Township on March 21, 1906. He died only two years and three months later on June 27, 1908. Edvin was baptized on April 29, 1906. His sponsors were Hans Stavig, Lena Stavig, Edwin Stavig, and Mabel Holm.

Iver and Serina's seventh child was born — Laura Mathilda Vevang

Laura was born on the Vevang family farm in March of 1908 and graduated from Roslyn High School in 1926. Laura was still in the Vevang family household in the 1930 census. Laura furthered her education with a one-year teacher's program from Northern Normal and Industrial School in Aberdeen, South Dakota—earning her degree in 1927 and teaching in rural schools. She married Henry Hanson in 1932 and they had four children. Lorraine was born in 1933, Henry Jr. in 1935, and twins David and Douglas in 1942. Laura and Henry lost their daughter, Lorraine, when Lorraine was 14 years old. Their son David died just four days after he was born. Laura served on the Day County Board, was a Deputy County Auditor for Webster, and was also appointed Webster City Finance Officer from 1970 to 1979 when she retired. Henry was a Day County Treasurer and Auditor, and a Webster City Auditor. He was also self-employed as an accountant. Henry passed away at age 86 in 1984, and Laura at age 83 in 1991.

1908 Family Photo
From left: Hilda, Serina holding Laura, Julius, Ingvald, Elmer, and Iver holding Selmer.
Edvin died June 27, 1908, before this photo was taken.

Iver and Serina's eighth child was born — Ella Heninga Vevang

Ella was born on the Vevang family farm in October 1909 and graduated from Roslyn High School in 1928. She completed a one-year normal course of study at Augustana College in Sioux Falls, South Dakota. Ella was a school teacher in a one-room schoolhouse near Pickerel Lake, close to Roslyn. She later attended Swedish Nursing School in Minneapolis, Minnesota, and received a diploma in 1934. In 1935, she was living in Watertown, South Dakota. From there, Ella headed east, determined by a coin toss on whether to go east or west. She traveled and spent time with family, settling in Roanoke, Virginia as a nursing instructress at the Roanoke Hospital for two years. In 1938, Ella married John Edgar Lee Montgomery and they made their home in Rocky Mount, Virginia. They had three children. Serina was born in 1939, Johnny in 1942, and William in 1953. John Ed died in 1965 at age 67, and Ella died in 1999 at age 89.

The Thirteenth United States Federal Census taken in 1910
Nutley Township, Day County, South Dakota

Vevang	Iver A.	Head	M	W	44
	Serina	Wife	F	W	38
	Julius	Son	M	W	12
	Hilda	Daughter	F	W	11
	Elmer	Son	M	W	9
	Ingvald	Son	M	W	7
	Selmer	Son	M	W	5
	Laura	Daughter	F	W	2
	Ella	Daughter	F	W	6/12
Gaara	Halvor	Lodger	M	W	36

Iver, Serina, Julius, Hilda, Elmer, Ingvald, Selmer, Laura, and Ella were in the Vevang family home in 1910. They also had a lodger, Mr. Halvor Gaara, who was a teacher at their country school.

Iver and Serina's ninth child was born — Alida Vevang

Alida was born on the Vevang family farm in December 1910. She is not listed in the school records as graduating from high school, but she was an intelligent woman. Alida was still in the Vevang family household in the 1930 census at the age of 19. She later cared for Iver and Serina in their retirement years when they moved to Roslyn. Alida moved to Minneapolis and worked for a company that made molds. In about 1970, she developed some health problems thought to be caused by environmental issues where she worked. Alida could no longer work and could not live alone, so her sister, Laura, took care of her in Webster until her death on August 23, 1971 at age 60. She never married.

Hilda (back center), Selmer (first from the left in the front row), and Ingvald (taller boy on Selmer's left) with their class at the Nutley Township Rural School in Day County South Dakota in 1911.

Iver and Serina's tenth child was born — Jacob Vevang

Jacob was born on the Vevang family farm in Nutley Township, Day County, South Dakota on July 19, 1912, and died on July 21, 1912, just two days after his birth. He was born between Alida and Myrtle. One can only imagine their sad day. He is buried in the Roslyn Cemetery.

Vevang family farm in 1911
From left: Laura, Iver, Selmer, Serina holding Alida, Ella, and Hilda
Julius and Ingvald are in the buggy, and Elmer is holding the reins of the horse to the far right.

Iver and Serina's eleventh child was born — Myrtle Hazel Vevang

Myrtle was born on the Vevang family farm in August of 1914 and was included in the 1915 census. She graduated from Roslyn High School in 1934 and attended beauty school. She lived in New Jersey with her brother Selmer and his family and was included as a member of their household in the 1940 census. Selmer, her brother, escorted her on her dates with Myrtle's soon-to-be husband, Charles. Myrtle married Charles Henry Watkins in November of 1940 in Elizabeth, New Jersey. They had four children. Bruce was born in 1943, Cheryl in 1945, and James and Marilyn in 1948. Charles died in 2004 at age 90, and Myrtle died in 2008 at age 93.

Iver and Serina's twelfth child was born — Lawrence Arthur Vevang

Lawrence was born on the Vevang family farm in October of 1915. He attended school in Roslyn, SD until the age of approximately 15. He married Margaret Rose Pitzl in December of 1941. Three days later, on December 7th, they heard the news that Pearl Harbor in Honolulu, Hawaii had been bombed by the Japanese. The country was preparing for war. Lawrence went to the Draft Board to register for enlistment. Iver, Lawrence's father, went with Lawrence to explain that Lawrence was needed to farm their land. The country needed the farming operation to continue full steam through the war, so Lawrence was excused from the military. Lawrence and Margaret lived with Iver and Serina until 1942 when Iver and Serina moved to their home in Roslyn. Lawrence and Margaret had two children. Bonita was born in 1943, and Larry in 1945. Lawrence died in October of 2016; eleven days shy of his 101st birthday. Margaret passed away in August 2020 at age 101.

The Vevang Sisters in 1915
Ella, Hilda holding Myrtle, Laura, and Alida (sitting)

1917. Laura is sitting, Ella is standing on the left, and Alida on the right.

Ingvald is taking a picture in front of the mirror on the vehicle.

1916. Myrtle and Serina holding Lawrence

In about 1916 Iver purchased his first automobile, an Oakland. The first time he drove it, he ran into the porch pillar (the porch was not enclosed at that time). There was only slight damage to the porch, but Iver never drove again, leaving the driving to his sons. Over the years, the family had an assortment of automobiles: a 1928 Chevrolet purchased by Ingvald, a 1931 Chevrolet, a 1932 Model A Ford purchased by Lawrence with some monetary help from his father, a 1938 Chevrolet purchased by Lawrence, and a Chevrolet Fleet that Lawrence also purchased.

Vevang Family Portrait in 1919

Standing from left:
Laura, Elmer, Hilda, Myrtle, Julius, Ingvald, Selmer

Sitting from left:
Ella, Serina, Lawrence, Iver, Alida

**The Fourteenth United States Federal Census taken in 1920
Nutley Township, Day County, South Dakota**

Vevang, Iver A.	Head	O	m	m	w	54
—— , Serina	Wife			h	w	47
—— , Julius S.	Son			m	w	23
—— , Elmer L.	Son			m	w	18
—— , Engvald	Son			m	w	17
—— , Selmer	Son			m	w	15
—— , Laura M.	Daughter			f	w	11
—— , Ella H.	Daughter			f	w	10
—— , Alida	Daughter			f	w	9
—— , Myrtle H.	Daughter			f	w	5
—— , Lawrence A.	Son			m	w	4 3/12

The first child to leave home was Hilda Marie Vevang. On December 20, 1919, Hilda married Edwin Casper Olson.

SWANSON & LOSETH HARDWARE

The first hardware store in Roslyn was built by Henry and Anton Gilbertson in 1914. Later Anton left for California and Iver Vevang became Henry's partner. The name was then *Gilbertson and Vevang.* They sold it to D. LaSalle in 1918, and in 1920 it was sold to Andrew Swanson and E.C. Loseth, the latter being from Veblen. *Swanson and Loseth Hardware* sold John Deere implements, radios, all kinds of hardware and Minnesota paints. Mr. Swanson conducted this business with the assistance of C. Nelson. In 1947 he sold it to Clarence Nelson. In 1963 it was sold to Elser and Marlyn Rye. It was destroyed by fire in 1964. It was located on the west side of Main Street.

Iver Vevang and Henry Gilbertson were partners in the hardware business. Henry was the father to Hazel Gilbertson. Just a few years later, Hazel married Julius Vevang on July 3, 1921.

Also in 1921, Hilda and Edwin began having children—Iver and Serina's first four grandchildren.

Julius and Hazel
Vevang

**Spencer Hiram Olson
born October 19, 1921**

**Rosalie Eugene Olson
born March 17, 1923**

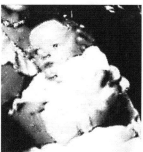

**Calvin Irving Olson
born December 30, 1930**

**Viola Delores Olson
born January 15, 1932**

Life on the Farm During the 1920s and 1930s
Written by Ingvald Vevang

Dad was born in Vevang, Norway in 1865. This was the same year Lincoln was shot. In 1888, he came to the United States and started to work on farms north of Roslyn. My mother was born in Hustad, Norway in 1872 and came to the United States in 1892. My mother and dad were married in 1896 and they bought a farm northeast of Roslyn where they lived for 46 years and raised ten children. They first lived on a farm in Raritan Township. There were a lot of farms around the country in those days.

There was a farm you might say on every square mile, a lot of young folks around. And as to my own life on the farm, in my early life, my folks raised ten children on the farm. I was fourth from the oldest. We went to an old country school north of the farm to get part of our education. Of course, in those days we farmed with horses. We even went to Webster with a team of horses, hauled grain to Webster. Got up early in the morning and loaded grain to Webster.

Now I'm going to start off with life on the farm in the spring. We usually got up at 6:00 in the morning and went down to the barn to feed 10-13 heads of horse's hay, and a gallon of oats a piece. Then I usually harnessed the horses and Dad milked cows and other chores. When we got the horses harnessed, curried and everything, we went up for breakfast. Around 7:30 we went out in the field with two rigs, one usually dragging and the other one seeding grain. It was quite peaceful on the farm in those days. We didn't get to town except for a couple of times a year. We lived and enjoyed life on the farm. We used to milk about 15 cows and fed the milk back to the calves after we took the cream out.

Threshing on the Farm

The big time of the year was threshing. We went out with the big steam rig. We used to leave Monday morning with a team of horses and a hay rig and a good fork and go to the neighbors and pitch bundles; we exchanged help. We used to sleep in barns or anywhere that we could throw a blanket down. Dad bought his first car in 1916. From

then on things started to speed up a little bit around the farm. At least we got to Webster occasionally more often and Roslyn, too. I want to go back a bit further to hauling grain to Webster, pre-Roslyn years. We used to haul grain to Webster. We used two teams. I remember one time when Dad had one team and I drove the other. I don't think I was over twelve years old. Dad of course was up in front with a load on and I was behind. I followed him all the way to Webster and back again. We left early in the morning and got back late in the evening, way after dark. It was a big deal to be able to drive a team to Webster in those days. Of course, the big time on the farm in those days came when the threshing machine came in the fall; especially when we had a good crop. The women folk used to bring lunch out in the forenoon around 10:00 and we'd come home for dinner. Then about 3:30 in the afternoon they'd bring lunch out for us again. We'd come home for supper at about 7:30 or so. It was a lot of work for women folk in those days.

We had about eight bundle teams and three grain haulers; then a separator man, an engineer, and a water man. It got to be 13, 14, 15, 16 men to cook for. We used to go out and sleep in the barns and we young fellows used to tell stories, lay up in the hay mound, and tell stories half the night. It was hard for the older fellows to get us up in the morning. So, it was quite a job. And when we got through threshing the fall work started. We usually plowed two gang plows. Five horses on each gang and sometimes with the long rounds, why we'd fit the lines on the handles on the plow and get out and walk behind; just to have something to do. Get a little exercise. And it was kind of nothing to do to occupy your mind. You were daydreaming an awful lot—building air castles. And of course, we went back to get ready for wintertime on the farm. Hauled hay. We used two hay rigs, two teams. About three of us used to haul the hay to get the barn filled up for winter.

Church

Going to Church; especially in the summertime. We had a buggy with two seats on with horses. It was approximately two and a half miles to church up on the hill down south. In wintertime, of course, we went once in a while, but not every Sunday. We used a bobsled with a quilt to keep our feet warm.

School

When we went to school, the old country schoolhouse. I don't know how many of us went to school there, but it must have been seven or eight of us at one time. And then the folks had to take care of the schoolteacher, too. She used to board a room there. So, it was quite a time….

Horses

We usually raised colts on the farm, Dad did… and of course, when they got to be three years old, we had to break them. That was quite a job. We used to put a harness on them for half a day and let them stand with the harness on to get used to the harnesses. The next day Father would take an older horse as a mate and hook them onto a wagon then turn them away from the buildings. Then when we got them hooked to the wagon, we'd jump in, and off we went at a dead gallop; just as fast as they could run. Then they'd run until they got tired, then down to a trot, and pretty soon they'd be walking.

Pretty soon you'd tell them to stop, and they'd stop. Get out and pat them a little bit and talk to them. Then we could drive them back home again. The next day we'd probably do the same thing over again. But we probably wouldn't have to drive the young colt so hard that second day; until they get used to it. It wasn't too hard a job to break them. Of course, we worked the broodmares.

I remember one time in the spring I was dragging with six horses. I unhooked for dinner and went home. I noticed that one of the mares wasn't feeling good, so it was about time for her to deliver. So, I unhooked her, took the harness off and turned her out in the hay land there. I figured if she was having a colt, she'd have it, if not she'd come home. So, I drove the other five horses home. After a while in the afternoon, I went out there and here she was with a new colt. He was getting his first meal already. Dad used to raise two or three colts on the farm every year. Sometimes he'd sell some of them. He had 12 or 13 horses. Of course, he had to raise some of them.

Elmer with a farm horse

Elmer was also good with horses. He was the best one of the boys with horses. We never took the horses to the blacksmith shop to have them shod. We usually did that in the fall. One of the best teams, we used to have them shod in front. Sometimes we'd put shoes on the teams but mostly with just the best team we had, we put shoes on front. We used to take a front foot and put it between our legs and file them down or use a rasp to get the shoe to fit. Then we'd nail it on… five nails in each shoe—each side of the shoe. That was so they could go on ice.

I'll go back a little further. I talked about it before. One year we were harvesting with two binders. It was an awfully hot dry spell that harvest. It was up to 100–102ºF every day. And we tried to protect our horses, but they got hurt one day. I had a three-year-old on my rig. Next morning, we started out about 11 o'clock. I noticed that the horse was slowing up and I knew there was something wrong with him, so I unhooked. Dad was running the other outfit, so I told him that we'd better get this horse home. So, we started home with all five horses. We got him in the barn okay, but the horse died in about two hours from too much heat. We felt bad about it for the simple reason that it was the first time an animal died from the heat while we were farming out there.

Another interesting time on the farm years ago was when we had Christmas in the old country schoolhouse. We'd hook up a horse on a bobsled and go and take in the Christmas program. They used to have a Christmas tree with candles. We'd drive down there, unhooked the horses, tie them to the bobsled, cover them up with blankets to keep them warm while the program was going on. Enjoyable times they were. Some of the best times of the year were around Christmas time. Another thing we used to do on the farm was to put bells on the reins of the horses in wintertime. It sounded really good, and of course, it was a must to braid the tails on the horses and put them in a pug, so they got short. We trimmed the mane in kind of an arch shape and put bells on the hang of the horses.

When we went to Webster with a team when I was a kid, we used to have a hitch rack along the street and sidewalks to tie the horses to. Down where the Standard Oil Station is, we used to have a big tank of water. We used to water our horses. You didn't see a car in the street. Just horses, teams, buggies, and wagons.

I'm going to go back again to the time when I was on the farm with my folks. I bought a steam rig to thresh with. That was quite a big thing in those days. We ran quite a few teams. I used Spencer Olson to haul water for me. He's quite a guy. One time he drove out in the slough too far with the tractor pulling the water tank and got stuck. We had to shut down the whole rig because we were out of water. Then we had to go and pull him out... lots of fun in those days.

To start off, the first year I had Lawrence haul water for me when he was a youngster. Of course, he shoveled coal in the engine once in a while. I had Ted Haaseth to run the separator, I ran the engine and Lawrence hauled water. It worked well...pretty fair crop. I'll go back to the days when I had my own threshing rig again. I ran the steam rig for about ten years. My rig was the only one in the country running later years with a steam engine. I had a lot of customers. People stand around hours watching the engine run. I had one guy from Minnesota with a movie picture camera. He was out there two-three hours one day taking pictures all the way from the engine where the coal went in, water went in the engine, the belt followed the rotary belt, to the machine, to the blower: guys pitching into the machine and striking out to the blower. He got a kick out of it...

29

THIS SIDE FOR CORRESPONDENCE

This is the kind of steam engine Ingvald Vevang bought in Watertown 1926. I drove it home it took me 2 days. I thrashed 10 year with it.

AL PRESS, INC., NORTH CHICAGO

In 1926, while still on the Vevang farm, Ingvald Vevang bought a Case steam engine thresher in Watertown, South Dakota. He and his brother, Selmer, drove it home taking them two days. Ingvald threshed for ten years. Ing wrote on the back of a postcard to note the purchase of his steam engine thresher.

Ingvald Vevang Thrashing Outfit in 1926

1932
From left:
Hanson,
Christenson,
Selmer Vevang,
Nels,
Lawrence Vevang,
Lester,
Ken Baukol,
Walter Rasmussen,
J. Hasseth,
Ingvald Vevang,
Ted Hasseth

Ingvald
Vevang
with his
threshing
crew

Selmer Vevang is the first man from the left with the hat and white shirt, Lawrence Vevang is the eighth from the right, and Ingvald Vevang, the fifth from the right.

Roslyn South Dakota, Diamond Jubilee, p.38. Published by The Reporter and Farmer, Webster SD

1920s. Myrtle and Lawrence are on the left. Alida with the necklace. Ella is the first on the right and Laura is second from right.

From the writings of Ingvald Vevang

I am going to jump back again to the time I was home with the folks. I must mention my sisters once in a while. They used to help us with certain things on the farm. Especially during haying time. All my sisters would do the raking. It'd help us an awful lot. We gave them a team of good horses. Alida did some of it and Myrtle was good at it. If you talked nice to Myrtle, she'd help us just about every time. They helped quite a bit, too. One of the boys ran the bucker, one by the haystack, running the hay stacker. Dad used to be in the stacks, so things went smooth...

Ingvald and Lawrence are the first and the third from the left

1920s. Ella, unidentified, Laura, and Alida

Ingvald relaxing in his
1924 Model T Ford

1926. Selmer with Myrtle, Spencer,
Lawrence. Rosalie is on the wheel.

1928. Selmer on top of the car, Ella second
down from Selmer, Elmer and Hilda third and
fourth from left, Laura next to Hilda. Rosalie
Olson on the ground to the right.

1925. Vevang Farm

1929. Serina Hustad Vevang's family, the Stavigs and Tornesses. Standing: Third from left is Serina, fifth is Hilda
and sixth is Iver. Ingvald is second from right, and Ed Olson is first from right. Sitting on the left: Elmer, Spencer Olson
and Rosalie Olson. Sitting in center are from left: Laura, Alida, and Ella Vevang.

Out for a good time
The two on the right are Sam and Laura Vevang. They are
driving around the countryside, enjoying a refreshment.

A gathering at the Vevang farm in about 1929 or 1930 with their cars all lined up. Most had Model A Ford cars.

The Fifteenth United States Federal Census taken in 1930
Nutley Township, Day County, South Dakota

In the 1930 census, both Elmer and Selmer had left the household. Elmer attended barber school in Minneapolis and then started his barbering business while boarding in the Mattie Gilbertson home. Selmer attended and graduated from Augustana College in Sioux Falls, South Dakota. Iver Vevang (64, farmer), was the head of the household. His wife Serina (58) and their children, Ingvald (27), Laura (22), Ella (20), Alida (19), Myrtle (15), and Lawrence (14) were also in the home.

Vevang	Iver J	Head	O		R	Yes	M	W	64
	Serina	Wife				x	F	W	58
	Ingvald	Son				x	M	W	27
	Laura M	Daughter				x	F	W	22
	Ella	Daughter				x	F	W	20
	Alida	Daughter				x	F	W	19
	Myrtle H	Daughter				x	F	W	15
	Lawrence G	Son				x	M	W	14

33

Rosalie and Uncle Ingvald in 1931

Sisters Alida Vevang and Myrtle Vevang
with unidentified woman in the middle

Brother and Sister
Ingvald Vevang and Myrtle Vevang

Sisters Myrtle Vevang and Laura Vevang

Mother and Daughter
Serina and Myrtle

Laura at the front door of the Vevang home

Sisters Ella and Laura

Iver doing daily chores

Serina feeding the chickens

July 16, 1931

The barn on the Vevang farm was damaged during a summer storm.

1931. Elmer marries Elna Olson

1932. Laura marries Henry Hanson

Elna and Laura

1933. Selmer marries Bernice Sholl

From left: Henry Hanson Sr., Laura Vevang Hanson holding Lorraine Hanson, Serina Hustad Vevang, Ingvald Vevang, Selmer Vevang, Alida Vevang, Bernice Sholl Vevang, Myrtle Vevang, and Iver Vevang

Darlis Janet Vevang
born March 18, 1933
to Elmer and Elna Vevang

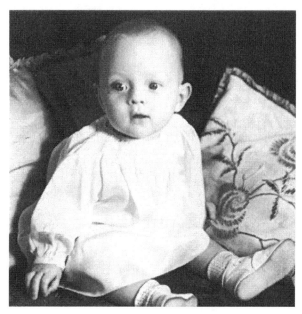

Lorraine Harriet Hanson
born April 21, 1933
to Laura and Henry Hanson

Warren Elmer Vevang
born October 23, 1934
to Elmer and Elna Vevang

1934. Henry Hanson holding Lorraine, and Elmer Vevang holding Darlis

Written Between the Lines of Ingvald Vevang's 1926 Ledger Book

1933 was the beginning of the drought. There was a lot of dust in the spring. There was a fair hay crop, but no other crops. 1934 was just as bad. There was barley that year, but no hay. Sold most of the cattle to the government. Had 27 head of calf left in the fall of 1934. Most of the farmers in the country were on relief.

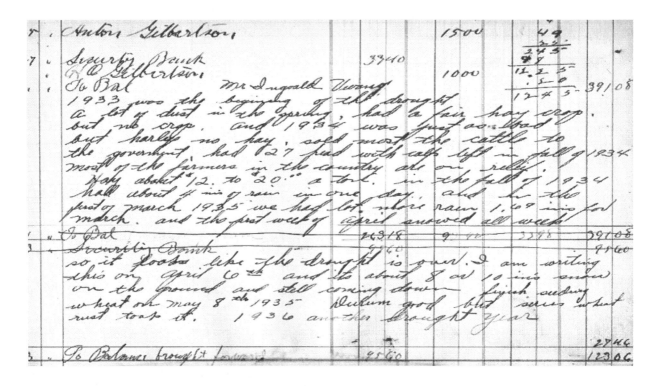

Selmer's drawings and doodles in his brother's ledger book.

Lorraine Hanson's first birthday in April 1934
Lorraine is held by an unidentified person.
The four children of Hilda and Ed Olson: Rosalie,
Spencer, Calvin, and Viola are to the right

Beverley Joan Vevang
born February 22, 1935 to
Selmer and Bernice Vevang

Henry Mark Hanson Jr.
born August 6, 1935
to Laura and Henry Hanson Sr.
Henry is with his sister, Lorraine

Shirley Elaine Vevang
born May 7, 1936
to Selmer and Bernice Vevang
Shirley is with her Aunt Myrtle,
and sister, Beverley

Allen Gene Vevang
born September 25, 1936
to Elmer and Elna Vevang

Iver and Serina's 40th Wedding Anniversary
1896-1936

Serina and Iver

Standing from left: Ella Vevang, Elmer Vevang, Selmer Vevang, Julius Vevang, Ingvald Vevang, Lawrence Vevang and Hilda Vevang Olson

Sitting in front from left: Laura Vevang Hanson, Serina Hustad Vevang, Myrtle Vevang, Iver Vevang and Alida Vevang

Iver and Serina, with Serina's sister, Beret Hustad Holm, and Beret's husband, Iver Holm

Iver and Serina's first eleven grandchildren on the Vevang farm in 1937

Standing from left: Darlis Vevang, Spencer Olson, Viola Olson, Rosalie Olson and Calvin Olson
Sitting: Shirley Vevang, Allen Vevang, Beverley Vevang, Warren Vevang, Henry Hanson Jr., Lorraine Hanson

On the Vevang farm 1937

Back: Serina, Iver, Selmer Vevang, Elna Olson Vevang, Hilda Vevang Olson, Ed Olson, Henry Hanson Jr.,
Henry Hanson Sr., Sigvart Olson (Hilda's father-in-law), Ingvald Vevang, Lawrence Vevang and Spencer Olson
Front row: Elmer Vevang, Rosalie Olson, Shirley Vevang, Beverley Vevang, Darlis Vevang, Warren Vevang, Allen
Vevang, Alida Vevang, Lorraine Hanson, Laura Vevang Hanson, Rosalie Olson, Calvin Olson, and Myrtle Vevang

A day on the Vevang farm in 1938

From left: Iver Vevang, Alida Vevang, Elna Olson Vevang, Ingvald Vevang,
Selmer Vevang, Bernice Sholl Vevang, and Lawrence Vevang
Front: Shirley Vevang and Beverley Vevang

Selmer with his daughters, Beverley and Shirley

Ingvald with his nieces, Beverley and Shirley.

Shirley and Beverley with the farm dog, Bobbie, and other farm animals

Myrtle Vevang

Brother and Sister, Ingvald and Myrtle

Ingvald Vevang

Julius Vevang

Laura and Henry Hanson Sr.

Ingvald, Julius, and Elmer

Brothers Selmer, Ingvald, Lawrence, Elmer, and Julius

Myrtle Vevang, Anne (Myrtle's friend), and Ella Vevang Montgomery

Ingvald bought a saxophone in 1925 for $145

Ing next to the piano (and doilies) at the Vevang home where it sits today (left), and a Chevrolet Coupe (right).

Ingvald

Ingvald with a Cabriolet

Brothers Ingvald and Selmer

Elmer (far left), Ingvald (middle), and Selmer (far right)

Ingvald, Myrtle, Ella, and Henry

Sister and brother, Ella and Ing

On June 1, 1938, Ella Heninga Vevang married John Edgar Lee Montgomery in Elizabeth, New Jersey.

Serina Vevang Montgomery was born March 6, 1939 to Ella and John Ed Montgomery.

Myrtle Vevang

Sisters Alida and Myrtle

Myrtle and Ingvald in front of the Vevang family home

United States of America a Declaration of Intention
State of South Dakota in the Circuit Court County of Day County of Webster, SD
October 3, 1940

ORIGINAL
(To be retained by clerk)

No. 8 1 3

UNITED STATES OF AMERICA

DECLARATION OF INTENTION
(Invalid for all purposes seven years after the date hereof)

State Of South Dakota, | *In the* Circuit _____ Court
County Of Day | *ss:* *of* Day County *at* Webster, S.D.

I, Iver Vevang
now residing at Route 2, Roslyn Day County South Dakota,
occupation Farmer, aged 74 years, do declare on oath that my personal description is:
Sex male, color white, complexion fair, color of eyes blue
color of hair gray, height 5 feet 6 inches; weight 155 pounds; visible distinctive marks
none
race Scandinavian; nationality Norwegian
I was born in near Christansund Norway, on Nov. 5th 1865.
I am married. The name of my wife or husband is Serina
we were married on June 1st 1896 at Grenville South Dakota,; she or he was
born near Christansund on Feb 10th 1872, entered the United States
at Sault Ste Marie Mich, on Fall 1892, for permanent residence therein. and now
resides at Roslyn South Dakota, I have 10 children, and the name, date and place of birth,
and place of residence of each of said children are as follows: _____

I have _____ heretofore made a declaration of intention: Number _____ on Nov. 15th 1893
at Webster, South Dakota,
my last foreign residence was near Christansund Norway
I emigrated to the United States of America from Christansund Norway
my lawful entry for permanent residence in the United States was at Sault Ste Marie Mich.
under the name of Iver J. Vevang, on
on the vessel train

I will, before being admitted to citizenship, renounce absolutely and forever all allegiance and fidelity to any foreign prince, potentate, state, or sovereignty, of whom or of which I may be at the time of admission a citizen or subject; I am not an anarchist; I am not a polygamist nor a believer in the practice of polygamy; and it is my intention in good faith to become a citizen of the United States of America and to reside permanently therein; and I certify that the photograph affixed to the duplicate and triplicate hereof is a likeness of me.

I swear (affirm) that the statements I have made and the intentions I have expressed in this declaration of intention subscribed by me are true to the best of my knowledge and belief: So help me God.

Iver Vevang

Subscribed and sworn to before me in the form of oath shown above in the office of the Clerk of said Court, at Webster, South Dakota, this 3rd day of Oct., anno Domini, 19 40. Certification No. _____ from the Commissioner of Immigration and Naturalization showing the lawful entry of the declarant for permanent residence on the date stated above, has been received by me. The photograph affixed to the duplicate and triplicate hereof is a likeness of the declarant.

(DO NOT ATTACH PHOTOGRAPH TO THIS COPY OF DECLARATION)

Steve Pearson

[SEAL]

Clerk of the Circuit _____ Court.

By _____, Deputy Clerk.

Form 2202—L-A
U. S. DEPARTMENT OF LABOR
IMMIGRATION AND NATURALIZATION SERVICE
14—X—13216

I, Iver Vevang now residing at Route 2, Roslyn, Day County, South Dakota, occupation farmer, aged 74 years, do declare on oath that my personal description is: sex male, color white, complexion fair, color of eyes blue, color of hair gray, height 5 feet 6 inches, weight 155 pounds, visible distinctive marks none, race Scandinavian, nationality Norwegian, I was born near Christansund Norway, on November 23rd 1865. I am married. The name of my wife is Serina. We were married on June 1, 1896, at Grenville (Church), South Dakota. She was born near Christansund on February 10, 1872, entered the United States at Sault Ste. Marie Michigan, in the Fall of 1892, for permanent residence therein and now resides in Roslyn South Dakota.

I have heretofore made a declaration on intention: on November 15th, 1893, at Webster, South Dakota. My last foreign residence was near Christansund Norway. I emigrated to the United States of America from Christansund Norway. My lawful entry for permanent residence in the United States was at Sault Ste. Marie Michigan under the name of Iver J. A. Vevang on the vessel train.

I will, before being admitted to citizenship, renounce absolutely and forever all allegiance and fidelity to any foreign prince, potentate, state, or sovereignty, of whom or of which I may be at that time of admissions a citizen or subject; I am not an anarchist; I am not a polygamist nor a believer in practice of polygamy; and it is my intention in good faith to become a citizen of the United States of America and to reside permanently therein; and I certify that the photograph affixed to the duplicate and triplicate hereof is a likeness of me. I swear (affirm) that the statements I have made and the intentions I have expressed in this declaration of intention subscribed by me are true to the best of my knowledge and belief: So help me God.

The above document was completed by Iver in Webster at the Clerk of Courts office on the same day that Serina completed hers in the fall of 1940. It is thought that information that was on Serina's document was also put on Iver's document in error. It is believed that Iver entered the United States at the port in New York. The document below was completed in 1893, when Iver was 28 years old. It states his entry through New York.

United States of America a Declaration of Intention
State of South Dakota in the Circuit Court County of Day County of Webster, SD
October 3, 1940

TRIPLICATE
(To be given to declarant)

No. 8 1 4

UNITED STATES OF AMERICA

DECLARATION OF INTENTION
(Invalid for all purposes seven years after the date hereof)

State of South Dakota, } ss: In the Circuit Court

County of Day } of Day County at Webster, S.D.

I, Serina Vevang
now residing at Route 2, Roslyn Day County South Dakota,
occupation Farmer Housekeeper, aged 68 years, do declare on oath that my personal description is:
Sex female, color white, complexion fair, color of eyes blue
color of hair gray, height 5 feet inches; weight 180 pounds; visible distinctive marks
none
race Scandinavian; nationality Norwegian
I was born in near Christansund Norway, on February 10th 1872
I am married. The name of my wife or husband is Iver
we were married on June 1st 1896, at Granville, South Dakota; she or he was
born at near Christansund, on Nov. 23rd 1865, entered the United States
at Sault Ste. Marie Mich., on Fall 1892, for permanent residence therein, and now
resides at Roslyn South Dakota. I have 10 children, and the name, date and place of birth,
and place of residence of each of said children are as follows:

I have not heretofore made a declaration of intention. Number, on
at
my last foreign residence was near Christansund Norway.
I emigrated to the United States of America from Christansund Norway
my lawful entry for permanent residence in the United States was at Sault Ste. Marie Mich.
under the name of Serina Rustad, on Fall 1892
on the vessel Train

I will, before being admitted to citizenship, renounce absolutely and forever all allegiance and fidelity to any foreign prince, potentate, state, or sovereignty, of whom or of which I may be at the time of admission a citizen or subject; I am not an anarchist; I am not a polygamist nor a believer in the practice of polygamy; and it is my intention in good faith to become a citizen of the United States of America and to reside permanently therein; and I certify that the photograph affixed to the duplicate and triplicate hereof is a likeness of me.

I swear (affirm) that the statements I have made and the intentions I have expressed in this declaration of intention subscribed by me are true to the best of my knowledge and belief: So help me God.

Serina Vevang

Subscribed and sworn to before me in the form of oath shown above in the office of the Clerk of said Court, at Webster, South Dakota, this 3rd day of October, anno Domini, 19 40 Certification No. from the Commissioner of Immigration and Naturalization showing the lawful entry of the declarant for permanent residence on the date stated above has been received by me. The photograph affixed to the duplicate and triplicate hereof is a likeness of the declarant.

Steve Pearson

SECURELY AND PERMANENTLY AFFIX
PHOTOGRAPH HERE

[SEAL]

Clerk of the Circuit Court.

I, Serina Vevang now residing at Route 2, Roslyn, Day County, South Dakota, occupation farmer housekeeper, aged 68 years, do declare on oath that my personal description is: sex female, color white, complexion fair, color of eyes blue, color of hair gray, height 5 feet, weight 180 pounds, visible distinctive marks none, race Scandinavian, Nationality Norwegian, I was born near Christansund Norway, on February 10, 1872. I am married. The name of my husband is Iver. We were married on June 1st, 1896, at Grenville (Church), South Dakota. He was born near Christansund on November 23rd, 1865, entered the United States at Sault Ste. Marie Michigan, in the Fall of 1892 for permanent residence therein and now resides at Roslyn South Dakota.

My last foreign residence was near Christansund Norway. I emigrated to the United States of America from Christansund Norway. My lawful entry for permanent residence in the United States was at Sault Ste. Marie Michigan under the name of Serina Hustad, in the fall of 1892 on the vessel of a train.

I will, before being admitted to citizenship, renounce absolutely and forever all allegiance and fidelity to any foreign prince, potentate, state, or sovereignty, of whom or of which I may be at that time of admissions a citizen or subject; I am not an anarchist; I am not a polygamist nor a believer in practice of polygamy; and it is my intention in good faith to become a citizen of the United States of America and to reside permanently therein; and I certify that the photograph affixed to the duplicate and triplicate hereof is a likeness of me. I swear (affirm) that the statements I have made and the intentions I have expressed in this declaration of intention subscribed by me are true to the best of my knowledge and belief: So help me God.

The above document was completed by Serina in Webster at the Clerk of Courts office on the same day that Iver completed his in the fall of 1940. The information is in error as to when and where Iver entered the country. Serina entered the United States in 1892, while Iver entered the United States in May of 1888 through the port in New York. This information was entered in error on Serina's document.

Form AR-3 Registration Number 2091548

ALIEN REGISTRATION RECEIPT CARD

Serina Vevang

UNITED STATES DEPARTMENT OF JUSTICE
IMMIGRATION AND NATURALIZATION SERVICE
ALIEN REGISTRATION DIVISION
WASHINGTON, D. C.

To the Registrant:
Your registration under the Alien Registration Act, 1940, has been received and given the number shown above your name. This card is your receipt, and is evidence

Serina Hustad Vevang's Alien Registration Receipt Card

The Alien Registration Act was passed by Congress in 1940. The Act made it illegal for any resident or citizen of the United States of America to teach or advocate the violent overthrow of the U.S. government. The law also forced non-citizens to register with the U.S. government so that the government would be able to track them and their un-American ideas which may or may not lead to the overthrow of the government.

Warren Vevang with his grandparents, Iver and Serina

Myrtle and Charles Watkins

Myrtle with her niece, Darlis Vevang

Family Gatherings in 1940

From left: Margaret Pitzl, Alberta Syverson, Alida Vevang, Unidentified,
Darlis Vevang, Viola Olson, Unidentified, Hilda Vevang Olson

Back: Sigvart Olson, Iver Vevang, Hilda Vevang Olson, Serina Hustad Vevang, Ed Olson,
Alida Vevang holding Serina Montgomery **Front:** Calvin Olson and Viola Olson

From left: Viola Olson, Myrtle Vevang, Alida Vevang, Ella Vevang Montgomery
holding Serina Montgomery, and Alberta Syverson

Weddings

Myrtle married Charles Henry Watkins
November 20, 1940

Ingvald married Alberta Syverson
December 6, 1940

Lawrence married Margaret Rose Pitzl
December 4, 1941

Ingvald, Alberta, and Lawrence on the Iver Vevang farm in 1940

Brothers Ingvald and Lawrence

Ingvald and Alberta as husband and wife

In approximately 1940, Iver purchased a two-story house in Roslyn that he rented out, apparently with the thought of moving into the house when he was ready to retire. The house, facing west, located on the southeast corner of Carlton and Main Street, was one of the most attractive houses in town with nice woodwork, a good-sized yard, and a small garage. They moved there on March 7, 1942, leaving their son, Lawrence, to operate the farm. Lawrence and Margaret Vevang eventually purchased the farm. It is still in the family and is now owned by Larry and Bonita—Lawrence and Margaret's children.

Iver Vevang with Rosalie Olson and Serina after retiring from the farm

Sandra Kae Vevang

On December 29, 1941, Ingvald and Alberta Vevang had a daughter they named Sandra Kae. She was stillborn and is buried in the Roslyn Lutheran Church Cemetery.

Paul Sholl Vevang born June 9, 1942 to Selmer and Bernice Vevang. He is with his cousin, Johnny (right).

John (Johnny) Edgar Lee Montgomery Jr. born July 7, 1942 to Ella and John Ed Montgomery. Johnny is wearing his father's christening dress.

Twins

David August Hanson and Douglas Iver Hanson were born to Laura and Henry Hanson on December 18, 1942. David died four days after his birth.

Douglas Iver Hanson born December 18, 1942 to Laura and Henry Hanson

Charles Bruce Watkins born January 25, 1943 to Myrtle and Charles Watkins

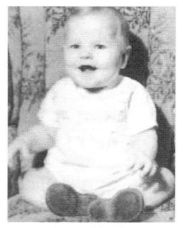

Timothy Iver Vevang born May 9, 1943 to Selmer and Bernice Vevang

Linda Ann Vevang born June 11, 1943 to Ingvald and Alberta Vevang

From left: Margaret Pitzl Vevang holding Bonita Vevang, Alberta Syverson Vevang holding Linda Vevang, and Darlis Vevang holding Douglas Hanson

Bonita Justyne Vevang born August 2, 1943 to Lawrence and Margaret Vevang

From left: Lawrence Vevang holding Bonita Vevang, Ingvald Vevang holding Linda Vevang, and Darlis Vevang holding Douglas Hanson

Serina and Iver with Johnny and Serina

Beverley, Serina, Johnny and Shirley at the Vevang family farm

1944. Back from left: Warren, Lorraine, Darlis, and Henry
Front: Serina, Johnny, Linda, and Douglas

Serina, Johnny, and Bruce

1945. Iver Vevang (first on the left), Henry Hanson Sr. (fourth from left) with Lawrence Vevang to the right of him, and the small boy in front is Allen Vevang

Larry Mathias Vevang born February 19, 1945 to Lawrence and Margaret Vevang

Rosalie married Donald Danielson on May 2, 1944
Daughter of Hilda and Edwin Olson, Rosalie was the first grandchild of Iver and Serina to marry.

Dennis Ingvald Vevang born May 12, 1945 to Ingvald and Alberta Vevang

James Sholl Vevang born July 14, 1945 to Selmer and Bernice Vevang

Sonja May Danielson born August 3, 1945 to Rosalie and Donald Danielson
She was the first great-grandchild of Iver and Serina Vevang.

Cheryl Ann Watkins born October 27, 1945 to Myrtle and Charles Watkins

Golden Wedding Anniversary

1896-1946

Roslyn Couple Honored On Golden Anniversary

Mr. and Mrs. Iver Vevang, long time residents of Roslyn vicinity, celebrated their golden wedding anniversary Sunday afternoon with a program and reception at the Roslyn Lutheran church. Approximately 200 relatives and friends gathered for the occasion, including all their 10 children, all sons-in-law and daughters-in-law except one, 23 grandchildren and one great grand child.

The sermon was given by Pastor O. M. Simundson, and other numbers of the program included: Duet, "Faith of Our Fathers," by Beverly and Shirley Vevang; musical reading, "Old Fashioned Wedding" by Pearl Baukol, accompanied by Clara Hagen; solo, "Sweeter as the Years Go By," by Serena Montgomery; reading, Edgar Guest's "Home" by Darlis Vevang; greeting in Norse from a nephew, Rev. Holm, read by a sister Mrs. Helen Jensen; and short talk by Rev. Selmer Vevang, son of the honorees.

A reception was held in the church parlors and an informal program given with Rev. Simundson acting as toastmaster. Magnus Stavig of Sisseton, who was a witness at the marriage of Mr. and Mrs. Vevang 50 years before, spoke briefly, also Julius Vevang, eldest son; Mrs. Selmer Vevang and John Montgomery for the in-laws, and Spencer Olson for the grandchildren. Greetings were read from a son-in-law Charles Watkins of Chicago; Mrs. Laura Hammer of Faribault, Minn., wife of a former pastor; Rev. S. Dale, former pastor, and wife of St. James, Minn.; from Bethlehem Lutheran church and Mr. and Mrs. Hanson, of Elizabeth, N. J., and Mabel Fordahl of California.

Refreshments were served after the program by the Roslyn Ladies Aid. Mrs. John Montgom-

(Continued on Page 7)

Golden Wedding

(Continued from Page 1)
ery cut the wedding cake, the day being also her own eighth wedding anniversary.

Open house was held at the Vevang home in the evening.

Guests from a distance, included: Mr. and Mrs. Edwin Stavig, Rosholt; Mr. and Mrs. Christ Pederson and family, Enderlin, N. D.; Magnus Stavig, Mr. and Mrs. Elmer Holm, Mr. and Mrs. Elmer Hustad and family, Mr. and Mrs. Andrew Anderson, Mr. and Mrs. Ed Berg, Mr. and Mrs. Carl Stenberg, Mr. and Mrs. Abel Hellevang and daughter, and Mrs. Herickstad, all of Sisseton; Mrs. Julius Holm, Mrs. Tom Lensegrav and Mrs. Irving Woodworth of Webster; Rev. and Mrs. Albert Holm of Arlington; Mr. and Mrs. Pete Olson, Mrs. K. J. Olson, Mr. and Mrs. Virgil Olson of Britton; Mr. and Mrs. George Pitzl and Math Pitzl, of Eden.

Mr. and Mrs. Vevang (nee Serina Hustad) were married at Grenville Lutheran Church on June 1, 1896, by Rev. Johan Granskau. Best man was Tom Hustad, brother of the bride now living at Britton but unable to attend the Golden Wedding due to illness. Another witness was Magnus Stavig of Sisseton, the bride's nephew who was present for the Golden Wedding.

The couple made their home on a farm a mile and a half south of the present site of Roslyn for two years, then moved to their farm northeast of Roslyn in Nutley township where they lived about 44 years. Four years ago, they moved into Roslyn where they now reside.

They have 10 children: Julius, Watertown; Hilda (Mrs. Ed Olson) Minneapolis; Elmer, Roslyn; Ingvald, Webster; Rev. Selmer, Galesville, Wis.; Laura (Mrs. H. M. Hanson), Webster; Ella (Mrs. John Ed Montgomery), Rocky Mount, Va.; Alida at home; Myrtle (Mrs. Chas. Watkins), Chicago; and Lawrence, who lives on the home farm.

MR. AND MRS. IVER VEVANG

Reporter and Farmer
Webster, South Dakota

Back from left: Elmer Vevang, Hilda Vevang Olson, Julius Vevang, Alida Vevang,
Selmer Vevang, Laura Vevang Hanson, Ingvald Vevang and Lawrence Vevang
Front: Ella Vevang Montgomery, Iver Vevang, Serina Hustad Vevang, and Myrtle Vevang Watkins

A bow pin was given to Serina on their
Golden Anniversary. Cheryl Watkins
Tanaka now has the pin.

Ella and John Ed Montgomery

Serina and Iver

From left: Iver Vevang, Donald Danielson holding Sonja Danielson,
Serina Hustad Vevang, Rosalie Olson Danielson, Hilda Vevang Olson, and Edwin Olson

Back from left: Ella Vevang Montgomery, Alida Vevang, Unidentified, Donald Danielson, Elna Olson Vevang,
Laura Vevang Hanson, John Edgar Lee Montgomery, Henry Hanson Sr., Edwin Olson, Unidentified, Alberta Syverson
Vevang, Selmer Vevang **Second row from left:** Spencer Olson, Margaret Pitzl Vevang, Hilda Vevang Olson, Rosalie
Olson Danielson, Myrtle Vevang Watkins, Serina Hustad Vevang, Iver Vevang, Elmer Vevang, Lawrence Vevang
Children standing from left: Shirley Vevang, Allen Vevang in back of John Edgar Lee Montgomery Jr., Warren Vevang,
Henry Hanson Jr. **Children front row:** Older grandchildren are Darlis Vevang kneeling, Serina Montgomery in front of
Serina Hustad Vevang, Viola Olson on the end, and the younger grandchildren are difficult to identify.

66

Back row from left: Myrtle Vevang Watkins, Hilda Vevang Olson, Hazel Gilbertson Vevang, Elna Olson Vevang, Laura Vevang Hanson, Bernice Sholl Vevang, Alida Vevang, Serina Hustad Vevang, Iver Vevang, Ella Vevang Montgomery **Front row from left:** Henry Hanson Sr., Julius Vevang, Lawrence Vevang, Elmer Vevang, Ingvald Vevang

Elmer Vevang, Selmer Vevang, John Ed Montgomery

Johnny Montgomery, Bruce Watkins, Cheryl Watkins, Serina Montgomery

Bonita Vevang, Serina Montgomery, Larry Vevang

Bruce Watkins and Douglas Hanson

Lorraine Harriet Hanson died on May 10, 1947, at age 14

Lawrence Vevang at his niece's grave

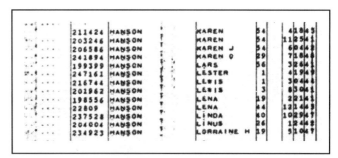

South Dakota Death Notice

A Western Union Telegram sent from Selmer to Myrtle
"Lorraine died, call Laura today, also me for ride."

Pallbearers at Lorraine's Funeral
From left: Lawrence Vevang, Melvin Hanson, Elmer Vevang, Albert Hanson, Ingvald Vevang, and Carl Hanson

Serina Montgomery

Visiting the Iver Vevang family in South Dakota
From left: John Ed, Alida, Serina, and Johnny

On a Summer Day in about 1948

Iver Vevang is sitting on the right. Ingvald Vevang, John Ed Montgomery, and Lawrence Vevang are laying in front (left to right). Sitting on left: Serina Montgomery, Alberta Syverson Vevang, Linda Vevang, Larry Vevang, Margaret Pitzl Vevang, Bonita Vevang, and Serina Hustad Vevang is sitting behind the tree.

Vevang Family Reunion in 1949

Standing from left: Myrtle Vevang Watkins holding James Watkins, Charles Watkins holding Marilyn Watkins, Alida Vevang, Margaret Pitzl Vevang, Alberta Syverson Vevang, Serina Hustad Vevang, Iver Vevang, Henry Hanson Sr., and Lawrence Vevang. **Front from left:** Larry Vevang, Bruce Watkins, Douglas Hanson, Bonita Vevang, and Laura Vevang Hanson

Standing from left: Myrtle Vevang Watkins, Charles Watkins, Ingvald Vevang, Margaret Pitzl Vevang, Alberta Syverson Vevang, Serina Hustad Vevang, Iver Vevang, Henry Hanson Jr.
Front from left: Alida Vevang holding Marilyn Watkins, Bruce Watkins, Douglas Hanson, Laura Vevang Hanson holding James Watkins, Bonita Vevang, Larry Vevang, and Henry Hanson Sr.

Twins
James Alan Watkins and
Marilyn Louise Watkins
born June 23, 1948 to
Myrtle and Charles Watkins

They are pictured with their
grandparents, Iver and Serina

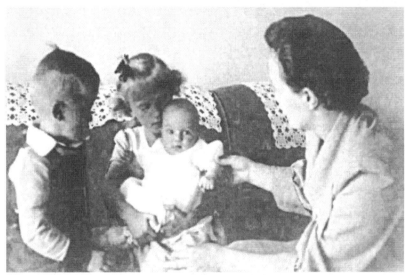

Pamela Jean Vevang
born July 1, 1949
to Ingvald and Alberta Vevang

Dennis, Linda holding Pam, Alberta

Serina Hustad Vevang
with her great-grandchildren,
Sonja Danielson and Ronald Danielson

Seated on couch from left: Bonita Vevang, Iver Vevang, Serina Hustad Vevang and Linda Vevang
Front from left: Dennis Vevang, Douglas Hanson, and Larry Vevang

From left: Ingvald Vevang, Alberta Syverson Vevang, Margaret Pitzl Vevang,
Lawrence Vevang, Selmer Vevang, Serina Hustad Vevang, and Iver Vevang

Iver and Serina at Ingvald's Webster home in their later years

November 25, 1951
Serina at the Ingvald Vevang home with Pamela and Dennis

Serina and Iver at the Elmer Vevang family home in Roslyn.
They lived on Hamilton Avenue.

OBITUARY

Serina Hustad Vevang

Mrs. Serina Hustad Vevang, youngest child of the late Mr. and Mrs. Hans Hustad, was born in Hustad, Norway February 10, 1872. She arrived in America in September 1892 at the age of 20. On June 1, 1896, she was united in marriage to Iver Vevang at the Grenville Lutheran Church with Rev. Johannes Granskou officiating.

The year of their marriage the newlyweds settled on a farm three miles southwest of Roslyn. Four years later this was sold and the present farm in Nutley Township was purchased. Here Mrs. Vevang lived with her husband for 42 years, giving birth to twelve children: experiencing the sorrow of her son, Edvin, dying at the age of two, and her son Jacob, at the age of two days. In this home, she also had the joy and work of rearing ten living children. On March 7, 1942, Mr. and Mrs. Vevang retired from the farm to make their home in Roslyn, South Dakota.

In her busy near-pioneer life, Mrs. Vevang always found time to do what she could for her church realizing the importance of the teaching of God in helping her and her family.

At 2:45 Sunday morning, January 20, 1952, she died at the age of 79 years, 11 months, and 20 days, leaving to mourn her passing her 86-year-old husband, Iver, one brother, Thomas, ten children, 25 grandchildren, and three great-grandchildren. Surviving children are: Julius of Watertown; Mrs. Ed Olson (Hilda), Minneapolis; Elmer, Roslyn; Ingvald, Webster; Selmer, Galesville, Wisconsin; Mrs. Henry M. Hanson (Laura), Webster; Mrs. John Ed Montgomery (Ella), Rocky Mount, Virginia; Alida, Roslyn; Mrs. Charles Watkins (Myrtle) Western Springs, Illinois; Lawrence, Roslyn.

Funeral services were held at the Roslyn Lutheran Church at two o'clock on January 25th. Pallbearers were Mike Stavig, Ingvald Nerland, Henry Baukol, John Gullickson, Jake Schad and Ted Gilbertson. Out of town friends and relatives attending the services were: Mrs. Abel Hellevang, Mrs. R. Herigstad, Mr. and Mrs. Elmer Hustad and Alton, Mrs. Martin Olson, Mr. and Mrs. Melvin Hanson, Arne Hellevang all of Sisseton; Mr. and Mrs. Elmer Holm, Waubay; Mrs. Eddie Berg of Sioux Falls; Mr. and Mrs. I.H. Woodworth of Webster, All the sons and daughters were present and five (out-of-state) grandchildren, Mrs. Don Danielson, Viola Olson and Darlis Vevang of Minneapolis: Warren and Allen Vevang of Moorhead, Minnesota.

Serina Hustad Vevang's Funeral
January 25, 1952

Serina died at the age of 79

Iver and Serina are buried in the
Roslyn Lutheran Church Cemetery near
Roslyn, South Dakota

Ella Vevang Montgomery's handwritten obituary of her mother

Mrs. Serina Hustad Vevang

youngest child of the late Mrs. & Mrs. Hans Hustad

was born in Hustad, Norway

February 10, 1872. She arrived

in America in September 1892

at the age of 20.

On June 1st 1896 she

she was united in marriage

to Iver Vevang, at the Grenville

Lutheran Church, Pastor John

Gronshow officiating.

The year of their marriage

the newly-weds settled on a farm

some three miles south west of

Roslyn.

Four years later this farm was

sold and the present home farm

purchased.

In this farm home Mrs. Vevang

lived with her husband for 42 years,

giving birth to 12 children, experiencing

the sorrow of having her son

II

Edwin die at the age of 2 and
and son Jacob at the age of 2 days.

In this home she also had
the joy and the work of rearing
her 10 living children.

On march 7, 1942, Mr. + Mrs.
Vevang retired from the farm to
make their home in Roslyn.

In her busy, near pioneer
life Mrs. Vevang always found
time to do what she could for her
church realizing the importance
of the teachings of God in
helping her and her family.

At 2:45 o'clock, Sunday
morning, January 20, 1952
Serina Hustad Vevang died,
leaving to mourn her passing
her 86 year old husband, Iver.
One brother Thomas, 10 children
25 grandchildren and 3 great-

III

children,

The surviving children are;

Julius	— Watertown
Hilda, Mrs Ed Olson	Minneapolis
Elmer	Roslyn
Ingvald	Webster
Selmer	Gilesville, Wis.
Laura; Mrs. Henry Houson	Webster
Ella; Mrs J. E. Montgomery	Rocky mount, Va
Alida	Roslyn
Myrtle, Mrs Chas Watkins	— Western Spring Ill!
Lawrence	Roslyn

Besides her large family mrs. Evang leaves to mourn her passing a large number of relatives, neighbors and friends.

Saying Goodbye to Serina

Five Vevang Brothers
Elmer Vevang, Lawrence Vevang, Julius Vevang, Ingvald Vevang, Selmer Vevang

Five Vevang Sisters
Hilda Olson, Laura Hanson, Ella Montgomery, Alida Vevang, Myrtle Watkins

From left in back: Allen Vevang, Elmer Vevang, Warren Vevang, Julius Vevang, Selmer Vevang, Lawrence Vevang, Edwin Olson, Ingvald Vevang, Henry Hanson Sr. and Henry Hanson Jr.
Front from left: Larry Vevang, Dennis Vevang, and Douglas Hanson

Warren Vevang, Darlis Vevang, and Allen Vevang

Back: Darlis Vevang, Rosalie Olson Danielson, Viola Olson
Front: Linda Vevang and Bonita Vevang

From left: Rosalie Olson Danielson, Hilda Vevang Olson, Laura Vevang Hanson, Evelyn Miller Olson, Alida Vevang, Ella Vevang Montgomery, Hazel Gilbertson Vevang, Myrtle Vevang Watkins, Viola Olson, Margaret Pitzl Vevang, Elna Olson Vevang, Darlis Vevang and Alberta Syverson Vevang
Front: Linda Vevang and Bonnie Vevang

From left: Linda Vevang, Myrtle Vevang Watkins, Pamela Vevang, Alberta Syverson Vevang, Viola Olson, Darlis Vevang, Ella Vevang Montgomery, and Rosalie Olson Danielson

Playing in the Snow

Myrtle and Ella are ready to throw snowballs at their suspicious brother, Elmer

Myrtle Vevang Watkins and Ella Vevang Montgomery

Summertime

July 4th, 1953
A family gathering on the Vevang farm

Back row: Garry, Gordon, and Norma Syverson (Alberta Vevang's brother), Ingvald Vevang, Charles Watkins, Myrtle Vevang Watkins, Elna Olson Vevang, Alida Vevang, Iver Vevang, Alberta Syverson Vevang, Henry Hanson Sr., and Laura Vevang Hanson **Front row:** Pamela Vevang, Bonita Vevang, Unidentified, Dennis Vevang, Larry Vevang, Bruce Watkins, Doug Hanson, Sonja Danielson, and Linda Vevang **Seated:** Unidentified, Allen Vevang, Henry Hanson Jr., Warren Vevang, Elmer Vevang, and Lawrence Vevang

Henry Hanson Sr., Ingvald Vevang,
Elmer Vevang, and Lawrence Vevang

**William Lee Montgomery born July 10, 1953
to Ella and John Ed Montgomery**

Iver's Last Days

Iver with his sons: Ingvald, Lawrence, and Selmer

James Watkins, Alida, Iver,
Marilyn Watkins, and Myrtle

In back from left: Warren Vevang, Unidentified, Henry Hanson Sr., Arent Hoines, Henry Hanson Jr., Jenny Olson, Elna Olson Vevang, Mrs. Gullickson (who lived next door to the Vevang's in Roslyn), and Ida Beline Holm Hoines (a first cousin of the Vevang siblings through Serina Hustad Vevang's sister, Beret Hustad Holm)

In back of Iver from left: Lawrence Vevang and Anna Melina Oland Olson (Elna Olson Vevang's mother)

In front from left: Larry Vevang, Bonita Vevang, Alida Vevang, Pamela Vevang on Iver's lap, Linda Vevang, Laura Vevang Hanson, Unidentified, Alberta Syverson Vevang

The End of an Era

Iver passes away at the age of 88

Following is a letter written by Selmer to his brothers and sisters. The letter is about the last wishes their father had. Selmer had just been with his dad and had given him his Holy Communion. Iver told his family that he was looking forward to his passing on. Selmer, along with Alida, talked with Iver about his last wishes. On the morning that Selmer left for home, he told his father that he was a good father to them all. Iver said that he tried his best with his family.

Seattle 88, Washington
6304 Ryan Street,
December 18, 1953

Dear folks:
Being this is a letter to be sent out to all my brothers and sisters, I am
using the easiest method, which will be the mimo machine.
I returned, from a visit with dad, yesterday morning. Had a verynice trip and
was pleased to hear from Alida and Elmer that dad had improved. He still spends
most of the time in bed, with the best of care from Alida. He was active in his
mind and had many questions about many things, some of the distant past and
some about the present time.
I gave him the Holy Communion on Monday evening. He was pleased about being
able to receive the Sacrament. In his conversation he was looking forward to his
passing as do most Christians, with the calm assurance that it is to be expected.
The morning I took my leave from him I thanked him for being a good father to us
all, and told him it was my prayer that God would bless him. His answer was that
he had tried his best with his family.
I think we will all agree that that "best of his" has been very good for us
all.
With Alida with me in the room, I asked him who he would like to serve as the
administrator of whatever property he might leave. I also asked him about a number of other things, and I was surprised to note his tinking on these things we
had simply let drift.
I then arranged the following items. I trust you will look upon these matters
in the spirit in which I arranged them. Some of these matters were requested by
dad, others were suggested to him by me.
He told me he wanted Elmer to serve as the administrator. I then typed a
paper to the effect that it was dad's wish to have Elmer serve as the administrtor.
Dad signed this paper. In order to avoid the costs of lawyers and the probate
court, the $3,000.00 note dad has from Lawrence and the two shares he has in the
Roslyn creamery, were assigned to Elmer. Dad signed both these papers also. These
papers state whatever may be left is to be divided equally among dad's living
children by Elmer.
It was also agreed that Elmer is to receive any payment Lawrence may make on
this note, he will then deposit these payments to dad's checking account to be
used by Alida as in the past. This way we may be able to be sure Alida and dad
have whatever money they may need.
Alida and I then asked him about the different things in the house, such as
heirlooms. Alida then showed him most of these items which she thought to be
hairlooms. With some of the articles dad had very difinit ideas as to who he
wanted to give them to. With others Alida and I suggested who should receive
them in order to give some to each. None of these things have any monetary
value but I am sure we will all value them for sentimental reasons, be they in
our own homes or the homes of our brothers or sisters. By doing this this way
we may have the remembrance that dad gave them to us. I was pleased to note that
dad seemed to enjoy it as the different items were showed him and as it was assigned
to the different ones of his children.
The things we have given the folks may be taken back by the giver, or that
person may give it to someone else. In the event that item was to be left in the
house, it was to belong to Alida, and not to be claimed later on.
Here is the list:
Julius ————— Dad's and Mother's wedding present cup.
One wall plate
Hilda ————— Family Bible and Song book,
Small white rocker
I cup and saucer

```
Elmer ————— 1 cut glass jelly dish.
               1 table cleaner set

Ingvald ————— Cup (wedding present )

Selmer ————— 1 covered potatoe dish
               watch (not working)

Laura ————— Spinning wheel
               1 cut glass butter dish and sugar bowl

Ella ————— Old picture album (music box one)

Alida ————— Big rocker
               Cut glass fruit dish
               Cup and saucer

Myrtle ————— Silver butter dish (wedding present)

Lawrence ————— Farm picture
               Clock

Grandchildren
    Rosalie ————— 1 fancy sugar spoon
    Viola ————— Norwegian wall plate

    Darlis ————— Dad's and Mother's wedding picture

    Henry Jr. ————— Butter knife and sugar spoon

    Beverley ————— Cake and meat fork

    Serina ————— Gravy Ladle

   One spoon each to Bonnie, Linda and Chyrel.
```

Doilies and hand-work to be given to grandchildren as Alida may determine. Same with any remaining fancy dishes.

The silver set, the folks received for their Silver Wedding, consisting of nine forks, nine spoons and nine knives, (a few items missing) to be divided one set to each of us except Alida who said she would sooner have a large spoon in place of one of these sets.

You may think I should not have done the things I did in these matters but in my work, I have seen misunderstandings enter families, where these things have been left to drift or to chance.

If dad had been more demonstrative in expressing his feelings I am sure he would mention his deep love for us all. There is no doubt in my mind but that the greatest thing God has given us all through our parents, is the respect we have for that which is right in the eyes of God. I remember so well mother saying one time, "I have a nice family and they all married nice people". I know we will all agree with this sentiment, especially about those we married. In behalf of dad, I thank you in-laws, for your kindness toward the folks and toward us all.

        Love to you all,   Sam.

Long Time Resident of Roslyn Area Dies

Reporter and Farmer
Webster, South Dakota

Long Time Resident Of Roslyn Area Dies

(Roslyn News)

Iver Vevang, long time resident of Roslyn and vicinity, passed away at his home Sunday evening at 5:15 at the age of 88 years. He had been in failing health since last October and his daughter Alida has been caring for him. His wife preceded him in death in January of 1951.

Funeral services are being held this afternoon (Thursday) at 2 o'clock from the Roslyn Lutheran church with Rev. O. M. Simundson, a former pastor, officiating

He is survived by ten children, Julius of Watertown, Mrs. Ed Olson (Hilda) of Minneapolis, Ingvald and Mrs. H. M. Hanson (Laura) of Webster, Rev. Selmer of Seattle, Wash., Mrs. John Montgomery (Ella) of Rocky Mount, Va., Mrs. Charles Watkins (Myrtle) of Chicago, Ill., and Elmer, Lawrence and Alida of Roslyn. Two sons preceded him in death also.

Iver Vevang, longtime resident of Roslyn and vicinity, passed away at his home Sunday evening at 5:15, at the age of 88 years. He had been in failing health since last October and his daughter, Alida Vevang, has been caring for him. His wife, Serina Hustad Vevang, preceded him in death in January of 1952.

OBITUARY

Iver Andrew Vevang

Iver Andrew Vevang, the youngest son of Jakob and Sigrid Vevang, was born in Vevang Norway on November 23, 1865. In May of 1888, he arrived in America at the age of 22.

On June 1, 1896, he was united in marriage to Serina Hustad at the Grenville Lutheran Church by Rev. Johannes Granskou. They settled on a farm three miles southwest of Roslyn and four years later he sold his farm and bought one in Nutley Township where he and his wife lived for 42 years. While living in Nutley Township, they reared their ten children, five daughters and five sons, two sons having passed away.

In 1942 he retired from his farm and made his home in Roslyn until his death on Sunday afternoon, January 17, 1954, at 5:15 p.m. at the age of 88 years, one month and 25 days.

Funeral services were held Thursday afternoon, January 21 at 2:00 o'clock at the Roslyn Lutheran Church with Rev. O. M. Simundson, former pastor, officiating. Rev. S. Gulsvig of Britton sang the "Lord's Prayer" and Mrs. Elmer Berglund and Olga Rood sang a Norwegian song.

Burial was made in the Roslyn Cemetery. Pallbearers were four grandsons (Henry Hanson Jr., Spencer Olson, Allen and Warren Vevang), Jim Glosimodt, and Burdette Nerland. Honorary pallbearers: Ingvald Nerland, Mike Stavig, Jake Schad, Henry Baukol, Ted Gilbertson, John Gullickson.

Those attending from a distance: Milton and Magnus Stavig, Sisseton; Ed Stavig, Rosholt; Elmer Holm and Frank Rieder, Waubay; Henry Olson and Mrs. Clifford Olson, Britton.

His survivors include his ten children; Julius, Watertown; Hilda (Mrs. Ed Olson), Minneapolis; Elmer, Lawrence, Alida, Roslyn; Ingvald and Laura (Mrs. Henry M. Hanson), Webster; Selmer, Seattle, Washington; Ella (Mrs. John Ed Montgomery) Rocky Mount, Virginia; Myrtle (Mrs. Charles Watkins) Western Springs, Illinois; 26 grandchildren, four great-grandchildren. All the children were present at the funeral with the exception of Ella. His wife preceded him in death on January 20, 1952.

Standing: Henry Hanson Sr., Edwin Olson, Lawrence Vevang, Selmer Vevang, Rosalie Olson Danielson, Ingvald Vevang, Hazel Gilbertson Vevang, Hilda Vevang Olson, Julius Vevang **Seated:** Henry Hanson Jr., Allen Vevang, Laura Vevang Hanson, Evelyn Miller Olson, Myrtle Vevang Watkins, Margaret Pitzl Vevang, Alberta Syverson Vevang, Alida Vevang **Children in back row:** Linda Vevang, Larry Vevang, Dennis Vevang, Douglas Hanson **Children in front row:** Pamela Vevang, Ronald Danielson, Bonita Vevang

Standing: Laura Vevang Hanson, Elna Olson Vevang, Alida Vevang, Hazel Gilbertson Vevang, Alberta Syverson Vevang, Hilda Vevang Olson, Margaret Pitzl Vevang **Front:** Evelyn Miller Olson, Connie Olson, Rosalie Olson Danielson, Sonja Danielson, Bonnie Vevang, Linda Vevang

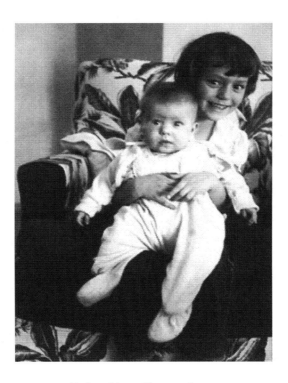

**Debra Diane Vevang born
November 10, 1954
to Ingvald and Alberta Vevang**

Debra is Iver and Serina's last grandchild.
She is seen here being held by her sister Pam.

In 1958 the Vevang Roslyn home was owned by Elmer and Elna Vevang
From left: Laura Vevang Hanson, Linda Vevang, Alida Vevang,
Hazel Gilbertson Vevang, Elna Olson Vevang, Alberta Syverson Vevang
Front from left: Pamela Vevang and Debra Vevang

Iver and Serina

Published by Day County Historical Research Committee
in *The History of Day County*, pg. 364

Iver Andrew Vevang, the youngest son of Sigrid Sivertsdatter Skotten and Jakob Jonsen Vevang, was born in Vevang, Norway, on November 23, 1865. In May of 1888 he arrived in America. Serina Hustad, youngest child of the late Mr. and Mrs. Hans Hustad, was born in Hustad, Norway, February 10, 1872. She arrived in America in September of 1892. On June 1, 1896, Serina was united in marriage to Iver Vevang at the Grenville Lutheran Church by Rev. Johannes Granskou.

The Vevangs settled on a farm three miles southwest of Roslyn and four years later they sold that farm and bought one in Nutley Township where they lived for 42 years.

To this union twelve children were born: Julius, who was born April 18, 1897, and married Hazel Gilbertson on July 3, 1921; Hilda, who was born January 12, 1899, and married Ed Olson on December 20, 1919; Elmer, who was born February 4, 1901, and married Elna Olson on November 15, 1931; Ingvald, who was born December 30, 1902, and married Alberta Syverson on December 6, 1940; Selmer, who was born August 12, 1904, and married Bernice Sholl on September 1, 1933; Laura, who was born March 18, 1908, and married Henry M. Hanson on June 14, 1932; Ella, who was born October 12, 1909, and married John Ed Montgomery on June 1, 1938; Alida, who was born December 13, 1910; Myrtle, who was born August 14, 1914, and married Charles Watkins on November 20, 1940; and Lawrence, who was born October 14, 1915, and married Margaret Rose Pitzl on December 4, 1941. Two children died in infancy.

On March 7, 1942, Mr. and Mrs. Vevang retired from the farm to make their home in Roslyn. Serina died January 20, 1952, and Iver died on January 17, 1954.

FAMILY

Iver Andrew Vevang b: 23 Nov 1865, Vevang, Norway; d: 17 Jan 1954; buried: Roslyn Lutheran Church Cemetery, Roslyn, Day County, South Dakota

Iver married **Serina Hustad Vevang** b: 10 Feb 1872, Hustad, Vevang; m: 01 Jun 1896, Grenville Lutheran Church, Day County, South Dakota; d: 20 Jan 1952; buried: Roslyn Lutheran Church Cemetery, Roslyn, Day County, South Dakota

CHILDREN
of Iver Andrew Vevang and Serina Hustad Vevang

Julius Selmer Vevang b: 18 Apr 1897; d: 15 Jul 1990; m: Hazel Mary Gilbertson b: 30 Mar 1901; d: 04 Feb 1994

Hilda Marie Vevang b: 12 Jan 1899; d: 30 Apr 1998; m: Edwin Casper Olson, b: 08 Feb 1891; d: 30 Nov 1983

Elmer Nicolai Vevang b: 04 Feb 1901; d: 15 Aug 1994; m: Elna Annette Olson b: 04 Nov 1911; d: 09 Nov 1994

Ingvald Vevang b: 30 Dec 1902; d: 17 May 1985; m: Alberta Katherine Syverson b: 21 Dec 1920; d: 03 Aug 1982

Selmer Edwin Vevang b: 12 Aug 1904; d: 29 Sep 1972; m: Bernice Marcel Sholl b: 09 Sep 1911; d: 12 Jul 2009

Edvin Vevang b: 21 Mar 1906; d: 27 Jun 1908

Laura Mathilda Vevang b: 18 Mar 1908; d: 24 Apr 1991; m: Henry Mark Hanson b: 29 Jul 1897; d: 02 May 1984

Ella Heninga Vevang b: 12 Oct 1909; d: 24 May 1999; m: John Edgar Lee Montgomery b: 02 Nov 1897; d: 26 Apr 1965

Alida Vevang b: 13 Dec 1910; d: 23 Aug 1971

Jacob Vevang b: 19 Jul 1912; d: 21 Jul 1912

Myrtle Hazel Vevang b: 14 Aug 1914; d: 22 Jul 2008; m: Charles Henry Watkins b: 21 Mar 1913; d: 11 Mar 2004

Lawrence Arthur Vevang b: 14 Oct 1915; d: 03 Oct 2016; m: Margaret Rose Pitzl b: 18 Feb 1919; d: 15 Aug 2020

CHAPTER III

JULIUS

Born
April 18, 1897
Vevang Family Farm
Raritan Township, Day County, SD

Died
July 15, 1990
Watertown, Codington County, SD
Laid to rest in Roslyn Lutheran Cemetery, Roslyn, SD

1898. Julius at one year old

JULIUS was the first child

born to Iver and Serina Vevang on April 18, 1897. Serina gave birth to Julius in their home at the age of 25, and Iver at the age of 31. At the time, Iver and Serina made their home on a farm in Raritan Township, Day County, South Dakota. Julius was baptized on May 16, 1897.

1908. Julius at age ten

No.	Barnets Navn.	Fødselsdatum.	Daabsdatum.	Forældrenes Navne.
1	Josefine Elise	22 Jan.	14 Mars	Nikolai og Bea Arntsen
2	Julius Selmer	18 April	16 Mai	Iver og Serina Vevang
3	Helen	10 Mars	16 Mai	Mathias og Aline Herland
4	Ole	18 April	7 Juni	Jørgen og Anna Nalum

U.S. Evangelical Lutheran Church in America Church Records

Sponsors: Lars and Maren Stavig, Magnus Stavig, and Ericka Hustad

The Twelfth United States Federal Census taken in 1900
Raritan Township, Day County, South Dakota

As noted in the Twelfth United States Federal Census taken in 1900, Julius was included in this census as living in Raritan Township, Day County, South Dakota. Hilda Marie was born in 1899, and shortly after this census the family of four moved to the Vevang family farm in Nutley Township.

The Thirteenth United States Federal Census taken in 1910
Nutley Township, Day County, South Dakota

Vevang Sever A.	Head	M	M	W	44	
Ferina	Wife	F		W	38	
Julius	Son	M		W	12	
Hilda	Daughter	F		W	11	
Elmer	Son	M		W	9	
Ingvald	Son	M		W	7	
Selmer	Son	M		W	5	
Laura	Daughter	F		W	2	
Ella	Daughter	F		W	6/12	
Gaara Halvor	Lodger	M		W	36	

By 1910, Julius was twelve years old, the oldest of seven children.

Julius was confirmed in 1911, at the age of 14

in the Lutheran Christian faith in the Roslyn Lutheran Church

1914. Julius at age 17

—1911—
William Henry Sunde
Alfred Thorwald Hagen
Sedolf Dedrick Danielson
Herman Aastrem
Cornell Oliver Haaseth
Ludvig Bernard Sunde
Julius Selmer Vevang
Olger Julius Loseth
Johnnie Clarence Arntson
Selmer Alfred Farmen
Ole Fredrick Haagenson
Helen Olette Brunsvik
Olga Josefine Loseth-Haaseth
Agnes Mina Hustad-Hustad
Ellen Anderson-Olson

1911. Julius and his brother Ingvald

Julius was registered for the United States World War I

Three registrations occurred for World War I between 1917 and 1918.

The first was held in June of 1917 for men ages 21-31.

The second was held June 5, 1918 for men who turned 21 since the first registration.

The third started in September of 1918.

Julius registered for the second draft on June 5, 1918, as he turned 21 in April.

U.S. World War I Draft Registration Cards 1917-1918

Julius Selmer Vevang

5th Air Service

Recruiting Squadron

Fort Wayne, Michigan

November 1918

Julius left the farm at the age of 21, but he was included in the 1920 census as living in the Iver Vevang household when he was 23. The only child not in the house was Hilda, as she married in 1919. Julius was stationed in Detroit, Michigan, serving in the United States Army. He was there for six months. Once he was discharged, he moved to Watertown, South Dakota.

Julius in 1918 at age 21

Julius is sixth from left in the kneeling row.

The Fourteenth United States Federal Census taken in 1920
Nutley Township, Day County, South Dakota

Vevang Iver A.	Head	1	O	m	m	w	54
, Serina	Wife				f	w	47
, Julius S.	Son				m	w	23
, Elmer L.	Son				m	w	18
, Engvald	Son				m	w	17
, Selmer	Son				m	w	15
, Fauna M.	Daughter				f	w	11
, Ella H.	Daughter				f	w	10
, Alida	Daughter				f	w	9
, Myrtle H.	Daughter				f	w	5
, Lawrence A.	Son				m	w	4 3/12

HAZEL MARY GILBERTSON

Born
March 30, 1901
Webster, Day County, SD

Died
February 4, 1994
Webster, Day County, SD
Laid to rest in Roslyn Lutheran Cemetery, Roslyn, SD

Hazel grew up in the Roslyn area. Julius and Hazel made their home in Watertown, South Dakota. Julius was already working in Watertown for the Minneapolis and St. Louis Railroad as a machinist, where he remained for 49 years. Hazel worked as a salesclerk in Schaller's Department Store, as noted in the City of Watertown Directory. Their vocations are also noted in the 1930 census of Watertown, Codington County, South Dakota.

Julius and Hazel moved to Webster after their retirement, where they built an identical house, the same as they had in Watertown. He was a member of the American Legion. Julius died on July 15, 1990, in Watertown, South Dakota, at the age of 93. Hazel died on February 4, 1994, at the age of 92. They had no children.

JULIUS & HAZEL VEVANG

Married July 3, 1921
Watertown, Codington County, South Dakota

RECORD OF MARRIAGE

South Dakota State Board of Health

HUSBAND	WIFE
JULIUS S. VEVANG	HAZEL GILBERTSON
WATERTOWN, CODINGTON COUNTY	ROSLYN, DAY COUNTY
AGE 24	AGE 20
AMERICAN	AMERICAN
BACHELOR	MAIDEN

The Fifteenth United States Federal Census taken in 1930
Watertown, Codington County, South Dakota

State _South Dakota_			Incorporated place _Watertown city_				Form 15-4 DEPARTMENT OF COMMERCE—BUREAU OF THE CENSUS FIFTEENTH CENSUS OF THE UNITED STATES: 1930 POPULATION SCHEDULE					
County _Codington_			Ward of city _First_	Block No.								
711	30	32	Vevang, Julius S.	Head	R	22.	R	No	M	W	32	
			Hazel M.	Wife-H			V	F	W	28		

Julius attended engineering school in Austin, Minnesota.

J. S. Vevang
AUTO SPEC.

Watertown, S. D.

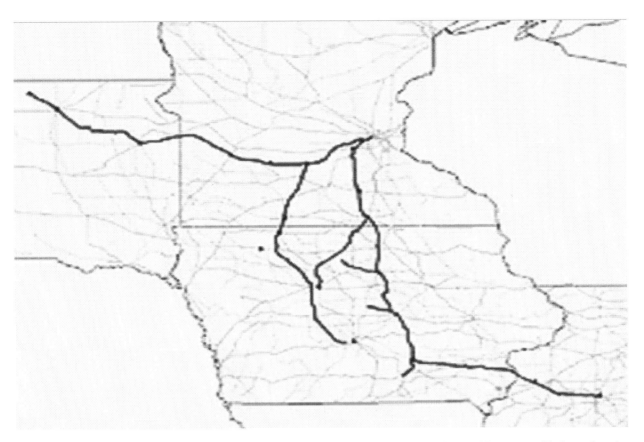

A map of the Minneapolis and St. Louis Railroad as shown around the time Julius began his career with the railroad. Bold black lines mark the tracks through South Dakota, Minnesota, and Iowa.

Train derailment near Morton, Minnesota in 1946

These photos were taken by Julius and are displayed on a story board in the Vevang home in Roslyn.

 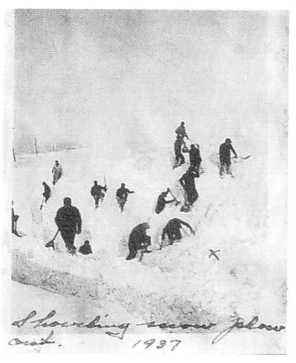

A train off the tracks during a 1937 snow storm

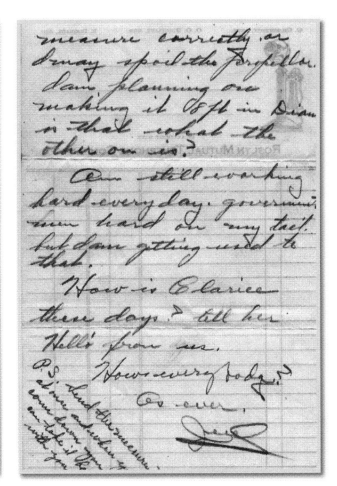

A letter was written on the back of this statement invoice from Julius to his brother, Ingvald. Dimensions were requested so that Julius could start working on the propeller for the boat he was making. While speaking with Lawrence in 2016, Lawrence referred to Julius' boat being made.

Julius was skilled in building things. He built the wind-powered battery charger that sat on the Vevang granary roof for many years before being brought down and placed on the ground. The battery charger is still on the farm as a tribute to Julius' talent. Julius built other items over the years.

OBITUARY

Julius Selmer Vevang

The funeral for Julius Vevang, 93, of Webster was Friday at St. John's Lutheran Church in Webster. The Rev. Vernon Severson officiated. Casket bearers were Willie Kungel, Alden Hanson, Larry Vevang, Jerry Forslund, Jim Dedrickson and Kimberly Dedrickson. Soloist was Milo Nielsen and organist was Phyllis Hanse. Mr. Vevang died Sunday, July 15, 1990, at Jenkins Methodist Home in Watertown.

Julius Selmer Vevang was born April 18, 1897, to Iver and Serina (Hustad) Vevang in Raritan Township, Day County, South Dakota. He was baptized and confirmed at Roslyn Lutheran Church. He attended country school in Nutley Township. He served during World War I in the U.S. Army and was stationed in Michigan. After his discharge he moved to Watertown. He worked for the Minneapolis and St. Louis Railroad.

He married Hazel Gilbertson on July 3, 1921, at Watertown. They lived there until his retirement from the railroad after 49 years of service. For the past 20 years they had lived in Webster. He was a member of St. John's Lutheran Church in Webster. He was also a member of the Herbert McKennett Post No. 40 American Legion.

Survivors include his wife of Webster: two brothers, Elmer Vevang and Lawrence Vevang, both of Roslyn; and four sisters, Hilda Olson of Minneapolis, Ella Montgomery of Rocky Mount, Va., Mrs. Charles (Myrtle) Watkins of Ocala, Fla., and Laura Hanson of Webster. He was preceded in death by his parents, four brothers and one sister.

Julius was laid to rest in Roslyn Lutheran Cemetery in Roslyn, South Dakota

IN MEMORY OF
JULIUS VEVANG
APRIL 18, 1897 - JULY 15, 1990

JULIUS SELMER VEVANG WAS BORN ON APRIL 18, 1897 TO IVER AND SERINA HUSTAD VEVANG ON A FARM SOUTHEAST OF ROSLYN, DAY COUNTY, SOUTH DAKOTA. HE WAS BAPTISED AND CONFIRMED AT THE ROSLYN LUTHERAN CHURCH. HE ATTENDED COUNTRY SCHOOL IN HUTLEY TOWNSHIP NEAR HIS HOME. HE SERVED DURING WORLD WAR I IN THE U. S. ARMY AND WAS STATIONED IN MICHIGAN.

AFTER HIS DISCHARGE FROM THE ARMY, JULIUS MOVED TO WATERTOWN, SOUTH DAKOTA WHERE HE WORKED FOR THE MINNEAPOLIS & ST. LOUIS RAILROAD. HE MARRIED HAZEL GILBERTSON ON JULY 3, 1921 AT WATERTOWN. THE COUPLE RESIDED IN WATERTOWN UNTIL HIS RETIREMENT FROM THE RAILROAD AFTER 49 YEARS OF SERVICE. THE COUPLE MADE THEIR HOME IN WEBSTER FOR THE PAST 20 YEARS.

JULIUS WAS A MEMBER OF ST. JOHN'S LUTHERAN CHURCH IN WEBSTER AND THE HERBERT MCKENNETT POST   AMERICAN LEGION.

HE PASSED AWAY ON SUNDAY, JULY 15, 1990 AT WATERTOWN, SOUTH DAKOTA AT THE AGE OF 93.

HE IS SURVIVED BY HIS WIFE OF WEBSTER; 2 BROTHERS, ELMER VEVANG & LAWRENCE VEVANG BOTH OF ROSLYN, S. DAK.; 4 SISTERS, MRS. HILDA OLSON OF MINNEAPOLIS, MN, MRS. ELLA MONTGOMERY OF ROCKY MOUNT, VA, MRS. CHARLES (MYRTLE) WATKINS OF OCALA, FL & MRS. LAURA HANSON OF WEBSTER, SD; AND SEVERAL NIECES & NEPHEWS. HE WAS PRECEDED IN DEATH BY HIS PARENTS, 2 BROTHERS & 1 SISTER.

SERVING AT THE SERVICE

PASTOR   VERNON E. SEVERSON
ORGANIST   PHYLLIS HANSE
SOLOIST   MILO NIELSEN
USHERS   OSCAR SIMONSON & JASPER FOSHEIM
SERVING LUNCH   WOMEN OF ST. JOHN'S
MINISTERS   ALL WHO HAVE COME

CASKET BEARERS

WILLIE KUNGEL, ALDEN HANSON, LARRY VEVANG, JERRY FORSLUND, JIM & KIM DEDRICKSON.

SERVICES
ST. JOHN'S LUTHERAN CHURCH
WEBSTER, SOUTH DAKOTA

FRIDAY, JULY 20, 1990   10:30 A.M.

THE FUNERAL SERVICE

ORGAN PRELUDE
ORDER FOR BURIAL OF THE DEAD   PAGES 206-211
LITURGY #3 & #4   PAGE 206
ENTRANCE HYMN   "WHAT A FRIEND"   NO. 439
"THE LITURGY OF THE WORD"   PAGE 207
LESSONS: JOB 19:23-27
          I CORINTHIANS 15:12-27
GOSPEL: JOHN 11:17-27
VOCAL SOLO   "HEAVEN IS MY HOME"
SERMONETTE "IF MORTALS DIE, WILL THEY LIVE AGAIN"
                                JOB 14:14A
VOCAL SOLO   "HOW GREAT THOU ART"
THE CREED   PAGE 209
THE PRAYERS   PAGE 209
THE COMMENDATION
HYMN   "AMAZING GRACE"   NO. 448
ORGAN POSTLUDE

REFRESHMENTS - TO BE SERVED IN THE CHURCH DINING ROOM IMMEDIATELY FOLLOWING THE FUNERAL SERVICE.

INTERMENT

BURIAL WILL BE IN THE ROSLYN LUTHERAN CEMETERY WITH MILITARY RITES BY RUDOLPH BAUKOL POST 253 AMERICAN LEGION.

OBITUARY

Hazel Mary Gilbertson Vevang

Hazel Vevang, 92, of Webster, died Feb. 4, 1994 at Lake Area Hospital in Webster. Funeral services were Feb. 7 at St. John's Lutheran Church in Webster with Rev. Vernon Severson officiating. Casket bearers were Larry Vevang, Burdette Nerland, Noel Nerland, Harlan Storley and Larry Smith. Organist was Suzanne Olawsky and soloist was Milo Nielsen. Ushers were Clarence Dedrickson and Jasper Fosheim. Burial was in the Roslyn Lutheran Cemetery near Roslyn.

Hazel Mary Gilbertson was born March 30, 1901 to Henry and Mathilda (Emberson) Gilbertson in Webster. She was baptized and confirmed at Roslyn Lutheran Church. The family lived in Webster and at Milbank for a short time, and she attended school in both places. In 1915, the family moved to Roslyn. She worked as a clerk at Monson's Store.

She married Julius Vevang July 3, 1921, in Watertown. After their marriage the couple made their home in Watertown. He was employed with the railroad. After his retirement they moved to Webster, where she had resided for the past 25 years. He died in July of 1990. For the past several years she had resided at Bethesda Home. She was a member of St. John's Lutheran Church. Survivors include one sister, Thelma Nerland of Roslyn. She was preceded in death by her parents, her husband and three sisters.

Hazel Vevang

Hazel Vevang, 92, of Webster, died Feb. 4, 1994 at Lake Area Hospital in Webster.

Funeral services were Feb. 7 at St. John's Lutheran Church in Webster with Rev. Vernon Severson officiating.

Casket bearers were Larry Vevang, Burdette Nerland, Noel Nerland, Harlan Storley and Larry Smith.

Organist was Suzanne Olawsky and soloist was Milo Nielsen. Ushers were Clarence Dedrickson and Jasper Fosheim.

Burial was in the Roslyn Lutheran Cemetery near Roslyn.

Hazel Mary Gilbertson was born March 30, 1901 to Henry and Mathilda (Emberson) Gilbertson in Webster. She was baptized and confirmed at Roslyn Lutheran Church. The family lived in Webster and at Milbank for a short time, and she attended school in both places. In 1915, the family moved to Roslyn. She worked as a clerk at Monson's Store.

She married Julius Vevang July 3, 1921, in Watertown. After their marriage the couple made their home in Watertown. He was employed with the railroad. After his retirement they moved to Webster, where she had resided for the past 25 years. He died in July of 1990. For the past several years she had resided at Bethesda Home.

She was a member of St. John's Lutheran Church.

Survivors include one sister, Thelma Nerland of Roslyn.

She was preceded in death by her parents, her husband and three sisters.

Dinner guests at the Elmer Vevang home following the funeral of Julius Vevang were Mr. and Mrs. Jim Miller, Viola Fellows, Rosalie Danielson, Hilda Olson, Mr. and Mrs. Jerry Forslund, Allen Vevang and Margaret Vevang and son Larry, all of Minneapolis; Jim Dedrickson, Keith Dedrickson, Alicia and Breanna, Sioux Falls; Mr. and Mrs. Claude Nelson, Sisseton; Mr. and Mrs. Elmer Nerland, Mr. and Mrs Oscar Torness of Milbank; Hazel Vevang and Laura Hanson of Webster and Lawrence Vevang.

Julius Vevang estate
1990

To settle the estate of Julius Vevang, there will be a public auction Saturday, Oct. 6, starting at 1 p.m., at 601 East Third Street in Webster. To be sold are household items, Fostoria dishes, yard tools and equipment and miscellaneous items. Paul Wagner is auctioneer and Security Bank & Trust is clerk. A listing will be published next week.

Reporter and Farmer
Webster, SD

CHAPTER IV

HILDA

Born
January 12, 1899
Iver Vevang Farm
Raritan Township, Day County, SD

Died
April 30, 1998
Edina, Hennepin County, MN
Laid to rest in Lakewood Cemetery, Minneapolis, MN

The Twelfth United States Federal Census taken in 1900
Raritan Township, Day County, South Dakota

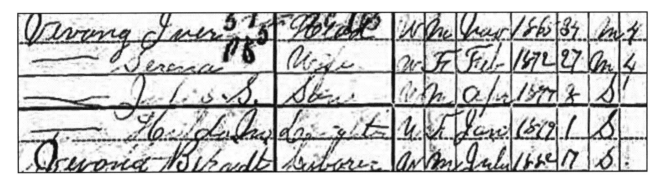

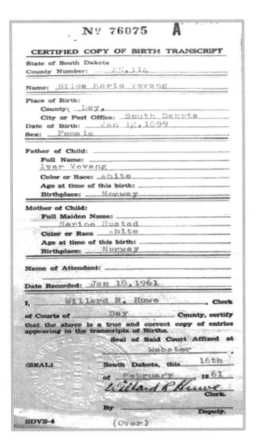

HILDA

was born in 1899 in the home of Iver and Serina in Raritan Township, Day County, South Dakota. In 1900 she lived with her father, mother and older brother, Julius. They later moved to the farm that we know as the Vevang family home.

CERTIFIED COPY OF BIRTH TRANSCRIPT

Name: Hilda Marie Vevang
Date of Birth: January 12, 1899
Place of Birth: Day County, South Dakota
Father of Child: Iver Vevang
Color or Race: White
Birthplace: Norway
Mother of Child: Serina Hustad
Color or Race: White
Birthplace: Norway
Date recorded: January 18, 1961
Certified by: Willard R. Huwe
Date of Baptism: February 19, 1899

	Dôbte.				Dôbte.		
Barnets Navn.	Fodselsdatum.	Daabsdatum.	Foreldrenes Navne.		Faddernes Navne.		
Hilda Marie	12 Jan.	19 Feb.	Iver og Serine Vevang		Thomas og Helen Hustad, Jens Hatle, Louise Stavig		

U.S. Evangelical Lutheran Church in America Church Records

Sponsors: Thomas & Helen Hustad (uncle & aunt), Jens Hatle (family friend), Louise Stavig (first cousin)

Hilda in 1908. Four more brothers were born to Iver and Serina; Elmer in 1901, Ingvald in 1902, Selmer in 1904 and Edvin in 1906. Laura was born in March of 1908 and Edvin died in June of 1908. Ella was born in 1909 and Alida in 1910. Hilda Vevang is pictured with her sister, Ella, outside of their home in 1911.

The Thirteenth United States Federal Census taken in 1910
Nutley Township, Day County, South Dakota

Vevang Iver A.	Head	M	W	44
Serina	Wife		W	35
Julius	Son	M	W	12
Hilda	Daughter	F	W	11
Elmer	Son	M	W	9
Ingvald	Son	M	W	7
Selmer	Son	M	W	5
Laura	Daughter	F	W	2
Ella	Daughter	F	W	4/12
Gaara Halvor	Lodger	M	W	36

Iver, Serina, Julius, Hilda, Elmer, Ingvald, Selmer, Laura, and Ella were in the Vevang family home in 1910.
They also had a lodger, Mr. Halvor Gaara, who was a teacher at their country school.

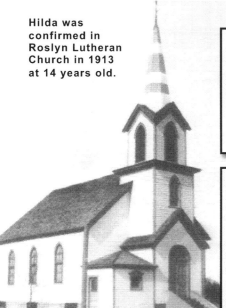

Hilda was confirmed in Roslyn Lutheran Church in 1913 at 14 years old.

—1913—
Melvin Hustad
Edward C. Hagen
Clemens Aastrom
Albert Melvin Stavig
Carl Edwin Danielson
Walter Wm. Reed

Nellie Stavig-Roach
Hilda Marie Vevang-Olson
Cora M. Kjorsvig-Wickstrom
Mabel Beatrice Sunde
Thilda Elnora Haaseth-Englund

Hilda with her school teacher, Helen Song

EDWIN CASPER OLSON

Private First Class
United States Army
World War I

Born
February 8, 1891
Nutley Township, Day County, SD

Died
November 30, 1983
Minneapolis, Hennepin County, MN
Laid to rest in Lakewood Cemetery, Minneapolis, MN

REGISTRATION CARD: Edwin Casper Olson, 26
He was a natural citizen born in Nutley Township, Day County, South Dakota. Edwin's occupation was that of a farmer, employed by himself in Nutley Township. He was exempt from draft on the grounds that he was a farmer.

Edwin is pictured in the center.

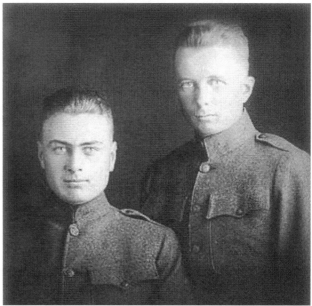

REGISTRAR'S REPORT: Edwin was of medium size with a stout build. His eyes were gray and his hair light brown. The registration card was signed and certified in Nutley Precinct, Day County, South Dakota. (Edwin was born in 1891, not in 1890 as recorded on his registration card).

Hilda Marie and Edwin Casper Olson Family History

Written by Sonja Danielson Cordray Quillen and Rosalie Olson Danielson

Hilda and Edwin's Wedding Reception at the Vevang Farm
From left: Sigvart Olson (Edwin's father), Iver Vevang (Hilda's father), Julius Vevang (Hilda's brother),
Edwin Olson, Hilda Vevang Olson, Selma Olson (Edwin's sister), Serina Hustad Vevang (Hilda's mother),
and Minnie Erickson Olson (Edwin's mother)

U.S. Evangelical Lutheran Church in America Records (1875-1940) Written in Norwegian

Groom, Edwin C. Olson (28) and Bride, Hilda M. Vevang (20) married on December 20, 1919.

Witnesses were Julius Vevang (Hilda's brother) and Selma Olson (Edwin's sister)

116

EDWIN & HILDA OLSON

Married December 20, 1919
Roslyn, Day County, South Dakota

RECORD OF MARRIAGE

South Dakota State Board of Health

HUSBAND	WIFE
EDWIN CASPER OLSON	HILDA MARIE VEVANG
ROSLYN, DAY COUNTY, SD	ROSLYN, DAY COUNTY, SD
AGE 28	AGE 20
AMERICAN	AMERICAN
BACHELOR	MAIDEN

The Fourteenth United States Federal Census taken in 1920
Nutley Township, Day County, South Dakota

	108	108	Olson	Sigvart	Head		O	m	m	w	53	m	1896	na	1895				Norway
			—	Minnie A.	Wife				f	w	58	m	1891	na	1895				Norway
			—	Edwin E.	Son			m	w	28	m							So. Dakota
			—	Selma	Daughter			f	w	24	s							So. Dakota
			—	Martin	Son			m	w	22	s							So. Dakota
			—	Alma S.	Daughter			f	w	19	s							So. Dakota
			—	Hilda M.	Daughter			f	w	20	m							So. Dakota

Spencer

Spencer and Rosalie

Hilda was the first child to leave home at just 20 years old. Her brothers, Elmer, Ingvald, Selmer, and Lawrence were about 18, 17, 15, and 4 years old, respectively. Hilda's sisters, Laura, Ella, Alida, and Myrtle were about 11, 10, 9, and 5 years old, respectively.

Hilda and Edwin Olson lived in Nutley Township, Day County, near Roslyn, South Dakota. In the 1920 census, Hilda and Ed were part of the Sigvart and Minnie A. Olson household. Also in the household were Ed's siblings, Selma (24), Martin (22), and Alma (19). Sigvart and Minnie were both born in Norway.

Sigvart and Edwin were farmers, Martin was a laborer, and Selma was a sales lady in a department store. The census notes that Hilda's father and mother, Iver and Serina, were born in Norway. It also noted that Hilda was able to speak English.

Hilda and Ed's first child, Spencer Hiram Olson, was born on October 19, 1921 on the Olson farm in Nutley Township. Their second child, Rosalie Eugene Olson, was born on March 17, 1923, also on the Olson farm. Their third child, Calvin Irving Olson, was born December 30, 1930. And their last child, Viola Delores Olson was born January 15, 1932.

The Fifteenth United States Federal Census taken in 1930
Nutley Township, Day County, South Dakota

Olson	Sigvart	Head	O				Yes	M	W	63
	Minnie	Wife W.					x	F	W	68
Olson	Edwin	Head	R		R	Yes	M	W	39
	Hilda	Wife W.					x	F	W	31
	Spencer H.	Son					x	M	W	8
	Rosalie E.	Daught			11		x	F	W	7

Edwin Olson (39) was noted as the head of the household with his wife, Hilda Olson (31), their children, Spencer H. Olson (8) and Rosalie E. Olson (7). Edwin's parents, Sigvart and Minnie, are also noted in the census.

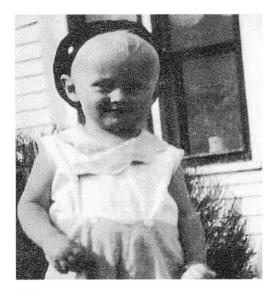

Calvin

Viola

Rosalie, Viola, and Spencer

Serina holding her granddaughter, Viola

Rosalie, Edwin, Hilda, and Spencer

Rosalie and Calvin

Calvin and Viola

Calvin and Viola

Spencer, Rosalie, and Viola were born on the Olson family farm in Nutley Township, Day County, South Dakota. Calvin was born on the Iver Vevang farm. Viola celebrated her birthday on the 16th until age 83 when she was told by the insurance representative that her date of birth didn't match her medical records and birth certificate. The official story is that she was born on the farm in the evening on the 15th and her dad didn't get to the courthouse until the next day. Hilda and Ed somehow chose the 16th as the day to celebrate her birthday.

In 1935, the Olson family decided to leave the country and move to the town of Waubay, as they could have Spencer in high school, Rosalie in seventh grade, and Calvin in first grade. Little Viola was not yet in school. Ed and Hilda could take their horses and a few cows with them, with space for a small dairy farm. Their place was on the edge of the town of Waubay. They sold milk to make their living.

Standing: Sigvart Olson, Spencer, and Hilda
Seated: Calvin and Viola
Sigvart lived with Hilda and Ed in Waubay.

Hilda tended to her children. She was involved in the Women's Circle at the Lutheran church they belonged to. Hilda was interested in sewing and would sew Rosalie's and Viola's pretty dresses, and do handwork in crochet and embroidery. Many of her pieces are still cherished. Hilda made homemade lefsa, bread and buns, cookies, and rosettes—all of which are enjoyed to this day by her great-grandchildren.

1935		
Card No. 552	Name Mrs. Hilda Olson Age 36	
Sex Female	County Day P.O. Waubay	
Color White	Town or Township Waubay Ward	
Married Yes	Occupation Do you own your home or farm { Yes No X	
Single	Birthplace Nutley Township Ancestry	
Widowed	Father's birthplace Norway	
Divorced	Mother's birthplace Norway	
Read Yes	Extent of Education 8 Gr. Graduate of	
Write Yes	Military Service: Civil War Spanish World	
Blind Deaf	State Company Regiment Division	
Insane Idiot	Maiden name of wife Year married 1919	
If foreign born, are you naturalized	Church affiliation Luthern Free Church	
Years in U.S. 36	Signed Assessor	
Years in S.D. 34	This card is a permanent record.	

122

The Sixteenth United States Federal Census taken in 1940
Waubay City, Waubay Township, Day County, South Dakota

Olson	Ed (X)	Head	0	M	W	49	
	Hilda	Wife	1	F	W	41	
	Spencer	Son	2	M	W	18	
	Rosalie	Daughter	2	F	W	17	
	Calvin	Son	2	M	W	9	
	Viola	Daughter	2	F	W	8	
Olson	Siamat	Grandfather	3	M	W	73	

In 1942, World War II was building. Spencer had finished barber school. He was working in a barbershop and living in Minneapolis, Minnesota. The Olson family decided to move to Minneapolis. Ed was employed at a defense plant. On Saturdays, Ed worked at Boyd's Furniture Transfer Co. After the war ended, Ed worked for the company full time. After retirement, Ed and Hilda purchased and renovated properties, working side by side. Rosalie completed Waba beauty school in Watertown, South Dakota, and was employed at a beauty salon as a hairdresser for six months. She acquired an allergic breakout of eczema on both hands, so she had to quit working and decided to move to Minneapolis.

Rosalie met a young army soldier stationed at Fort Snelling named Donald O. Danielson, formerly from Princeton, Minnesota. His sister, Berna Danielson, was in the women's military—WACS (Women Army Corp). Rosalie and Don fell in love and became engaged about a year later, marrying on May 2, 1944. Hilda worked a short time at Honeywell in Minneapolis. Rosalie found work, too, at the Honeywell defense plant for a couple of years. Spencer had enlisted in the U.S. Navy. His enlistment date was July 30, 1942. His release date was January 15, 1946. He was deployed to the Pacific.

Name: Spencer Hiram Olson
Gender: Male
Race: White
Age: 20
Relationship to Draftee: Self (Head)
Birthplace: Roslyn, South Dakota, USA
Birth Date: October 19, 1921
Residence Place: Minneapolis, Hennepin, Minnesota, USA
Draft Registration Date: February 15, 1942
Employer: Auto Electric Supply Company
Weight: 146
Complexion: Light
Eye Color: Blue
Hair Color: Brown
Height: 5'7"
Next of Kin: Ed Olson

Spencer H. Olson

1942
Mother and son, Hilda and Spencer

The Olson Family
Viola, Rosalie, Calvin, and Spencer
Hilda Vevang Olson and Edwin Olson

1944
Viola, Donald Danielson, Spencer, and Calvin
Minneapolis, Minnesota

1946
From left: Hilda, Calvin, Edwin, Spencer, Viola, and Rosalie holding Sonja Danielson

Christmas 1948
Standing: Calvin Olson and Donald Danielson
Middle row: Spencer Olson, Alida Vevang, and Edwin Olson
Front row: Evelyn Miller Olson, Rosalie Olson Danielson, Viola Olson, Hilda Vevang Olson

Edwin & Hilda's Golden Wedding Anniversary

1919 — 1969

Hilda and Ed

Ed and Hilda's Children
Viola, Spencer, Hilda, Edwin, Rosalie, and Calvin

Spencer, Rosalie, Evelyn Miller Olson, Donald Danielson,
Ed, Hilda, Marguerite Lee Olson, Calvin, and Viola

Robert Olson, Evelyn Miller Olson, Spencer Olson, Connie
Olson, and David Olson

Chuck Cordray, Sonja Danielson Cordray, Rosalie, Donald Danielson, and Ronald Danielson

OBITUARY

Hilda Marie Vevang Olson

Olson

Hilda M., age 99, of Mpls on April 30th. Preceded in death by husband, Edwin; sons, Spencer and Calvin; sons-in-law, Allen Fellows and Donald Danielson. Survived by daughters, Rosalie Danielson, Viola Fellows; daughters-in-law, Margie, Evelyn and her husband, Jim. Also survived by 12 grandchildren, 17 great-grandchildren, and 4 great-great-grandchildren. Services Monday 1 pm at the Morris Nilsen Chapel, 6527 Portland Ave S., Richfield. Visitation one hour prior to the service. Interment Lakewood. Deeply cherished by family and friends. Hilda will be greatly missed and fondly remembered. Memorials preferred to Nokomis Heights Lutheran Church Endowment Fund, and Alzheimer's Research in memory of her son.

Morris Nilsen Chapel
869-3226

Hilda M. Olson

Born in
Roslyn, South Dakota
January 12, 1899

Died on
April 30, 1998

At the Age of
99 Years   3 Months   18 Days

Services at
Morris Nilsen Funeral Chapel
6527 Portland Avenue South

Monday, May 4, 1998   1:00 P.M.

Clergy Officiating
Rev. Mark Nelson

Vocalists:
Richard Olson and Colleen Hiebeler

Organist: Jan Lindquist

Survived by
daughters, Rosalie Danielson and Viola Fellows; daughters-in-law, Margie and Evelyn and her husband, Jim;   twelve grand-children; seventeen great-grandchildren;   and four great great-grandchildren

Casketbearers

David Olson   Mark Olson
Kent Olson   Richard Olson
Kevin Olson   Robert Olson
            Steven Olson

Interment
Lakewood Cemetery

Hilda Marie Olson, age 99, of Minneapolis died on April 30, 1998. She was preceded in death by husband Edwin: sons, Spencer and Calvin: sons-in-law, Allen Fellows and Donald Danielson. Survived by daughters, Rosalie Danielson, Viola Fellows: daughters-in-law, Margie, Evelyn and her husband, Jim. Also survived by twelve grandchildren, 17 great-grandchildren and four great-great-grandchildren. Hilda Marie Vevang was born in Raritan Township, Day County, South Dakota, January 12, 1899, to Iver and Serina Hustad Vevang. She died at the age of 99 years, 3 months, and 18 days.

FAMILY

Hilda Marie Vevang b: 12 Jan 1899, Raritan Township, Day County, South Dakota; d: 30 Apr 1998, Edina, Hennepin County, Minnesota; buried: Lakewood Cemetery, Minneapolis, Hennepin County, Minnesota

Hilda married **Edwin Casper Olson** b: 08 Feb 1891, Nutley Township, Day County, South Dakota; m: 20 Dec 1919, Nutley Township, Day County, South Dakota; d: 30 Nov 1983, Minneapolis, Hennepin County, Minnesota; buried: Lakewood Cemetery, Minneapolis, Hennepin County, Minnesota

CHILDREN
of Hilda Marie Vevang and Edwin Casper Olson

Spencer Hiram Olson b: 19 Oct 1921, Olson farm, Nutley Township, Day County, South Dakota; d: 08 Mar 1981, Minneapolis, Hennepin County, Minnesota; buried: Lakewood Cemetery, Minneapolis, Hennepin County, Minnesota

Rosalie Eugene Olson b: 17 Mar 1923, Olson farm, Nutley Township, Day County, South Dakota; d: 11 Mar 2023, Clearwater, Pinellas County, Florida; buried: Fort Snelling National Cemetery, Minneapolis, Hennepin County, Minnesota

Calvin Irving Olson b: 30 Dec 1930, Iver Vevang farm, Nutley Township, Day County, South Dakota; d: 03 Dec 1972, Tucumcari, Quay County, New Mexico; buried: Lakewood Cemetery, Minneapolis, Hennepin County, Minnesota

Viola Delores Olson b: 15 Jan 1932, Olson farm, Nutley Township, Day County, South Dakota; d: 07 Aug 2023, Apple Valley, Dakota County, Minnesota; buried: Fort Snelling National Cemetery, Minneapolis, Hennepin County, Minnesota

SPENCER HIRAM OLSON

Born
October 19, 1921
Olson Farm
Nutley Township, Day County, SD

Died
March 8, 1981
Minneapolis, Hennepin County, MN
Laid to rest in Lakewood Cemetery, Minneapolis, MN

Spencer Hiram Olson

married

Evelyn Beatrice Miller

February 28, 1948

Minneapolis,
Hennepin County,
Minnesota

The Wedding Party

From left: Viola Olson, Rosalie Olson Danielson, Edna (Evelyn's sister), Olga (Evelyn's friend), Evelyn Miller Olson,
Spencer Olson, Calvin Olson, Jerry Forsberg, Donald Danielson, unidentified, Ring bearer in front is unidentified

Evelyn, Spencer, and Connie at the wedding of
Viola Olson and Allen Fellows in 1953.

Spencer and Evelyn with their children
David, Connie, Robert, Richard, and Kevin

From top and left to right: David, Richard,
Connie, Robert, and Kevin between his
parents, Evelyn and Spencer

OBITUARY

Spencer H. Olson

IN MEMORY OF

Spencer H. Olson

October 19, 1921 — March 8, 1981

SERVICES AT
NOKOMIS HEIGHTS LUTHERAN CHURCH
Minneapolis, Minnesota

Thursday, March 12, 1981 at 1:30 P.M.

CLERGYMAN
THE REVEREND RALPH H. ALMQUIST

INTERMENT
LAKEWOOD CEMETERY

ARRANGEMENTS WITH
LISTOE & WOLD CHAPEL

Spencer H. Olson, age 59, died on March 8th, 1981 (born October 19, 1921). Residence 6140 Morgan Ct. in Minneapolis.

Survived by wife, Evelyn; daughter Connie, Minneapolis; sons David, Robert, Richard, and Kevin, all of Minneapolis; parents, Mr. and Mrs. Edwin C. Olson, Minneapolis; sisters, Rosalie (Donald) Danielson, Richfield, and Viola Fellows, Burnsville. Preceded in death by brother, Calvin I. Olson.

Services Thursday 1:30 pm at Nokomis Heights Lutheran Church, Minneapolis, Minnesota. Memorials to Association for Alzheimer's & Related Diseases.

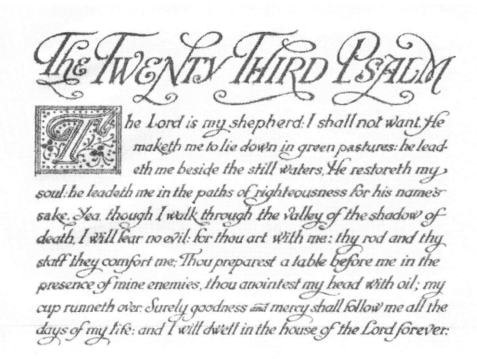

THE TWENTY THIRD PSALM

The Lord is my shepherd: I shall not want. He maketh me to lie down in green pastures: he leadeth me beside the still waters. He restoreth my soul: he leadeth me in the paths of righteousness for his name's sake. Yea, though I walk through the valley of the shadow of death, I will fear no evil: for thou art with me: thy rod and thy staff they comfort me. Thou preparest a table before me in the presence of mine enemies, thou anointest my head with oil; my cup runneth over. Surely goodness and mercy shall follow me all the days of my life: and I will dwell in the house of the Lord forever.

OBITUARY

Evelyn Beatrice Miller Olson Miller

Evelyn Beatrice Miller was born at home on October 31, 1926, to Peder and Thora Miller in Prairie Farm, Wisconsin. Thora was a first-generation immigrant, arriving in the US at the age of 13. Evelyn was the fifth of six children. She grew up in a farming community by Hay River and attended a one-room school for elementary and middle school, before going on to Clayton High School. This school was quite a distance from home. One of the stories Evelyn liked to tell was of the Armistice Day Blizzard in 1940. She and the other children were on the school bus heading home, but because of the blizzard they had to stop at farms along the way until the roads were passable. It took two days to get home!

Evelyn eventually moved to Minneapolis with her cousin, Celia, and her sister, Lily. She worked at Babson, Inc. Most weekends the girls would return home. However, one weekend she went to the Calhoun Ballroom on Lake and Hennepin instead. It was there she met Spencer Olson. From the stories told, it was mutual "love at first sight." They were married in 1948 and had five children together. They loved to go dancing and to travel. Evie loved music and would bring out her accordion to entertain at family gatherings. She was an amazing wife and mother. She was also a businesswoman, supporting her husband in the Mr. C business. Evelyn and Spencer were married for 33 years before Spencer passing in 1981.

In the early 1980s Evelyn reluctantly attended a class reunion at the request of her friends. Little did she know that here she would reconnect with an old friend, Jim Miller, whom she would eventually marry. They loved to dance, travel and go to the cabin. The cabin was without plumbing and electricity and they loved it. The annual pancake breakfast at the cabin was a highlight each year. They also loved to go snowmobiling. Evie and Jim were married for more than 20 years before Jim's passing.

Evelyn was preceded in death by her parents, siblings, husbands and one son, David. She will be remembered for her amazing strength under pressure, joy in all circumstances and her ability to laugh and have fun! She will be missed by her children, Connie Olson, Rob Olson (Joy), Rick Olson (Bonna) and Kevin Olson (Maureen); grandchildren, Stephanie Olson, Heather Olson, Alex Olson, Andy Olson, Jana Olson, Spencer Olson, Evan Olson and Brea (Olson) Petry (Alex); and great-grandchildren, Isaac, Bella, Genesis and Jeasten.

FAMILY

Spencer Hiram Olson b: 19 Oct 1921, Olson farm, Nutley Township, Day County, South Dakota; d: 08 Mar 1981, Minneapolis, Hennepin County, Minnesota; buried: Lakewood Cemetery, Minneapolis, Hennepin County, Minnesota

Spencer married Evelyn Beatrice Miller b: 31 Oct 1926, Prairie Farm, Barron County, Wisconsin; m: 28 Feb 1948, Minneapolis, Hennepin County, Minnesota; d: 5 Jan 2018, Minneapolis, Hennepin County, Minnesota; buried: Lakewood Cemetery, Minneapolis, Hennepin County, Minnesota

Spencer and Evelyn's children:
Constance Marie Olson b: 16 Oct 1949, Minneapolis, Hennepin County, Minnesota
David Bryon Olson b: 10 Feb 1952, Minneapolis, Hennepin County, Minnesota;
d: 13 Oct 2013, Minneapolis, Hennepin County, Minnesota
Robert Spencer Olson b: 15 Mar 1955, Minneapolis, Hennepin County, Minnesota
Richard Allen Olson b: 12 Feb 1960, Minneapolis, Hennepin County, Minnesota
Kevin Erick Olson b: 01 Feb 1965, Minneapolis, Hennepin County, Minnesota

Evelyn Beatrice Miller Olson married James E. Miller b: 06 Jun 1926, Clayton, Polk County, Wisconsin; m: 27 Dec 1986, Minneapolis, Hennepin County, Minnesota; d: 13 Mar 2008, Minneapolis, Hennepin County, Minnesota

CHILDREN AND GRANDCHILDREN

of Spencer Hiram Olson and Evelyn Beatrice Miller

Constance (Connie) Marie Olson

David Bryon Olson married Lee Ann Schulz: div.

David and Lee Ann's children:
Stephanie Ann Marie Olson b: 09 Sep 1982, Minneapolis, Hennepin County, Minnesota
Heather Lee Olson b: 25 Apr 1985, Minneapolis, Hennepin County, Minnesota

Stephanie Ann Marie Olson

Stephanie and Nathan David Roy Averill's child:
Jeasten Bryon Averill b: 21 Dec 2016, Grand Rapids, Kent County, Michigan

Heather Lee Olson married **Richard Ralph Calkins III** 11 Aug 2007, Minneapolis, Hennepin County Minnesota: div.

Heather and Richard's children:
Isaac Lee Calkins b: 02 Dec 2007, Minneapolis, Hennepin County, Minnesota
Isabella (Bella) Marie Calkins b: 19 May 2009, Minneapolis, Hennepin County, Minnesota

Heather's child with **Allen Jarvi**:
Genesis Jean Jarvi b: 09 Mar 2015, Grand Rapids, Itasca County, Minnesota

Isaac   Bella   Genesis

Robert Spencer Olson married **Mary Jo Flaherty** b: 01 Oct 1954, St. Paul, Ramsey County, Minnesota; m: 14 Oct 1983, Minneapolis, Hennepin County, Minnesota: div.

Robert and Mary Jo's children:
Alexander Robert Olson b: 29 Dec 1989, Minneapolis, Hennepin County, Minnesota
Andrew Robert Olson b: 14 Jan 1994, Minneapolis, Hennepin County, Minnesota; married **Emma Sand Ostby** b: 04 Jun 1993, Spicer, Kandiyohi County, Minnesota; m: 19 Aug 2023, Chaska, Carver County, Minnesota

Alexander   Andrew & Emma

Robert married **Joy Marie Shimmin** b:11 Jan 1964, Virginia, St. Louis County, Minnesota; m: 28 Apr 2001, Minneapolis, Hennepin County, Minnesota

Robert and Joy's child:
Jana Marie Olson b: 28 Nov 2004, Minneapolis, Hennepin County, Minnesota

Jana

Richard Allen Olson married **Bonna Rae Horn** b: 11 Jun 1959, Pillager, Cass County, Minnesota; m: 30 Jul 1983, Pillager, Cass County, Minnesota

Richard and Bonna's children:
Spencer David Olson b: 03 Aug 1989, Rochester, Olmsted County, Minnesota
Evan Richard Olson b: 01 Nov 1990, Minneapolis, Hennepin County, Minnesota
Brea Marie Olson b:18 Dec 1994, Minneapolis, Hennepin County, Minnesota

Spencer, Evan, and Brea

Spencer David Olson married **Samantha Nicole Crowther** b: 01 Apr 1990, adopted; m: 25 Sep 2020, Lake Harriet, Minneapolis, Hennepin County, Minnesota

Evan Richard Olson married **Jordan Marie Matesi** b: Jan 11, 1993, Flagstaff, Coconino County, Arizona; m: 21 Sep 2019, Asheville, Buncombe County, North Carolina

Evan and Jordan's children:
Lennox Winston Matesi Olson b: 27 Jan 2021, Winston-Salem, Forsyth County, North Carolina
Iona Jane Matesi Olson b: 27 Jun 2023, West Des Moines, Iowa

Brea Marie Olson married **Alex J. Petry** b: 18 Apr 1995, Minneapolis, Hennepin County, Minnesota; m: 19 Jul 2015, Semple Mansion, Minneapolis, Hennepin County, Minnesota

Brea and Alex's child:
Ayla Rae Petry b: 09 Jan 2023, Minneapolis, Hennepin County, Minnesota

From left: Spencer David Olson, Samantha Crowther, Bonna Horn Olson, Jordan Matesi-Olson (bride), Evan Olson (groom), Richard Olson, Brea Olson Petry, Alex Petry, and Sara Thornhill

Kevin Olson, Maureen Bodine, Robert Olson, Evelyn Miller, Richard Olson, Connie Olson

Kevin Erick Olson and girlfriend **Maureen Bodine**

ROSALIE EUGENE OLSON

Born
March 17, 1923
Olson Farm
Nutley Township, Day County, SD

Died
March 11, 2023
Clearwater, Pinellas County, FL
Laid to rest in Fort Snelling National Cemetery, Minneapolis, MN

Rosalie Eugene Olson

married

Donald O. Danielson

May 2, 1944

Minneapolis,
Hennepin County,
Minnesota

From left; Leon Brown, Donald Danielson, Rosalie Olson Danielson, Fern Brown, and Della Layng

Donald and Rosalie's first child,
Sonja May Danielson, was born in 1945.
Sonja was Iver and Serina's first great-grandchild.

Donald and Rosalie with Sonja

Viola with her niece, Sonja.
The little guy is a family friend.

Rosalie and Sonja holding
Ronald Danielson, born in 1949.

Standing: Evelyn Miller Olson, Calvin Olson, Alida Vevang, Hilda Vevang Olson, Viola Olson
Seated:Donald Danielson, Rosalie Olson Danielson holding Ronald Danielson.
Spencer Olson is kneeling in front and the little girl is Sonja Danielson

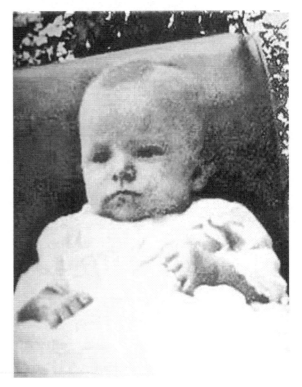

Ronald Stephan Danielson's Baptismal Day
Sponsors were Viola Olson, Alida Vevang, and Calvin Olson

Ronald and Sonja in 1954

Tinsel Decorations in the 1950s were common.
From left: Ronald, Donald, Rosalie, and Sonja

Sonja and Chuck married in 1964
and divorced in 1980

Charles J. III (Chuck) Cordray, age 66, died peacefully on February 20, 2010, after a battle with cancer. A graduate of Bloomington High School, Chuck spent his later years living in both Richfield and Orlando, where his daughters and five grandchildren live. Known for his keen wit which he retained to the end, Chuck was a sensitive, loving and fiercely loyal father, grandfather, brother, uncle and friend who will be dearly missed.

Michael David Quillen passed away on Jan. 1, 2023. He was a loving husband, father, grandfather, and great-grandfather. He attended Rose-Hulman Institute of Technology and finished his Engineering degree from Purdue University in 1977. He moved to St. Augustine, FL in 1983 where he practiced engineering for Tim Gabriel and Association, and later became a principle of Quillen, Mills, and Brody. He went on to the City of Clearwater for 25 years, 17 years as Director of Engineering, where he spearheaded many projects including the Memorial Causeway Bridge (2005). Michael retired in 2017.

Sonja and Michael
married in 1986

Donald and Rosalie are laid to rest at
Fort Snelling National Cemetery
in Minneapolis, Minnesota

Serina and Matthew Frizzell's Wedding
From left: Olsen Flanscha, Blake Flanscha, Taylor Valdes, Nixon MacDade, Matt (Groom) and Serina (Bride),
Nicole Cordray Valdes, Hal Valdes, Kennedy Valdes, and Grant Gassman

Kelsey and Trent Miller's Wedding
From left: Nicole Cordray Valdes, Kaili Park Cordray,
Kelsey Danielle Hanner (Bride), Sonja Quillen, and Joseph Daniel Wawrzyniak

FAMILY

Rosalie Eugene Olson b: 17 Mar 1923, Olson farm, Nutley Township, Day County, South Dakota; d: 11 Mar 2023, Clearwater, Pinellas County, Florida; buried: Fort Snelling National Cemetery, Minneapolis, Hennepin County, Minnesota

Rosalie married **Donald O. Danielson** b: 25 May 1917, Belmont, Golden Valley County, Montana; m: 02 May 1944, Grace Lutheran Church, Minneapolis, Hennepin County, Minnesota; d: 09 Feb 1991, Hennepin County, Minnesota

> Rosalie and Donald's children:
> **Sonja May Danielson** b: 03 Aug 1945, Minneapolis, Hennepin County, Minnesota
> **Ronald Stephan Danielson** b: 10 May 1949, Minneapolis, Hennepin County, Minnesota;
> d: 05 Aug 2004, Richfield, Hennepin County, Minnesota

CHILDREN AND GRANDCHILDREN
of Rosalie Eugene Olson and Donald O. Danielson

Sonja May Danielson married **Charles Joseph Cordray III** b: 20 Jan 1944, Minneapolis, Hennepin County, Minnesota; m: 11 Dec 1964, Minneapolis, Hennepin County, Minnesota: div.; d: 20 Feb 2010, Minneapolis, Hennepin County, Minnesota

> Sonja and Charles's children:
> **Nicole Daniela Cordray** b: 23 Jul 1965, Minneapolis, Hennepin County, Minnesota
> **Kaili Park Cordray** b: 20 Jan 1973, Korea: adopted

Sonja May Danielson married **Michael D. Quillen** b: 27 May 1952, Logansport, Cass County, Indiana; m: 03 May 1986, St. Augustine, St. John's County, Florida; d: 01 Jan 2023, Clearwater, Pinellas County, Florida

Nicole Daniela Cordray married **William (Hal) Haldon Valdes** b: 23 Aug 1966, Tampa, Hillsborough County, Florida; m: 31 Aug 1991, Tampa, Hillsborough County, Florida

> Nicole and Hal's children and grandchildren:
> **Taylor Brooke Valdes** b: 14 Sep 1993, Orlando, Orange County, Florida

> > Taylor's child with **Robert Cody MacDade** b: 18 Mar 1992, Winter Park, Orange County, Florida:
> > **Nixon Robert MacDade** b: 10 Feb 2013, Orlando, Orange County, Florida

> > Taylor's child with fiancé **Blake Robert Flanscha** b: 05 Sep 1981, New Hampton, Chickasaw County, Iowa:
> > **Olsen Bloom Flanscha** b: 09 Jan 2020, Orlando, Orange County, Florida

> **Serina Ryan Valdes** b: 27 Feb 1996, Orlando, Orange County, Florida
> married **Matthew (Matt) Keith Frizzell** b: 14 Nov 1994, Orlando, Orange County, Florida; m: 21 Oct 2023, Orlando, Orange County, Florida

> **Kennedy McCall Valdes** b: 14 Feb 1997, Orlando, Orange County, Florida

Kennedy, Taylor, Matt, Serina, Nicole, Hal

Kaili Park Cordray married **Michael Bryan Hanner** b: 14 Dec 1969, Chapel Hill, North Carolina; m: 12 Mar 1994, St. Petersburg, Pinellas County, Florida: div.

Kaili and Michael's child:
Kelsey Danielle Hanner b: 27 Jul 1994, St. Petersburg, Pinellas County, Florida

Kelsey married **Trent Wilson Miller** b: 19 Aug 1990, Tampa, Hillsborough County, Florida; m: 22 Jan 2023, Plant City, Hillsborough County, Florida

Kelsey and Trent's child:
Annabella Grace Miller b: 24 Oct 2019, Brandon, Hillsborough County, Florida

Kaili married **Michael Alexander Wawrzyniak** b: 11 Jan 1980, Monroeville, Allegheny County, Pennsylvania; m: 08 Dec 2001, Ocala, Marion County, Florida: div.

Kaili and Michael's child:
Joseph Daniel Wawrzyniak b: 12 Aug 2002, Ocala, Marion County, Florida

Ronald Stephan Danielson

From left: Joseph Wawrzyniak, Kelsey Hanner holding Annabella Miller, Kaili Cordray, Sonja Cordray Quillen, Rosalie Olson Danielson, Nixon MacDade, Taylor Valdes, Serina Valdes, Kennedy Valdes, Nicole Cordray Valdes

CALVIN IRVING OLSON

Born
December 30, 1930
Iver Vevang Farm
Nutley Township, Day County, SD

Died
December 3, 1972
Tucumcari, Quay County, NM
Laid to rest in Lakewood Cemetery, Minneapolis, MN

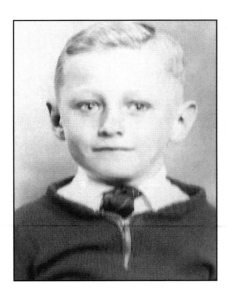

Calvin Irving Olson

married

Marguerite Clara Lee

July 16, 1951

Minneapolis,
Hennepin County,
Minnesota

Sonja Danielson, Calvin Olson's niece, seeing the couple off to their honeymoon.
They went to Marguerite's mother's lake home in Horseshoe Lake near McGregor, Minnesota.

Calvin and Marguerite with their grandparents
From left: Clara Lee, Iver Vevang, and Serina Hustad Vevang

Hilda Vevang Olson and Edwin Olson Family in 1952

Standing: Allen Fellows, Viola Olson Fellows, Alida Vevang, Donald Danielson,
Marguerite Lee Olson, Calvin Olson, Hilda Vevang Olson, and Edwin Olson

Sitting: Sonja Danielson, Rosalie Olson Danielson, Ronald Danielson,
Spencer Olson, and Evelyn Miller Olson

Marge and Cal

From left: Kent Olson, Marguerite Lee Olson,
Mark Olson, Calvin Olson, and Steven Olson
with dogs Jock (left) and Amby (right)

Hilda and Ed Olson's 50th Anniversary dinner
hosted at the Hopkin's House in 1969

Calvin, with Don Danielson and Spencer Olson

Calvin Olson dies in crash of light plane

Reporter and Farmer
Webster, South Dakota

Calvin Olson dies in crash of light plane

Relatives here received word of the plane crash Sunday which took the lives of five people at Tucumcari, N.M., including Calvin Olson, 41, of Minneapolis, a former resident of the Roslyn area.

Olson, who was former owner of Hopkins House Hotels in Minneapolis was presently senior vice president of Investment Dynamics of Minneapolis and was at the end of a flight from Minneapolis to Tucumcari in company with other company officials when their light plane crashed Sunday night.

Survivors include his wife and three sons; his parents, Mr. and Mrs. Olson (Hilda Vevang of Roslyn); one brother, Spencer Olson and two sisters, Mrs. Don (Rosalie) Danielson and Mrs. Viola Fellers, all of Minneapolis.

Relatives who plan to attend funeral services for their nephew are Mr. and Mrs. Elmer Vevang of Roslyn, Mr. and Mrs. Julius Vevang, Mr. and Mrs. Ingvald Vevang and Mr. and Mrs. Henry Hanson, all of Webster.

Relatives here received word of the plane crash Sunday which took the lives of five people at Tucumcari, NM, including Calvin Olson, 41, of Minneapolis, a former resident of the Roslyn area.

Olson, who was former owner of Hopkins House Hotels in Minneapolis was presently senior vice president of Investment Dynamics of Minneapolis and was at the end of a flight from Minneapolis to Tucumcari in company with other company officials when their light plane crashed Sunday night.

Survivors include his wife and three sons; his parents, Mr. and Mrs. Olson (Hilda Vevang, formerly of Roslyn); one brother, Spencer Olson and two sisters, Mrs. Don (Rosalie) Danielson and Mrs. Viola Fellows, all of Minneapolis.

The Twenty Third Psalm

The Lord is my Shepherd: I shall not want.
He maketh me to lie down in green pastures:
He leadeth me beside the still waters.
He restoreth my soul: He leadeth me in the
paths of righteousness for his name's sake.
Yea, though I walk through the valley of the
shadow of death, I will fear no evil:
for thou art with me: thy rod and
thy staff they comfort me.
Thou preparest a table before me in the
presence of mine enemies:
thou anointest my head with oil:
my cup runneth over.
Surely goodness and mercy shall follow
me all the days of my life: and I will
dwell in the house of the Lord for ever.

In Memory of
Calvin J. Olson
Born in
Roslyn, South Dakota, December 30, 1930
Passed Away
December 3, 1972
Services from
Werness Brothers Chapel
Minneapolis, Minnesota
Thursday, December 7, 1972   11:00 A.M.
Clergyman Officiating
Dr. A. Reuben Gornitzka
Soloist, Mr. Maurice Anderson
Organist, Mrs. Dorothy Scheibe
Survived by
Wife, Marguerite; Sons, Mark, Steven and
Kent; Parents, Mr. and Mrs. Ed C. Olson;
Brother, Spencer Olson; Sisters,
Mrs. Donald Danielson and
Mrs. Allen E. Fellows
Pallbearers

Raymond Duffy	Alphonse Fazendin
Herbert Mason	Dewey Paulsen
Donald Hagen	Joseph Knoblauch

Honorary Pallbearers

Carl Nygren	George Connor
James Dowling	James Harmon
James Meriwether	David Gravdahl
John Okerstrom	

Interment
Lakewood Cemetery

Thoughts of Death Encircle Crash and Survivors Hope to Return Home

Aberdeen American News, Aberdeen, SD, December 7, 1972

Tucumcari, N.M.—Bill Loder and Tom Anderson were hoping to return home to Minneapolis, Minn., Wednesday alive but were surrounded by thoughts of death. Loder, Anderson and nine others were on board a refurbished World War II Navy bomber that crashed Sunday night as it approached the runway at the Tucumcari airport.

Five members of a suburban Minneapolis firm died in the burning wreckage. Loder, Anderson and four others survived. The five badly-burned bodies were pulled from the demolished plane Monday and identified as Cal Olson, 41, senior vice president of Investment Dynamics Corp., Bloomington; Karen Drees, 30, Olson's secretary; Ken Harvey, 33, advertising director of the firm; Don Bennett, 44, the pilot, and Paul Ladwig, 28, the copilot. All were from the Minneapolis area.

Loder, while hospitalized in Tucumcari, Tuesday, recalled the aftermath of the crash. He said he remembers grabbing Robert Gisselbeck, one of the survivors, and pulling him out of the wreckage. "He was lying face down in the aisle and I had a hard time with him," Loder recalled. "You know," he said, "I told 'gis' he is going to have to lose weight before I go flying with him again. Boy was he heavy." Loder recalled.

But the humor was only momentary. When asked about Olson, Loder paused, then said: "I keep wishing I had grabbed hold of him when I first went out. He must have been near me somewhere. If I had just realized." Loder, 29, was still inside the plane when he regained consciousness after the crash. He was on his feet and dazed.

"I've got to get the hell out of here." Loder thought, then he crawled through a side of the plane that was ripped open. George Heaton, also 29, was outside the plane, possibly thrown out when the craft crashed. Moments later, Anderson, 32, and Gene Bingham came stumbling from the wreckage.

Heaton and Loder headed back toward the plane and pulled out Gisselbeck, 32, and Nancy Warner, 31, a secretary. They started back into the plane again but stopped. "Flames were everywhere," Loder recalled. "They were engulfing all the seats. The fumes and smoke, the heat, were so intensive we couldn't... well... it would have been an idiot's move to go back in again."

The survivors were all Investment Dynamics employees and from the Minneapolis area except Bingham, who lived in Tulsa, Okla. Anderson and Loder were listed in good condition Tuesday and were expected to be released Wednesday. Heaton was reported in good satisfactory condition and Gisselbeck, Bingham and Mrs. Warner in serious condition. The group was on a flight from Tulsa to Tucumcari in the company plane to inspect some property purchased recently by the firm. The Federal Aviation Administration was investigating the crash.

OBITUARY

Marguerite Lee Olson Hanken

Marguerite C. Hanken (Olson), age 89, of Edina, Minnesota, passed away July 18, 2021, in Minneapolis, MN, following a long illness and surrounded by her loving family. Marguerite is preceded in death by Calvin I. Olson, Robert J. Hanken, Hilda M. Lee, Kenneth F. Lee, and Robert Hanken Jr.

Marguerite was born in Minneapolis to Kenneth and Hilda Lee on November 1, 1931. She went to school at Holy Rosary and graduated from South High in Minneapolis in 1949. She married Calvin I. Olson on July 16, 1951, in Minneapolis. She worked in the payroll department for the Government in Virginia Beach while Calvin was out at sea on the USS Roanoke.

Aside from her prime endeavor supporting her husband, children, and families, Marguerite served as a den mother and active in a variety of philanthropic and charitable organizations. Most recently, she loved being a member of the Minneapolis Women's Club and St. Patrick's Church of Edina. Marge and Cal were popular and successful owners of the Hopkins House and Breezy Point Resort during the '60s and '70s.

After Cal's untimely death in 1972, Marge found love again and married Bob Hanken, owner of the Guest House Minneapolis and the Guest House Motor Inn Watertown. She spent the rest of her life enjoying families at their homes in Naples, FL, Edina, MN, and their lake home on Sylvan Lake in Brainerd, MN.

Marguerite is survived by Mark Olson, Steve (Carrie) Olson, Kent Olson, Krystal Olson, Calvin Olson (Lynne), Chad Olson (Elena), Katie (Jay) Brooks, Jared (Cherish) Olson, Brittany (Justin) Sorensen, Brandon Olson, Cynthia Hanken, John (Nancy) Hanken, David Hanken, Matthew Hanken, Cody Hanken. Memorials preferred to the Woman's Club of Minneapolis. A private family service will be held.

FAMILY

Cal and Marguerite

Calvin Irving Olson b: 30 Dec 1930, Iver Vevang farm, Nutley Township, Day County, South Dakota; d: 03 Dec 1972, Tucumcari, Quay County, New Mexico; buried: Lakewood Cemetery, Minneapolis, Hennepin County, Minnesota

Calvin married **Marguerite Clara Lee** b: 01 Nov 1931, Minneapolis, Hennepin County, Minnesota; m: 16 Jul 1951, Minneapolis, Hennepin County, Minnesota; d: 18 Jul 2021, Minneapolis, Hennepin County, Minnesota; buried: Lakewood Cemetery, Minneapolis, Hennepin County, Minnesota

Robert and Marguerite

Calvin and Marguerite's children:
Mark Lee Olson b: 12 Nov 1954, Minneapolis, Hennepin County, Minnesota
Steven Calvin Olson b: 20 Nov 1955, Minneapolis, Hennepin County, Minnesota
Kent Edwin Olson b: 04 Jan 1960, Minneapolis, Hennepin County, Minnesota

Marguerite married **Robert J. Hanken** b: 05 Aug 1917, Iowa; m: 28 Aug 1976; d: 15 Feb 1994, Naples, Collier County, Florida; buried: Fort Snelling National Cemetery, Minneapolis, Hennepin County, Minnesota

CHILDREN AND GRANDCHILDREN
of Calvin Irving Olson and Marguerite Clara Lee

Mark Lee Olson married **Kay Ann Lauritzen** b: 07 Mar 1957, Beaver Dam, Dodge County, Wisconsin; (d: 24 Sept 2021); m: 21 Jun 1980, Hopkins, Hennepin County, Minnesota: div.

Mark and Kay's children:
Krystal Ann Olson b: 30 Apr 1982, Minneapolis, Hennepin County, Minnesota
Calvin John Olson b: 10 Jan 1986, Minneapolis, Hennepin County, Minnesota
Chad Jerald Olson b: 27 Nov 1987, Minneapolis, Hennepin County, Minnesota

Krystal Ann Olson

Krystal's children:
Tai Marcus Le b: 03 Jan 2005, Edina, Hennepin County, Minnesota
Tori Bella Le b: 28 Oct 2009, Edina, Hennepin County, Minnesota

Calvin John Olson and partner **Lynne Marie Jones** b: 26 Jan 1986, Minneapolis, Hennepin County, Minnesota

Calvin and Lynne's children:
Scarlett Jo Olson b: 02 May 2016, Grapevine, Texas
Preston Edward Olson b: 14 Jul 2019, Grapevine, Texas

Chad Jerald Olson and partner **Elena Katherine Sorensen** b: 01 Sep 1997, Yaroslavl, Russia

Chad and Elena's children:
Jerald Carter Olson b: 11 Dec 2020, Waconia, Carver County, Minnesota
Isabella Maria Olson b: 22 Jul 2022, Waconia, Carver County, Minnesota

Steven Calvin Olson married **Carrie Jo Voldness** b: 05 Jul 1956, Silver Bay, Lake County, Minnesota; m: 29 Jul 1978, Mt. Olivet Lutheran Church, Minneapolis, Hennepin County, Minnesota

Steven and Carrie's children:
Katie Jo Olson b: 26 Nov 1981, Milwaukee, Milwaukee County, Wisconsin
Jared Lee Olson b: 22 Dec 1983, Hutchinson, Reno County, Kansas

Katie Jo Olson married **James Joseph Brooks** b: 27 Dec 1979, Bartlesville, Oklahoma; m: 02 Feb 2008, Nassau, Bahamas

Katie and James' children:
Avery Jo Brooks b: 15 Jan 2009, Olathe, Johnson County, Kansas
Emma Jean Brooks b: 04 Oct 2012, Olathe, Johnson County, Kansas

Jared Lee Olson married **Cherish Marie Smith** b: 25 Mar 1985, Park Rapids, Hubbard County, Minnesota; m: 06 Aug 2011, King's Gardens, Longville, Cass County, Minnesota

Jared and Cherish's children:
Owen James Olson b: 17 Feb 2013, Bemidji, Beltrami County, Minnesota
Livia Jean Olson b: 27 Aug 2015, Bemidji, Beltrami County, Minnesota

Kent Edwin Olson married **Penny P. Davies** b: 13 Dec 1961, Denver, Denver County, Colorado; m: 14 Aug 1982, Hopkins, Hennepin County, Minnesota: div.

Kent and Penny's children:
Brittany Christine Olson b: 14 Oct 1984, Hoffman Estates, Cook County, Illinois
Brandon Kent Olson b: 13 May 1988, Minneapolis, Hennepin County, Minnesota

Brittany Christine Olson married **Justin Earl Sorensen** b:16 Feb 1982, Waconia, Carver County, Minnesota; m: 16 Sep 2006, Victoria, Carver County, Minnesota

Brittany and Justin's children:
Natalie Christine Sorensen b: 31 May 2005, Shakopee, Scott County, Minnesota
Ryder James Sorensen b:15 May 2009, Waconia, Carver County, Minnesota

Brandon Kent Olson

VIOLA DELORES OLSON

Born
January 15, 1932
Olson Farm
Nutley Township, Day County, SD

Died
August 7, 2023
Apple Valley, Dakota County, MN
Laid to rest in Fort Snelling National Cemetery, Minneapolis, MN

Viola Delores Olson

married

Allen Eugene Fellows

September 19, 1953

Minneapolis,
Hennepin County,
Minnesota

Wedding Party
From left: Phyllis Bjornstad (friend of bride), Spencer Olson (brother of bride),
Margaret "Suzy" Fellows (sister of groom), Herbert 'Herb' Howe, (friend of groom), Viola Delores Olson (bride),
Allen Eugene Fellows (groom), Rosalie Olson Danielson (sister of bride),
Roland "Ron" Berg (friend of groom), Jeannie Chartier (friend of bride), Vaughn Green (friend of groom)

A passenger manifest of the United States Air Force flight on April 22, 1954 through the United States Department of Justice that is outward bound to Yokohama, Japan

Form 1-432 UNITED STATES DEPARTMENT OF JUSTICE IMMIGRATION AND NATURALIZATION SERVICE (Rev. 1-4-48)	Form approved. Budget Bureau No. 48-R361.	**LIST OF OUTWARD-BOUND PASSENGERS** (United States Citizens and Nationals)		LIST No. 12 of 17	
PAGE 12		Sailing from SEPE (Port)	22 April 1954 (Date) , 19		
S. S. USNS GEN HUGH J. GAFFEY		bound for port of YOKOHAMA			
(1)		(2)	(3)	(4)	

Line No.	Family Name—Given Name Address in United States	Age (Years)	Sex (F-M)	U. S. Passport No.	Place of Birth Date and Place of Naturalization	Length of Time Passenger Intends To Remain Abroad

This list of outward-bound passengers is for the ship that Viola took to join her six-month newlywed husband, Allen, already at Yokohama base Tachikawa in Japan while serving in the U.S. Air Force as a second lieutenant. She had never traveled outside of Minnesota and South Dakota, so this was a big trip! Taking Viola's car so it could be shipped to Japan as well, Aunt Alida drove Vi from Minneapolis to Seattle. Viola stayed with Sam's family for 3-4 days before boarding the ship. Sam took her to the port for boarding. It was about a nine-day journey. She shared a stateroom with another wife and her three children. One night during dinner, the seas were so rough they had to wet down the tablecloths to keep items from sliding off.

17	FAULHABER, Eleanor Stratford, N.J.	33	F	50570	Waterford Twp, N.J.	"
18	Judith P	9	F	"	Stratford, N.J.	"
19	Susan C	7	F	"	Camden, N.J.	"
20	Deborah A	15 mo	F	"	" "	"
21	FELLOWS, Viola D Minneapolis, Minn.	22	F	50795	Nutley Twp, S.D.	"
22	FLEMING, Catherine E New Brockton, Ala.	24	F	50572	Abbeville, Ala.	"
23	Deborah C	2	F	"	Dothan, Ala.	"
24	FOYE, Agnes D New Haven, Conn.	36	F	50888	New Haven, Conn.	"
25	Barbara M	6	F	"	New Haven, Conn.	"

The USAF PASSENGER MANIFEST is for the return trip to the United States ten months later, February 1955. Allen had been diagnosed with tuberculosis and whisked back to Fitzsimmons Army Hospital in Denver by way of Oahu, Hawaii. Viola's 36-hour return flight was broken up by a stopover in Oahu, where she got to see Allen briefly before she went on to Minneapolis. They sent him on an evac plane to Denver. Four months later she had tested possible positive for tuberculosis and was also admitted into the same hospital, but in the women's wing. She and Allen would wave to each other from across the courtyard but didn't get to visit with each other face to face for 18 months. Allen had surgery, part of his lung removed and made a full recovery. A moment in history was witnessed while at the hospital. President Eisenhower was in Denver on a visit to see his mother-in-law, Mrs. Doud. He was on the golf course when he suffered a heart attack and they took him to Fitzsimmons. Vi recalls seeing the ambulance and motorcade, lights flashing, and security detail as they brought him in. It was the talk of the hospital.

Allen Eugene Fellows Colonel

20TH TAC AIR SPT SQDN, 504TH TASG, 7TH AF

United States Air Force

Rank/Branch: O4/US Air Force

Date of Birth: 01 December 1931

Home City of Record: Minneapolis MN

Date of Loss: 20 March 1968

Country of Loss: Laos

Loss Coordinates: 162000N 1060000E (XD068059)

Status (in 1973): Missing In Action

Category: 4

Acft/Vehicle/Ground: O2A

Refno: 1099

Other Personnel In Incident: None missing

Allen Fellows had been in the Air Force for 18 years when he took his O2A observation plane into Laos on a mission. On 20 March 1968, a COVEY Forward Air Controller from the 20th Tactical Air Support Squadron, Major Allen E. Fellows, flying O-2A tail number 67-21338, departed Danang Air Base for a FAC mission in Laos. While in flight, and somewhere about 30 miles southwest of the city of Sepone, Laos, his aircraft disappeared and was never found. No trace of Fellows was found either. He simply disappeared over southern Laos somewhere in the vicinity of Ban Gnang. Search and rescue efforts failed to locate either the aircraft or Major Fellows, who was placed in Missing in Action (MIA) status. Fellows was carried as MIA for over ten years, receiving two promotions, to Lt. Colonel and then Colonel, before the Secretary of the Air Force approved a Presumptive Finding of Death on May 5, 1978.

Allen's family, like the families of the other men lost in the Vietnam War, waited for news. At the end of the war, a prisoner release occurred, but Allen, like the nearly 600 others lost in Laos where the U.S. "wasn't at war", was not released. The U.S. Government urged families to be patient as the CIA had a list of men held in Laos. Laos spokesmen indicated they held "tens of tens" of American prisoners in Laos, but as the years passed, not one of them came home.

Finally, in 1979, Allen's family held a memorial service at the encouragement of the U.S. Air Force, hoping that it would help bring closure. It didn't. Reports mounted that Americans were still alive. Family members were slowly forced to conclude that the U.S. Government had not been fully truthful with them. They feared their men had been abandoned. A decade after Allen's memorial service was held, reports relating to American prisoners, missing or unaccounted for, were still flowing in, having reached a total of over 10,000. Many experts believe that hundreds of Americans are being held, but negotiations to bring any of them home seem to have been inadequate.

Sources: http://www.pownetwork.org/bios/f/f006.htm — http://www.virtualwall.org/df/FellowsAE01a.htm

To live in the hearts we leave behind, is never to have died.

THOMAS CAMPBELL
"HALLOWED GROUND"

**FALLEN FLIER
MISSING FRIEND**

We thank you for the selfless devotion to our country and for your service in that ill-fated war. You and your fine family are fondly remembered by all whose path you crossed.

From a comrade in arms and family friend,

Harvey D. Gilzean

In Memory of Allen Eugene Fellows
Col US Air Force Vietnam
December 1, 1931 – March 20, 1968

Memorial in Fort Snelling
Minneapolis, Minnesota

Rosalie (81) and Vi (72)
August 2004

Rosalie (93) and Viola (84)
November 2016

Lesli Brook Paquette and Viola Olson Fellows at
Lawrence Vevang's funeral on October 10, 2016

Viola
October 2019

OBITUARY

Viola Delores Olson Fellows

Viola Delores Fellows, born to Hilda Marie and Edwin Casper Olson in Roslyn, South Dakota on the family farm on January 15, 1932, joining her loving siblings Spencer, Rosalie, and Calvin. Vi enjoyed playing with her brother Calvin at an early age. The siblings helped each other carry the milk to town and gathered the eggs every morning. The family left the farm, first moving to Waubay, South Dakota and then in 1942 landed in South Minneapolis where Ed and Hilda worked for the war effort. Vi and Cal walked to the movies on Lake Street together all summer long. Vi was active in her high school women's club, the Craws, was named to the homecoming court, and voted best smile in her senior year.

Vi met her future husband, Allen Fellows at Central High School in Minneapolis. They married on September 19, 1953, at St. James Lutheran Church. They had many adventures together during their travels around the world in service to the United States Air Force. Allen and Vi adored their two children, Christopher, and Lesli Brook. In March 1968 Allen was reported Missing in Action over Laos. Vi returned to Minneapolis to the warm and loving support of both the Olson and Fellows families. She never remarried, raising the children in Burnsville, Minnesota.

She enjoyed traveling with Lesli visiting family and friends, as well as going on wonderful vacations with her high school friends for many years. Being a wife and mother were the most important parts of Vi's life, roles that gave her much pride and joy. She was an excellent mom; supportive, kind, and generous with a great sense of humor. She always kept an elegant home, was a wonderful hostess, and enjoyed entertaining. It's been often said Vi lit up every room she went into.

Vi was a lover of: HGTV, crime TV shows, especially Blue Bloods, soap operas, Young and the Restless and Bold and the Beautiful, SWEETS!—any lemon dessert and milk chocolate, Dairy Queen Peanut Buster Parfaits, lefse! Cocktails, cigarettes and good conversation.

FAMILY

Viola Delores Olson b: 15 Jan 1932, Olson farm, Nutley Township, Day County, South Dakota; d: 07 Aug 2023, Apple Valley, Dakota County, Minnesota; buried: Fort Snelling National Cemetery, Minneapolis, Hennepin County, Minnesota

Viola married Allen Eugene Fellows b: 01 Dec 1931, Minneapolis, Hennepin County, Minnesota; m: 19 Sep 1953, St. James Lutheran Church in Minneapolis on Portland Avenue, Hennepin County, Minnesota; Allen went Missing in Action (MIA) in Laos on March 20, 1968

Viola and Allen's adopted children:
Christopher Olson Fellows b: 18 Sep 1958, Dayton, Montgomery County, Ohio
Lesli Brook Fellows b: 30 Apr 1965, Columbus, Montgomery County, Ohio

CHILDREN AND GRANDCHILDREN
of Viola Delores Olson and Allen Eugene Fellows

Christopher Olson Fellows

Christopher's child:
Caprina Christine Stenson b: 19 Jul 1985, Minneapolis, Hennepin County, Minnesota

Caprina's child:
Lillian Rose Stenson b: 02 May 2005, Minneapolis, Hennepin County, Minnesota

Lesli Brook Fellows married Greg O'Brien Paquette b: 17 Feb 1966, Edina, Hennepin County, Minnesota; m: 03 Oct 1999, San Diego, San Diego County, California

Lesli and Greg's child:
Ava (Remi) Marie Paquette b: 04 May 2001, San Diego, San Diego County, California

CHAPTER V

ELMER

Born
February 4, 1901
Vevang Family Farm
Nutley Township, Day County, SD

Died
August 15, 1994
Webster, Day County, SD
Laid to rest in Roslyn Lutheran Cemetery, Roslyn, SD

ELMER

was the third child born to Iver and Serina Vevang, and the first born in the Vevang family home in Nutley Township. He was baptized a month after birth, and confirmed by age 14 in 1915. In the far right photo, Elmer is to the right of his father, Iver.

Elmer was baptized in the Lutheran Christian faith on March 10, 1901

Sponsors: Iver and Beret Holm, Bernhard Vevang, and Ericka Hustad.

U.S. Evangelical Lutheran Church in America Church Records

The Thirteenth United States Federal Census taken in 1910
Nutley Township, Day County, South Dakota

Vevang	Iver A.	Head	M	W	44
	Serina	Wife	F	W	38
	Julius	Son	M	W	12
	Hilda	Daughter	F	W	11
	Elmer	Son	M	W	9
	Ingvald	Son	M	W	7
	Selmer	Son	M	W	5
	Laura	Daughter	F	W	2
	Ella	Daughter	F	W	6/12
Gaaras	Halvor	Lodger	M	W	36

Elmer Vevang was confirmed
in the Lutheran Christian faith
in the Roslyn Lutheran Church
in 1915 at age 14

—1915—
Alfred Aastrem
Solveig Hammer-Nilsen
Elmer Nicolai Vevang

1919

Vevang Family Portrait

Elmer was 18 years old

Standing: Laura, Elmer, Hilda, Myrtle, Julius, Ingvald, Selmer
Sitting: Ella, Serina, Lawrence, Iver, Alida

The Fourteenth United States Federal Census taken in 1920
Nutley Township, Day County, South Dakota

Vevang Iver A.	Head	O	m	m	w	54
Serina	Wife			F	w	47
Julius D.	Son			m	w	23
Elmer L.	Son			m	w	18
Ingvald	Son			m	w	17
Selmer	Son			m	w	15
Laura M.	Daughter			F	w	11
Ella H.	Daughter			F	w	10
Alida	Daughter			F	w	9
Myrtle H.	Daughter			F	w	5
Lawrence A.	Son			m	w	4 3/12

A Story about Elmer Vevang's Little Desk

Written by Warren Vevang (Elmer's Son)

It is a handmade, front drop-down writing surface, with a small inside drawer and a round mirror on top. There is a rather interesting story on this little desk. When Dad was a young boy, he (as well as all the Vevang kids) attended a small one-room schoolhouse, which was located about 1/4 mile north of the farm building and east of the tree claim. When Dad was attending the school, sometime between 1907-1916, a man taught at this school and lived at the Vevang home. During this time Dad had a job of going over to the schoolhouse each cold morning to start a fire in the wood stove to heat the classroom.

When this teacher left to go back to Norway, he gave this little desk to Dad in appreciation for him keeping the schoolhouse warm on those cold South Dakota mornings. Dad had referred to this man as a schoolteacher and then later he called him a parochial schoolteacher who also taught in Norwegian. I think about parochial school as having to do the Bible teachings. I don't remember Dad ever saying this teacher's name was Bernhard, or that he was a relative. As I recall, he just referred to "a schoolteacher." Could Bernhard have been the Norwegian Bible teacher?

Dad kept the little desk while growing up on the farm and then when he became a barber and opened his shop in Roslyn in 1925, it became a permanent fixture in the shop. He did his record keeping, bills, etc., on this desk until he quit barbering in 1989 due to a fall and a broken hip, 64 years spent at that desk. After that, Mother moved the desk to her home for safekeeping. She had it refinished, and during the refinishing process, the small round mirror was removed and behind it a newspaper clipping was found. The clipping was from the St. Paul Dispatch dated Sunday, October 30, 1899. From this I am guessing the desk was built in the St. Paul area in about 1899 or 1900.

I took everything out of the desk, rolled it over, turned it upside down and looked very carefully for any writing or carving that might indicate who owned the desk in the past. I found nothing other than a scrawled Elmer Vevang, Roslyn, S.D. 1925. Could Bernhard have purchased this desk and left it at the farm? The time frame seems to fit, however, I do not know when Bernhard left South Dakota. The desk made the trek to California with me when the Elmer Vevang home in Roslyn was sold in 1994. It stands quietly in a corner of our home, providing fond memories of Dad.

The Fifteenth United States Federal Census taken in 1930
Nutley Township, Day County, South Dakota

Gilbertson	Mattie	Head	H	O	3500			No	F	M 56
	Cora	M	Daughter						F	N 16
Vevang	Elmer		Roomer						M	N 29

At age 29, Elmer was a roomer at the home of Mattie Gilbertson,
Hazel Gilbertson Vevang's mother, in Roslyn, South Dakota.

ELNA ANNETTE OLSON

Born
November 4, 1911
Hillhead, Marshall County, SD

Died
November 9, 1994
Sioux Falls, Minnehaha County, SD
Laid to rest in Roslyn Lutheran Cemetery, Roslyn, SD

ELMER & ELNA VEVANG

Married November 15, 1931
Roslyn, Day County, South Dakota

RECORD OF MARRIAGE

South Dakota State Board of Health

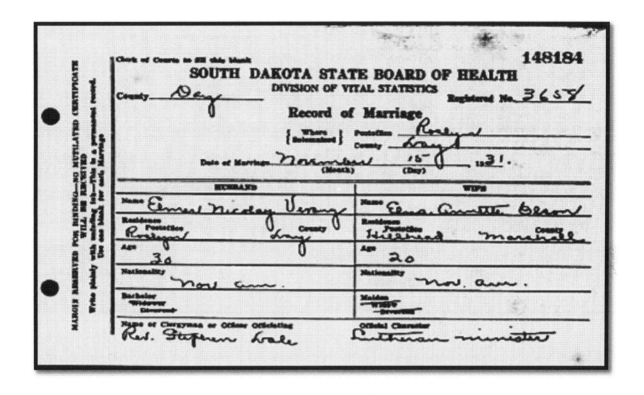

HUSBAND	WIFE
ELMER NICOLAI VEVANG	ELNA ANNETTE OLSON
ROSLYN, DAY COUNTY, SD	HILLHEAD, MARSHALL COUNTY, SD
AGE 30	AGE 20
NORWEGIAN AMERICAN	NORWEGIAN AMERICAN
BACHELOR	MAIDEN

Elmer Vevang and Elna Olson Vevang on the day they were married, and the day after.

U.S. Evangelical Lutheran Church in America Church Records — Marriage Records
Printed in Norwegian

No.	Vielsesdatum.	Brud og Brudgoms fulde Navne.	Alder (Aar.)	Hvor født.	Vidner.	Vielsessted.	Præst.	58
	11-15-1931	Elmer Nicolay Vevang	33	Roslyn, S.D.	Ingvald Vevang	Parsonage		
		Elna Annetta Olson	20		Myrtle Olson			

Elmer Vevang, Elna Olson Vevang (left) with witnesses Myrtle Olson
(sister of the bride) and Ingvald Vevang (brother of the groom)

Darlis Janet Vevang, Elmer and Elna's first child, was born in 1933, and baptized in the Lutheran church in Roslyn, South Dakota. Her sponsors were Alida Vevang and William Olson.

Elmer and Elna's second child, Warren Elmer Vevang was born and baptized in 1934. His sponsors were Mr. and Mrs. Theo Gilbertson, Ingvald Vevang, and Myrtle Olson Homolstead.

Allen Gene Vevang was born to Elmer and Elna in 1936. Lawrence Vevang and Alma Hemmah were his sponsors.

Darlis' Baptism Record

Warren's Baptism Record

Allen's Baptism Record

1937. Elmer Vevang with sons, Allen, and Warren   Elmer Vevang with his son Warren

The Sixteenth United States Federal Census taken in 1940
Roslyn, Day County, South Dakota

Vevang Elmer "N."	Head	◯	M	W	39
Elna G ⊗	Wife	1	F	W	28
Darlis J	Daughter	2	F	W	7
Warren E	Son	2	M	W	5
Allen G.	Son	2	M	W	3

Members of the Elmer and Elna Vevang home: Darlis (7), Warren (5), and Allen (3)

Warren and Darlis

Allen, Warren, and Darlis

Darlis

Warren and Allen

Elna, Allen, Darlis, Warren, and Elmer

Elmer and Elna Vevang

History of Day County by the Day County Historical Research Committee, p. 791-792

Elmer Vevang, son of Iver and Serina Hustad Vevang, was born in Nutley Township, and attended grade school in Nutley Township and in Roslyn. He attended barber school in Minneapolis. For a short time, he barbered in Minneapolis, Eden and Aberdeen. In 1925 he purchased the Roslyn Barber Shop from Melvin Einerson. Elmer has operated his shop for 55 years. In 1931 he married Elna Olson of Hillhead, who was born in Marshall County to Knute and Anna Oland Olson, attended rural school in Dumarce Township and high school in Aberdeen, South Dakota.

The Vevangs had three children. Darlis Vevang was born March 18, 1933. She attended school in Roslyn and Moorhead, Minnesota. In 1951 she graduated from Moorhead Minnesota High School, and in 1954 she graduated from Swedish Hospital School of Nursing, Minneapolis, Minnesota. She married Jim Dedrickson of Webster, South Dakota who is District Representative for the Lutheran brotherhood of Sioux Falls, South Dakota. They have four children, Kimberly, Vicki, Keith, and Kari.

176

Warren Vevang was born October 23, 1934. He attended school in Roslyn, and graduated from Moorhead Minnesota High School in 1952. After one year at South Dakota State University in Brookings, South Dakota, he enlisted in the U.S. Army. He served two years in Germany. In 1959, Warren graduated from San Jose State in California with a degree in business administration. He married Janice Hightower of San Jose, and they have two children, Valarie and Kevin.

Allen Vevang was born September 25, 1936. He attended school in Roslyn and Moorhead, Minnesota, graduated from Roslyn in 1954, enlisted in the Navy, and served three-and-a-half years. He later attended South Dakota State University in Brookings, South Dakota and San Jose State in California. In 1961 he graduated from the Mortuary School in San Francisco, California. He married Charlotte Knapp of Minneapolis, Minnesota. He is employed at McReary Funeral Home in Minneapolis, Minnesota.

The Elmer Vevang family lived on Hamilton Avenue in Roslyn. In 1950, they moved to Moorhead, Minnesota, at which time Elmer sold the home. They lived in Moorhead until June 1952. The family moved back to Roslyn. They lived in a trailer home behind the Iver Vevang house in the town of Roslyn. Elmer bought the home from Iver in about 1953. The home was sold in 1994. Elmer passed away in August of 1994 and Elna passed away in November of 1994.

The Elmer Vevang Family
Warren, Elna, Darlis, Elmer, and Allen are pictured on
Hamilton Avenue with the Swanson's home in the background.

**Darlis and Warren were confirmed in the Lutheran Christian faith
at the Roslyn Lutheran Church**

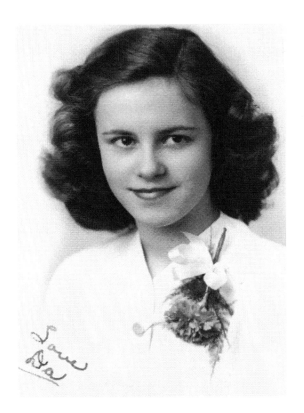

—1948—
Darlis Janet Vevang-Dedrickson
Jon Melvin Simundson
Marjorie Ann Berkeness
Glenn Durwood Hagen
Roger William Stavig
Maureen Claire Farmen-Holler

Darlis Janet Vevang confirmed: 1948

Baptized: April 30, 1933

Parents: Elmer and Elna Vevang

Sponsors: Alida Vevang and William Olson

—1949—
Joan Carol Gilbertson-Storley
Shirley Ann Hanson-Smith
Warren Elmer Vevang
Betty Jane Huggett-Walton

Warren Elmer Vevang confirmed: 1949

Baptized: November 25, 1934

Parents: Elmer and Elna Vevang

Sponsors: Mr. and Mrs. Theo Gilbertson,
Ingvald Vevang, and Myrtle Olson Homolstead

Warren, Darlis, and Allen

Elna and Elmer

Elmer Vevang Barber for 52 Years at 39

Reporter and Farmer, Webster, SD. July 9, 1975.

Ask Elmer Vevang of Roslyn how long he has been in the barbering business the next time you sit in his chair and he will tell you "52" years. Ask him how old he is and with a mischievous glint in his eye but a straight face his answer will be "39".

Of course, the figures don't add up, but if you want to quiz him a little more about his age you can do it at an open house in Roslyn this Saturday in honor of Elmer's 50 years of business there, the only Roslyn businessman at this point to achieve the mark. The event sponsored by his children will be from 2:00 to 5:00 p.m. at the senior citizens' building and the public is welcome.

Grew up near Roslyn

Elmer grew up near Roslyn. His father Iver farmed just two miles northeast of town and the barber was one of twelve children. He went to school at Roslyn and as a youngster discovered he had a knack for cutting hair.

Naturally, he experimented on his brothers and some of the neighbor kids. He found he liked it and decided to attend barber school at Minneapolis in 1923. He barbered there for a while, then cut hair at Swenson's Pool Hall in 1924, went to Aberdeen, moved to Eden and finally came back to Roslyn in 1925 where he bought the barbering business from Melvin Einerson that same year. Several different barbers worked for him until 1927 and then he continued cutting hair on his own after that.

His barbershop has changed somewhat during the past 50 years, but not a lot. It is in the same building he started in and the chair his customers sit in was purchased in 1930. His shop almost went up in smoke in November of 1964 when a fire destroyed Coyne's

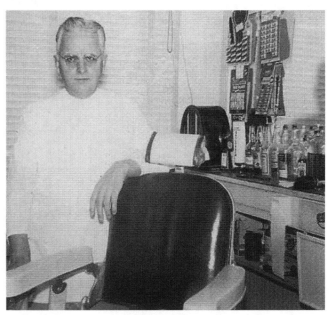

Elmer's barbershop almost went up in smoke. His shop was located on the west side of Main Street in Roslyn.

180

Elmer's hand-written sign on one of the walls of his barbershop. He notes the rise in the price of haircuts for adults and children.

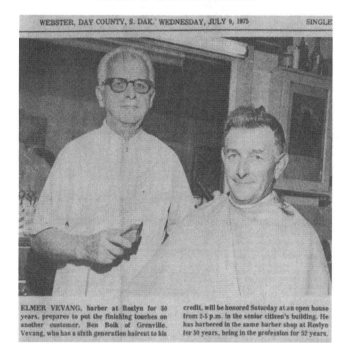

WEBSTER, DAY COUNTY, S. DAK. WEDNESDAY, JULY 9, 1975   SINGLE

ELMER VEVANG, barber at Roslyn for 50 years, prepares to put the finishing touches on another customer, Ben Boik of Grenville. Vevang, who has a sixth generation haircut to his credit, will be honored Saturday at an open house from 2-5 p.m. in the senior citizen's building. He has barbered in the same barber shop at Roslyn for 50 years, being in the profession for 52 years,

ROSLYN'S BARBER, Elmer Vevang, prepares to open the barber shop he has operated there for 50 years. His philosophy has always been "My customers are great, and if I treat them right they'll treat me right."   —Reporter and Farmer Photo

Meat Market, Rye Hardware and the City Liquor Store on the west side of Main Street. The blaze started in the hardware store and Vevang says that if the wind had continued to blow from the northwest instead of switching to the west while the fire was at its height, his shop would have gone too.

Haircuts were 25 cents

Elmer recalls that in those early days a haircut was about 40 cents and a shave 20 cents. When the depression set in, however, the price of haircuts during the 1930s dropped to 25 cents. "Haircuts today are $2, and it was tough going in the good old days, but my wife and I managed okay and were able to put all three of our children through college," he notes. Barbers today make their living on haircuts, with a razor shave almost a thing of the past due to the electric and safety razors, but on occasion, he still gets a chance to shave a customer. In the earlier days, he had a few customers who came in each day for a shave, while some came in every second or third day and others splurged for a shave once a week.

Sixth-generation haircut

It was just recently that he recorded a sixth-generation haircut. The select list reads John Monshaugen, Julia Hanson, Clare Formen, Maureen Holler, Karen Miotke, and Tracy Miotke. Barbering wasn't just shaves and haircuts years ago…. Elmer was called upon for other services too. He remembers pulling a tooth or two and helping quite a few people get something out of their eye down through the years—all at no charge.

His early years of barbering found him at the shop six days a week, including nights, sometimes to midnight, and occasionally even on Sundays. In 1950 he went to Moorhead, Minnesota for seven months to work for another barber, but occasional visits back to Roslyn convinced him he should return to his old hometown.

181

After 1951, he opened only Saturday and Wednesday nights and for the last 10 years, he has been open only during the day, closing on Mondays. For 14 years he also went to Pierpont one day a week to provide barbering services there, but he quit that routine in 1967.

His wife explains that her husband's health has always been good, and he has missed very few days at the barbershop due to illness. "He's always happy when he is busy, but I can remember some occasions when I wasn't too happy about the hours he kept," she mused. She told about one time when only two customers showed up the entire day and she figured it was useless for him to go back to the shop after supper. As it turned out, he gave 14 cuts that evening and didn't get home until 2 AM. "Needless to say, I didn't get a very welcome reception when I got home," Elmer chuckled.

Getting second wind

The barber figures he is just getting his second wind in the barbering business and plans to continue as long as his health allows. "I read a feature about a 78-year-old barber in Portland recently who is still cutting hair and figure I can match him," he says. Vevang went on, "That fellow said he went to work at 5 and quit at 11, chasing women after that. Heck, I don't chase women…. They chase me." He laughed.

Mrs. Vevang claims her husband has to continue barbering because "He already made his first million, and now he has to make mine." He argues that point, however, and explains he doesn't think the cigar box he uses for a cash register is indicative of a millionaire. "There's never been enough money in the box for anyone to want to steal it, and besides people here are too honest for that," Vevang lamented. The 39-year-old barber's motto is "hair today, gone tomorrow." Elmer plans to be at the open house Saturday, but he takes his barbering seriously. Thus, his children wouldn't be surprised if their father took time out from festivities to give someone a haircut, if they really needed and asked for one.

After all, how can you argue with a fellow who has been in the barbering business 52 years, 50 in the same town, says he is 39, plans to add a seventh-generation haircut to his clip list some day and goes by the successful philosophy of "My customers are great, and if I treat them right, they'll treat me right."

The community of Roslyn presented Elmer with this beautiful engraving, noting that Elmer provided a community service to the people of Roslyn.

Elmer certainly treated his customers right, and the community reciprocated.

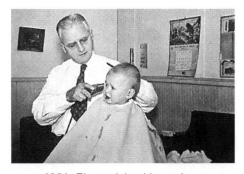

1951. Elmer giving his nephew, James Watkins, a haircut.

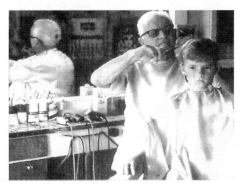

1968. Elmer giving his grandson, Kevin Vevang, a haircut.

Elmer Vevang and Elna Olson Vevang married 50 Years

November 15, 1981

Elmer and Elna with their children.
From left: Allen Vevang, Darlis Vevang Dedrickson, Elna, Elmer, and Warren Vevang

OBITUARY

Elmer N. Vevang

Roslyn – The funeral for Elmer N. Vevang, 93, Roslyn, will be at 2 p.m. Friday at Roslyn Lutheran Church. The Rev. Dean Nelson will officiate. Burial will be in the Roslyn Cemetery with Mohs Funeral Home in Webster and Werness Funeral Home in Minneapolis in charge of arrangements.

Visitation will be from 5 p.m. to 9 p.m. Thursday and 10 a.m. to 11:30 a.m. Friday at Mohs Funeral Home in Webster. There will also be visitation one hour prior to the service on Friday at the church in Roslyn. He died Monday, Aug. 15, 1994, at Lake Area Hospital in Webster.

Elmer N. Vevang was born Feb. 4, 1901, to Iver and Serina (Hustad) Vevang of Roslyn in Nutley Township, near Roslyn. He grew up and attended school in Nutley Township. He attended Barber College in Minneapolis in 1923. He barbered a short time in Minneapolis, Aberdeen and Eden. In 1925, he bought the Roslyn Barber Shop. He married Elna Olson on Nov. 15, 1931, in Roslyn. He barbered until February 1989. He had been a resident of the Strand-Kjorsvig Community Rest Home since April 1989. He was a member of the Roslyn Booster Club and Roslyn Lutheran Church.

Survivors include his wife of Roslyn; two sons, Warren Vevang of Scotts Valley, Calif., and Allen Vevang of Bloomington, Minn.; one brother, Lawrence Vevang of St. Paul, Minn.; Three sisters, Mrs. Ella Montgomery of Roanoke, Va., Mrs. Hilda Olson of Minneapolis and Mrs. Charles (Myrtle) Watkins of Florida; six grandchildren; and five great-grandchildren. He was preceded in death by one daughter, and several brothers and sisters. Casket bearers will be Harlan Storley, Irvin Mydland, James Dedrickson, James Sherman, Sidney Gullickson, Nord Monson and Sherman Johnson.

OBITUARY

Elna A. Olson Vevang

Roslyn – Elna A. Vevang, 83, Roslyn, died Wednesday, Nov 9, 1994, at The Good Samaritan Luther Manor in Sioux Falls.

Her funeral will be at 2 p.m. Saturday at Roslyn Lutheran Church. The Rev. Dean Johnson will officiate. Burial will be in the Roslyn Cemetery with Mohs Funeral Home in Webster in charge of arrangements.

Visitation will be from 2 p.m. to 7 p.m. today at the funeral home in Webster, and one hour prior to the service on Saturday at the church in Roslyn.

Elna A. Olson was born Nov. 4, 1911, to Knute and Anna (Oland) Olson in Hillhead, S.D. She attended elementary school in the Hillhead area and high school in Aberdeen.

She married Elmer N. Vevang on Nov. 15, 1931, in Roslyn. She was employed at Day County Hospital in Webster for several years. She resided in Roslyn for 63 years. She had been a resident of The Good Samaritan Luther Manor in Sioux Falls for the past two years. She was a member of many civic organizations in Roslyn and of Roslyn Lutheran Church.

Survivors include two sons, Warren Vevang of Scotts Valley, Calif., and Allen Vevang of Bloomington, Minn.; one sister Mrs. Myrtle Brown of Fremont, Calif.; one brother, Virgil Olson of Rapid City; six grandchildren, and five great-grandchildren.

She was preceded in death by her husband on Aug. 15, 1994, one daughter, and several brothers and sisters.

Honorary casket bearers will be Sidney Gullickson, Chester Sellevold and Sherman Johnson. Casket bearers will be James Dedrickson, Clarence Dedrickson, Harlan Storley, Nord Monson, James Sherman and Irvin Mydland. Organist will be Mrs. Doris Monson, and vocalists will be Bonnie Strand and Gary Strand.

FAMILY

Elmer Nicolai Vevang b: 04 Feb 1901, Nutley Township, Day County, South Dakota; d: 15 Aug 1994, Lake Area Hospital, Webster, Day County, South Dakota; buried: Roslyn Cemetery, Roslyn, Day County, South Dakota

Elmer married **Elna Annette Olson** b: 04 Nov 1911, Hillhead, Marshall County, South Dakota; m: 15 Nov 1931, Roslyn Lutheran Church, Roslyn, Day County, South Dakota; d: 09 Nov 1994, The Good Samaritan Luther Manor, Sioux Falls, South Dakota; buried: Roslyn Cemetery, Roslyn, Day County, South Dakota

CHILDREN
of Elmer Nicolai Vevang and Elna Annette Olson

Darlis Janet Vevang b: 18 Mar 1933, Peabody Hospital, Webster, Day County, South Dakota; d: 23 May 1990, Sioux Falls, Minnehaha County, South Dakota; buried: Woodlawn Cemetery, Sioux Falls, South Dakota

Warren Elmer Vevang b: 23 Oct 1934, Peabody Hospital, Webster, Day County, South Dakota

Allen Gene Vevang b: 25 Sep1936, Peabody Hospital, Webster, Day County, South Dakota; d: 31 Aug 2012, Edina, Hennepin County, Minnesota; buried: Resurrection Cemetery, Mendota Heights, Minnesota

DARLIS JANET VEVANG

Born
March 18, 1933
Webster, Day County, SD

Died
May 23, 1990
Sioux Falls, Minnehaha County, SD
Laid to rest in Woodlawn Cemetery, Sioux Falls, SD

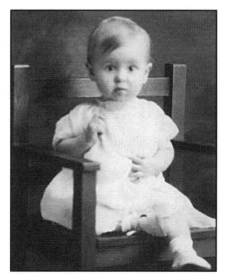 

Darlis Janet Vevang

married

James (Jim) LeRoy Dedrickson

October 3, 1954

Roslyn Lutheran Church
Roslyn,
Day County,
South Dakota

Wedding Party
From left: Carol Erickson, Joan Gilbertson, Idella Dedrickson, Darlis Vevang, James Dedrickson, Clarence Dedrickson, Robert Dedrickson, Allen Vevang, and the flower girl (front), Connie Olson

Three Cousins
One Dress

Three Vevang cousins wore the same wedding dress. Each made it their own.

Viola Olson Fellows married in 1953
Darlis Vevang Dedrickson married in 1954
Shirley Vevang Gillard married in 1958

Viola Olson Fellows   Darlis Vevang Dedrickson   Shirley Vevang Gillard

Kimberly (Kim) James Dedrickson was born in 1955
Vicki Lynn Dedrickson was born in 1957
Keith Allen Dedrickson was born in 1958
Kari Annette Dedrickson was born in 1966

Kim Dedrickson and Vicki Dedrickson

From left: Keith, Vicki, Kim, and Kari (front)

The Dedrickson Family
Standing from left: Keith, Vicki, Kim
Sitting from left: Kari, Darlis, Jim

OBITUARY

Darlis Janet Vevang Dedrickson

Darlis Janet Vevang was born March 18, 1933, at Webster, South Dakota, to Elna and Elmer Vevang. She attended school at Roslyn for eleven years and in 1950 moved with her family to Moorhead, Minnesota, where she graduated from Moorhead High School in 1951. Darlis attended the Swedish Hospital School of Nursing in Minneapolis, Minnesota and graduated in 1954. On Oct. 3, 1954, she was united in marriage to James "Jim" Dedrickson at Roslyn, South Dakota. Darlis' goal and dream in life was to be a registered nurse and to care for the sick. Darlis began her career in 1954 as a Registered Nurse at the Peabody Memorial Hospital, Webster, South Dakota. In 1955 Darlis and Jim moved to Mountain View, California, where Darlis worked at the Palo Alto Hospital.

In 1957 the family moved back to Webster, South Dakota, where Darlis worked at the Day County Memorial Hospital. Her duties were Director of Nursing and Surgery. In 1971 the family moved to Sioux Falls, South Dakota. Darlis worked at Sioux Valley Hospital and later at McKennan Hospital working part-time until 1988, when poor health forced her to retire.

She was a member of Our Savior's Lutheran Church where she served on numerous committees. She also served as a volunteer Red Cross worker and did other volunteer work in the community. Darlis' love and devotion for her Lord and Savior was her foundation on which she would minister to the family, her friends, and all who came in contact with her.

She leaves in mourning her husband; two sons, Kim James and Keith Allen of Sioux Falls; two daughters, Mrs. Randy (Vicki Lynn) Sturm and Kari Annette Dedrickson of Sioux Falls; three grandchildren, Alicia and Breanna Dedrickson, Minneapolis, Minnesota, Matthew Juhl, Sioux Falls, South Dakota, her parents, Elna and Elmer Vevang, Roslyn; her two brothers, Warren Vevang of Santa Cruz, California, and Allen Vevang of Minneapolis, Minnesota; and her many relatives whom she loved so dearly and a host of friends.

OBITUARY

James (Jim) Dedrickson

From left: Kim, Vicki, Keith, and Kari

James (Jim) Dedrickson, 87 passed away on March 22, 2018 at Tidewell Hospice in Venice, Florida with his family at his side.

Jim was born on December 19, 1930, in Bristol, South Dakota. He attended Webster, South Dakota, schools and played basketball for the Webster Bearcats who won consecutive state basketball titles in 1946, 1947 and 1948. They were inducted into the South Dakota Hall of Fame in 2012. He then attended Northern State College in Aberdeen, South Dakota.

Jim was in the National Guard and served in the tank division in Alaska until he was honorably discharged in 1952.

Jim was united in marriage to Darlis Vevang on October 3, 1954, and from this union four children were born, Kim, Vicki, Keith and Kari. Darlis passed away on May 23, 1990. Jim and Darlis lived in Webster and California before moving to Sioux Falls where Jim started selling insurance for Lutheran Brotherhood for 37 years before retiring in 1998. Jim married Judy Connor on February 28, 1992. They have many happy memories of travels to Hawaii, Germany, Italy, Ireland and other Scandinavian countries.

Jim was the head of the building fund at Our Savior's Lutheran Church when the new addition was built. He sang in the choir in Webster and at Our Savior's and was a member of the American Legion for over 50 years. In his active life, he loved being at Pickerel Lake during the summer and enjoyed fishing and boating as well as hunting with his family and friends.

In 2010 Jim and Judy purchased a villa in Venice, Florida, where he enjoyed riding his three-wheel bike on the flat land. He kept track of how many miles he rode in his little blue bike book. Most winters he would ride hundreds of miles just riding the same road back and forth by their home.

Grateful for having shared his life are: his wife, Judy of Sioux Falls; his children, Kim Dedrickson of Sioux Falls, Vicki (Jon) Lacey of San Diego, California, Keith Dedrickson and Kari Jamtgaard of Sioux Falls; step-children, Jill (Troy) Erlandson and Tim Connor; three grandchildren, Alicia Dedrickson and Bre Dedrickson and Matt (Alysia) Juhl; 1 step granddaughter, Kaylynn Erlandson.

FAMILY

Darlis Janet Vevang b: 18 Mar 1933, Peabody Hospital, Webster, Day County, South Dakota; d: 23 May 1990, Sioux Falls, Minnehaha County, South Dakota; buried: Woodlawn Cemetery, Sioux Falls, South Dakota

Darlis married **James LeRoy Dedrickson** b: 19 Dec 1930, Bristol, Day County, South Dakota; m: 03 Oct 1954, Roslyn Lutheran Church, Roslyn, Day County, South Dakota; d: 22 March 2018, Tidewell Hospice in Venice, Sarasota County, Florida; buried: Woodlawn Cemetery, Sioux Falls, South Dakota

    Darlis and Jim's children:
    Kimberly (Kim) James Dedrickson b: 16 Oct 1955, Webster, Day County, South Dakota
    Vicki Lynn Dedrickson b: 09 Jul 1957, Santa Clara, Santa Clara County, California
    Keith Allen Dedrickson b:10 Jun 1958, Webster, Day County, South Dakota
    Kari Annette Dedrickson b: 20 Dec 1966, Webster, Day County, South Dakota

James LeRoy Dedrickson married **Judy Wulff Connor** b: 23 Mar 1942, Madison, Lake County, South Dakota; m: 28 Feb 1992, Sioux Falls, South Dakota

CHILDREN AND GRANDCHILDREN
of Darlis Janet Vevang and James LeRoy Dedrickson

Kimberly (Kim) James Dedrickson

Vicki and Jon

Vicki Lynn Dedrickson married **Mark Douglas Juhl** b: 01 Mar 1952, Miller, Hand County, South Dakota; m: 17 Jun 1977, Sioux Falls, Minnehaha County, South Dakota: div.; d: 06 Feb 2021, Sioux Falls, South Dakota

    Vicki and Mark's child:
    Matthew Allen Juhl b: 18 Sep 1982,
    Sioux Falls, Minnehaha County, South Dakota, adopted

Vicki Lynn Dedrickson married **Jonathon Patrick Lacey** b: 15 Dec 1963, Sioux Falls, Minnehaha County, South Dakota; m: 04 Nov 2000, Manoa Falls, Oahu, Hawaii; d: 12 Sep 2020, San Diego, San Diego County, California

Alysia and Matthew

Matthew Allen Juhl married **Alysia Joy Swenson**
b: 08 Jun 1982, Dell Rapids, Minnehaha County,
South Dakota; m: 05 Jul 2006, Las Vegas,
Clark County, Nevada

Matthew and Alysia's children:
Dominick Thomas Juhl b: 22 Jul 2003,
Sioux Falls, South Dakota
Morgan JoAnne Swenson b: 02 Nov 2004,
Sioux Falls, South Dakota
Aiden Russell Juhl b: 14 Nov 2004,
Sioux Falls, South Dakota
Danika Lynn Juhl b: 29 Nov 2006,
Sioux Falls, South Dakota

Dominick

Morgan

Danika and Aiden

Keith Allen Dedrickson married **Christine Lynn Goettsch** b: 19 May 1960, Sioux City,
Woodbury County, Iowa; m: 29 Jul 1978, Sioux Falls, Minnehaha County, South Dakota:
div.

Keith and Christy's children:
Alicia Marie Dedrickson b: 21 Oct 1978,
Sioux Falls, Minnehaha County, South Dakota
Breanna Lynn Dedrickson b: 03 Nov 1980,
Sioux Falls, Minnehaha County, South Dakota

Breanna

Alicia

Alicia Marie Dedrickson married **Brian James Koberstein** b: 29 Dec 1976,
Milwaukee, Milwaukee County, Wisconsin; m: 17 Feb 2019, St. Paul, Ramsey
County, Minnesota

Brian's son:
Harrison Michael Koberstein
b: 10 Sep 2013, Minneapolis, Hennepin County, Minnesota

Alicia and Brian's children:
Evelyn Marie Koberstein
b: 20 Aug 2020, Minneapolis, Hennepin County, Minnesota
Judah Marson Koberstein
b: 23 Oct 2023, Minneapolis, Hennepin County, Minnesota

Evelyn, Alicia, Judah, Brian, and Harrison

Breanna Lynn Dedrickson married **Alexis Shaffer McKinley** b:12 Aug 1981,
La Mirada, Los Angeles County, California; m: 8 Sept 2018, Hudson, St. Croix
County, Wisconsin

Breanna and Alex's children:
Griffin Alexander Dedrickson
b: 16 Nov 2018, Edina, Hennepin County, Minnesota;
d: 16 Nov 2018, Edina, Hennepin County, Minnesota
Mack Zander Dedrickson
b: 31 Dec 2019, Minneapolis, Hennepin County, Minnesota
Sander William Dedrickson
b: 06 Jun 2022, Minneapolis, Hennepin County, Minnesota

Griffin

Alexis, Breanna holding
Sander, and Mack

Kari Annette Dedrickson Jamtgaard married **Kendall Jamtgaard** m: 12 Jun 1992: div.

At Keith Dedrickson's Pickerel Lake home near Grenville, South Dakota in 2016

Back row: Michael Downs, Kim Dedrickson, Jon Lacey, Warren Vevang and Keith Dedrickson
Front row: Valarie Vevang Downs, Kari Dedrickson Jamtgaard, James Dedrickson,
Judy Dedrickson, Vicki Dedrickson Lacey, Jan Hightower Vevang,
Breanna Dedrickson, Alicia Dedrickson

WARREN ELMER VEVANG

Born

October 23, 1934

Webster, Day County, SD

Warren Elmer Vevang

married

**Janice (Jan) Evelyn
Hightower**

November 15, 1957

San Jose,
Santa Clara County,
California

Wedding Bells

Mr. and Mrs. William E. Hightower
request the honour of your presence
at the marriage of their daughter

Janice Evelyn

to

Mr. Warren Elmer Vevang

on Friday, the fifteenth of November
nineteen hundred and fifty-seven
at eight o'clock in the evening

Baptist Temple
1920 Park Avenue
San Jose, California

Reception immediately
following the ceremony

Warren, Jan, and their children, Valarie and Kevin

Warren and Jan Vevang Family

In front from left: Jan, Sawyer, Porter, Warren, and Heather. Back row from left: Danielle, Aspen, Colton, Scott, Wes, LeiLani, Kevin, Valarie, Michael.

From left: Wesley Hodson, Heather Downs Hodson holding Sawyer Hodson, Michael Downs, Danielle Downs, Kevin Vevang, LeiLani Morris Vevang, Janice Hightower Vevang, Warren Vevang and Valarie Vevang Downs in 2011.

Making lefse has become a family tradition. From left: Sawyer Hodson, LeiLani Morris Vevang, Heather Downs Hodson, Janice Hightower Vevang, Danielle Downs Preizler, Valarie Vevang Downs and Colton Preizler

Warren and Jan Vevang's trip to Vevang, Norway in 2010
Written by Jan Vevang

Iver and Serina Vevang   Jakob Vevang

Friday, Max and Margaret, descendants of Jakob Vevang, drove us to the community of Vevang where we walked around a bit and saw the home where Warren's great-grandfather and grandfather Vevang lived. The house was built over 200 years ago.

We then drove the Atlantic Road, which is a unique highway that zigzags across eight bridges and rock fills from island to island right out to the ocean's edge. The road begins just outside Vevang, crossing the notorious waters of Hustadvika Bay, and was voted Norwegian Structure of the Century.

We took another drive out to Vevang to look over the community and the fishing docks a little more. While driving past the Vevang house we saw the owner was in the yard and we stopped to talk to her. Her husband came out and we introduced ourselves to them, telling them that Warren's great-grandfather and grandfather had lived in that house. Their names are Osa and Arild Noss (no relation) and they invited us in to see the house which they had purchased five years ago. They have worked very hard at restoring it and are planning to open it as a Bed and Breakfast by 2011.

Warren brought out some pictures he had taken in Vevang when he visited in 1955 and some old photos of his grandparents. Arild disappeared and soon came back with a cigar box of some old pictures he had saved from the previous owner who was a Vevang. One of the pictures was an original wedding photo of Warren's grandparents, Iver Vevang and Serina Hustad, and a photo of Warren's great-grandfather, Jakob Vevang, which he gave to us to keep since they were of Warren's family, not his. As we were leaving, Osa and Arild insisted that we stop for coffee on Monday when we go to Kristiansund. This day was probably the highlight of our trip as it was so meaningful to Warren to see Vevang and his grandfather's home 55 years later. Warren had visited Vevang Norway in 1955.

FAMILY

Warren Elmer Vevang b: 23 Oct 1934, Peabody Hospital, Webster, Day County, South Dakota

Warren married **Janice Evelyn Hightower** b: 29 Mar 1939, Phoenix, Maricopa County, Arizona; m: 15 Nov 1957, San Jose, Santa Clara County, California

Warren and Jan's children:
Valarie Lynn Vevang b: 19 Aug 1958, San Jose, Santa Clara County, California
Kevin Warren Vevang b: 21 Jun 1960, San Jose, Santa Clara County, California

CHILDREN AND GRANDCHILDREN
of Warren Elmer Vevang and Janice Evelyn Hightower

Valarie, Danielle, Heather, Michael

Valarie Lynn Vevang married **Michael Connell Downs** b: 02 Dec 1958, Fresno, Fresno County, California; m: 14 Aug 1982, First Baptist Church of Santa Cruz, Santa Cruz County, California

Valarie and Mike's children:
Danielle Ashley Downs b: 20 Apr 1985, San Jose, Santa Clara County, California
Heather Christine Downs b: 02 Apr 1988, Santa Cruz, Santa Cruz County, California

Danielle Ashley Downs married **Scott Alexander Preizler** b: 10 May 1984, Mt. Kisco, Westchester County, New York; m: 03 Oct 2015, El Dorado Hills, El Dorado County, California

Danielle and Scott's children:
Colton Connell Preizler b: 13 Oct 2016, Carmichael, Sacramento County, California
Aspen Alexandria Preizler b: 6 May 2019, Sacramento, Sacramento County, California

Danielle, Aspen, Colton, Scott

Heather Christine Downs married **Wesley David Hodson** b: 12 Aug 1987, Springfield, Lane County, Oregon; m: 12 Mar 2011, Oahu, Hawaii

Heather and Wesley's children:
Sawyer Rose Hodson b: 05 Sep 2011, Folsom, Sacramento County, California
Porter Michael Hodson b: 09 Aug 2013, Folsom, Sacramento County, California

Heather, Sawyer, Wesley, Porter

Kevin Warren Vevang married **LeiLani Louise Morris** b: 19 Dec 1950, Klamath Falls, Klamath County, Oregon; m: 04 Feb 1990, Catalina Island, California

ALLEN GENE VEVANG

Born
September 25, 1936
Webster, Day County, SD

Died
August 31, 2012
Edina, Hennepin County, MN
Laid to rest in Resurrection Cemetery, Mendota Heights, MN

Portraits of Allen Gene Vevang

Roslyn Grade School 1944-1945
Allen Vevang is standing in the second row, second from right

Allen served in the Navy aboard the hospital ship USS Consolation and received his mortuary training at San Francisco School of Mortuary Science. Allen was devoted to his profession and spent his entire career in the funeral business. Allen married Charlotte Ann Knapp—his best pal and loving wife of 40 years. Charlotte was born 19 Sep 1935 in Minneapolis, Hennepin County, Minnesota.

Allen Gene Vevang

married

Charlotte Ann Knapp

March 24, 1972

Edina,
Hennepin County,
Minnesota

The Call and The Smell of The North: Lutefisk

By Blaine Harden, *New York Times*
The Dallas Morning News
Thursday, December 26, 2002, p. 13A

MINNEAPOLIS – Allen Vevang, an undertaker of Norwegian descent, does not like to lunch alone, especially during the holidays. If Charlotte, his wife of 30 years, would join him, he says he would be filled with joy. But she refuses, as long as he insists on eating lutefisk.

So, it was in Christmas week that Mr. Vevang found his solitary way to Pearson's Restaurant, a Minneapolis institution that caters to the seasonal cravings of Scandinavian-Americans. His lunchtime plate was piled high with mashed potatoes, creamed squash and the translucent, lye-soaked cod that reliably causes his wife (of German descent) to eat elsewhere. "Some people say lutefisk has a very fishy taste and an unpleasant smell," said Mr. Vevang, 61, looking doleful as he chewed his gelatinous fish, which he had anointed, in the Norwegian way, with copious amounts of melted butter. "To me, it tastes like Christmas. My present to myself is to come to this restaurant and eat it, even if I have to do it alone."

All along the lutefisk zone – a vast swath of the United States stretching from Chicago to Seattle – it is again the season to rejoice in and quarrel over a food that stinks up hundreds of Lutheran church basements and injects menu-planning torment into hundreds of thousands of mixed marriages.

On one side of this tormented mix are Scandinavians like Mr. Vevang who lunched alone. Their mothers raised them to believe in lutefisk (pronounced LOOT-uh-fisk) as the quivering embodiment of the holiday spirit. On the other is a restive horde of spouses, children and in-laws (a surprisingly large number of whom have Scandinavian blood). They never eat lutefisk, object raucously to its odor and rarely allow themselves to be mollified by the inevitable peace offering of Swedish Meatballs.

Notwithstanding the familial tension, experts say that by New Year's Day, Americans will have cooked and eaten more than 1 million pounds of lutefisk. To locate the fish schism, one needs to look no farther than the restaurant that on Monday sated Mr. Vevang's hunger for tradition. "I serve it, but I won't eat it," said Carrie Cooney; the waitress at Pearson's who carried lunch to Mr. Vevang. "My wife is Norwegian, but we got the rules straight when we were married – no lutefisk," said Larry Nelson, the manager at Pearson's.

"I am not comfortable with the color texture," said Maureen Pearson, wife of the restaurant's owner. Her husband declined to say if he ate lutefisk. "I refuse to comment on the grounds that it might be bad for business," said Marston Pearson. He did say that the lutefisk trade has increased splendidly in his restaurant in recent years. The principle reason, he said, is the apparent reluctance of lutefisk eaters (and haters) to stink up their own kitchens. The odor of cooked lutefisk-an enduring aroma that melds the rankness of overripe fish with the industrial-strength stench of a soap factory—is something of an obsession in better homes throughout the lutefisk zone.

In the Minneapolis Star Tribune this month, a reader from Milaca, Minn., offered her favorite solution. It was Atmos Klear, a fragrance-free odor remover available at hardware stores. As interesting as the reader's cure was her description of how it saved the spirit of Christmas. "I was able to eliminate the smell of the lutefisk I prepare each year, while maintaining the vibrant odor of our fresh Christmas tree," the reader wrote. "Nobody smelled that terrible odor in my home ahead of time." "All this harping about odor is disproportionate and unfair," said Roger Dorff, the recently retired president of Olsen Fish, a company based in Minneapolis that processes about half the lutefisk eaten in North America. "You know, if I boil shrimp at home, it also smells," said Mr. Dorff, who this year handed the presidency of Olsen Fish to his son, Chris.

The Lye Method

Rather than talk about the smell, Mr. Dorff preferred to talk about tradition and purity in the processing of lutefisk. He explained that lutefisk literally means lye fish. It is an ancient Norwegian method of preserving the summer's catch and it was widely practiced by poor Norwegians, many of whom ended up migrating to the United States.

The fish is cod or lingcod caught in the North Sea. It used to be hung in the sun on racks, but now it is dried in kilns, which keeps birds from pecking at it and defecating on it. Once dried, cod becomes stock fish, a whitish or yellowish substance with the texture of leather and the rigidity of cardboard.

Olsen Fish imports its stockfish from Norway and begins soaking it in September. It receives alternating baths of fresh water, lye water and fresh water. When it is rinsed of lye and rehydrated to plumpness, lutefisk is vacuum-packed for church suppers and Christmas dinners. (Lye leaves a distinctive ashy taste, which many people find offensive and which can cause heartburn.) The traditional way of preparing lutefisk is to boil it. But boiling it too long turns it to fish water; so many modern cooks steam it or bake it.

About two-fifths of the lutefisk consumed in the United States and Canada, Mr. Dorff said, is put away at church suppers and gatherings of Scandinavian-dominated fraternal groups like the Sons of Norway. The rest is eaten at home. "The big eaters are the ones at the church suppers," Mr. Dorff said. "They will eat a pound or two of it at a sitting and they often go to several church suppers during the lutefisk season, which begins in late September."

But the big eaters, who tend to be Scandinavian men on the high side of 60, are disappearing. "When an old guy dies, then you lose 8 to 10 pounds of lutefisk consumption per year," said Mr. Dorff, who is 64. "Younger people are not as interested and they certainly don't eat that much lutefisk, although we are attempting to appeal to them."

That attempt includes hot, buttery lutefisk giveaways at summer gatherings of young people in Minnesota and Wisconsin, which are the premier lutefisk states. The others in the lutefisk zone are Illinois, Iowa, North and South Dakota, Montana and Washington. There is also the Lutefisk TV dinner, a mass-marketing ploy invented by Mike's Field of Mike's Fish in Glenwood, Minn., and imitated by Olsen Fish. Believing that there are a substantial number of Norwegians who would eat lutefisk year-round, Mr. Dorff made a sizable wager on TV dinners four years ago.

Microwaveable

Olsen Fish bought 1,500 cases of microwave-safe plastic packs, each containing 12 segmented dinner plates. His employees filled a few hundred of them with mashed potatoes, peas and six ounces of lutefisk. The frozen vacuum-sealed dinners were distributed to select supermarkets in Minnesota, where, for the most part they did not sell.

"Each year, it has gone down, down, down," Mr. Dorff said, speaking of TV dinner sales. That is not the case, though, with the overall lutefisk market. "It is holding steady at about a million pounds a year," Mr. Dorff said. "And if it snows early in the season, sales pick up. People like to eat lutefisk when there is snow on the ground."

An Old Storytelling Session

In 2006, an Old Storytelling session was held in Roslyn, South Dakota. It was emceed by Duane Bergland, hosted by Bob and Sally Kjorsvig at the Creamery building. It was filmed by Beverly Farmen of Farmen Productions from Groton, South Dakota.

Allen Vevang, the youngest son of Elmer and Elna, shared stories of growing up in the small Norwegian town of Roslyn. The 19-minute video can be seen at this link on YouTube. https://www.youtube.com/watch?v=1hevPOfYaZ8&app=desktop

Allen shares the story of how his article about lutefisk was published all over the country and even in Norway. It was published on Christmas Day. Allen talks of his father, Elmer's barbershop. The barbershop was moved to the Webster, Day County Museum where it can be seen as it was on Elmer's last day of business. Allen also shared colorful stories of his own vocation, that of being 'an undertaker'. Allen shared his talent of telling a story and finding the humor in everyday life—he always had a smile on his face, a twinkle in his eyes, and he made the people around him laugh.

Allen Vevang Tribute

In some families, aunts and uncles do not have a chance to spend time with their nieces and nephews as they grow up. Not so with our Uncle Allen and Aunt Charlotte. We are Allen's late sister's children: Kim, Vicki, Keith, and Kari. Uncle Allen was every kid's dream for an uncle. He rocked us when we were babies and loved to hold us on his lap when we were toddlers. There was excitement in the house when Allen was coming to visit. Not only for the neat gifts he would bring, but just for the anticipation of watching the shiniest black car we had ever seen pull up in our driveway. This tall dark handsome man that dressed like Cary Grant would jump out of the car, walk up to us kids wearing the blackest, shiniest shoes, and with his loud voice yell, "Hi kids! Come give Uncle Allen a hug!" Then he would laugh. Uncle Allen didn't have to read us bedtime stories. His stories were much better and as we got older, the stories kept getting better and better. Our Uncle Allen will be sincerely missed. Our family has so many fond memories of him and we cherish the times we spent together.

From Vicki: Allen would try anything and one of my fondest childhood memories was of watching Allen learn to water ski. The boat pulled him out of the water okay, but then the water show began. Allen skied on one ski, then two skis, then one ski, then sitting on the skies and up again. He skied with one hand and then two-handed and never fell—and then the drop off! He missed the dock, but then coasted right up to the beach. We were all laughing so hard we were in tears. Allen loves our children, too. He loved having Bre, Alicia, and Matt over. I named my son Matthew Allen after Uncle Allen. I was so proud of Allen.

From Keith: When we were little, Allen would take us out in the country and teach us how to drive while we were sitting on his lap. We have great memories of going duck hunting together or sitting in the pastures for hours shooting gophers. Allen was a great role model and a great influence on many of us growing up. He always enjoyed being around family and made it a priority to attend family reunions, athletic events, and graduations. As many of you know, Allen could start a conversation with anyone. Rarely was there a waitress or flight attendant that wasn't captured by his friendliness; he truly enjoyed getting to know people and connecting with them. Allen loved history and sharing his knowledge. Alicia and Bre were studying for a history test one evening at his house and Allen asked the kids to read the questions to him. To the girls' surprise, he knew all of the answers to the test. They asked him how he knew all of that and he responded simply, "I love history." As nephews and nieces, we all share a history with Allen and his spirit will live on through our stories, pictures and memories of him.

From Kim: Of course, not everyone has an uncle who is a mortician. That being said, most of our visits with Allen in Minneapolis consisted of visiting the beautiful cemeteries in Minneapolis, stopping at mortuaries and meeting Allen's co-workers and, of course, witnessing the admiration Allen had for the dead, and the respect given to each and every soul that was in Allen's hands. He loved his work.

From Kari: I was 8 or 9 years old and Allen and I were lying in the middle of the field with my BB gun in hand, waiting for a gopher to pop his little head up, and I would hear Allen say, "Shoot it now, Kari! Shoot it now!" But we were laughing so hard the little gopher always got away. I will always remember Allen's smile. He had the best smile. When our mother passed away, Allen was always there for us kids. He would take our telephone calls anytime and loved to have us come visit. We are all fortunate to have known him. Everyone, including us kids, will miss Allen deeply.

OBITUARY

Allen Gene Vevang

In Memory of

Allen Gene Vevang

September 25, 1936 ~ August 31, 2012

Allen Vevang, 75, of Bloomington, Minnesota, died August 31, 2012, with his family and friends at his side. Allen died peacefully in his sleep, after a short, but courageous battle with cancer. His parents, Elmer and Elna and his sister, Darlis Vevang Dedrickson preceded him in death.

Allen is survived by Charlotte, his best pal and loving wife of 40 years; brother Warren (Jan); nephews and nieces; close cousins; and a host of friends.

Allen was born in Webster, South Dakota, graduated from Roslyn High School in 1954, and represented Roslyn at South Dakota Boys State. He served in the Navy aboard the hospital ship USS Consolation, attended South Dakota State and received his mortuary training at the San Francisco School of Mortuary Science. Al was devoted to his profession and spent his entire career in the funeral business, including ownership of Listoe-Wold Funeral Home in St. Paul.

He was a member of the Jaycees, Optimist Club, Saga Kluben, and the Bloomington Lions Club chairing the Out of Sight Program. Allen loved traveling, being at the lake, fishing, sports, WW II history and airplanes, but most of all he loved being with family and friends.

Funeral Mass was Saturday, September 8th at St. Edward Catholic Church, 9401 Nesbitt Ave. S., Bloomington, Minnesota. Visitation two hours prior to Mass at church. Private interment. Allen's kind nature and sense of humor touched many hearts. He will be dearly missed.

PALLBEARERS

Jerry Baumberger	Richard Monson
Marvin Rosholt	Ron Schmidt
Elgin Van Anken	Tom Will

*May the road
rise up to meet you,
May the wind be always
at your back,*

*May the sun shine warm
upon your face,
And the rain fall soft
upon your fields*

And until we meet again

*May God hold you
in the palm of his hand.*

Irish Blessing

CHAPTER VI

INGVALD

Born
December 30, 1902
Vevang Family Farm
Nutley Township, Day County, SD

Died
May 17, 1985
Apple Valley, Dakota County, MN
Laid to rest in Webster Cemetery, Webster, SD

Ingvald was baptized in the Lutheran Christian faith on February 15, 1903

Sponsors: Ole and Kjerstine Aas, Ole Stavig and Anna Stavig

Ingvald	*1903* 30 Deb. 1902 15 Feb	Iver & Serina Vevang	*1903.* Ole & Kjerstine Aas, Ole Stavig, Anna Stavig.

U.S. Evangelical Lutheran Church in America Church Records

The Thirteenth United States Federal Census taken in 1910
Nutley Township, Day County, South Dakota

Vevang Iver A.	Head	M	W	44
Serina	Wife	F	W	38
Julius	Son	M	W	12
Hilda	Daughter	F	W	11
Elmer	Son	M	W	9
Ingvald	Son	M	W	7
Selmer	Son	M	W	5
Laura	Daughter	F	W	2
Ella	Daughter	F	W	6/12
Gaara Halvor	Lodger	M	W	36

Ingvald in 1908, age 6

Julius and Ingvald in 1911

Ingvald in 1919, age 17

The Fourteenth United States Federal Census taken in 1920
Nutley Township, Day County, South Dakota

Vevang Iver A.	Head	O	m	m	w	54
Serina	Wife			F	w	47
Julius S.	Son			m	w	23
Elmer L.	Son			m	w	18
Engvald	Son			m	w	17
Selmer	Son			m	w	15
Laura M.	Daughter			F	w	11
Ella H.	Daughter			F	w	10
Alida	Daughter			F	w	9
Myrtle A.	Daughter			F	w	5
Lawrence G.	Son			m	w	4 3/12

—1917—
Emil Anker Haagenson
Reuben Nerland
Ingvald Vevang
Beatrice Sofie Teigen-Storley
Annie Elisabeth Reed
Hilda Reed-Hagen
Laura Emilie Hendrickson

Ingvald was confirmed in 1917, at the age of 14

Confirmation Class of 1917, Roslyn Lutheran Church, Day County, South Dakota. Ingvald is seated on the right.

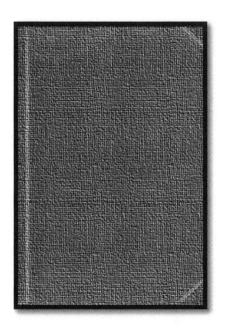

INGVALD was a deep thinker. From a young age he wrote down information about his life. He wrote wherever he could. The picture here is of his ledger book, and that is where he wrote—between the lines.

Ingvald wrote about his jobs and the wages he made. He only schooled through the eighth grade. It was common in those days for the boys to not further their education as they needed to farm the land and bring in other income for the benefit of their families. A summary of Ingvald's many jobs and wages received.

In 1916, at the age of 14, he made $0.45 per hour threshing—$92.00 total. At age 16, he hauled the mail for two weeks at $5.09 per day. At age 17, he ran the Nutley road grader one week at $4.50 per day. Ingvald was the engineer on a 20x40 Case tractor plowing for two weeks at $8.50 per day.

Ingvald worked at the Lincoln Hotel in Watertown, SD for two months running the elevator. At 18 years old, he ran a Titan tractor for one week. In the fall of 1922, Ingvald started to work in the railroad shop in Watertown as a machinist. After two months of service, he made $190-$230 per month. Ingvald worked there for 18 months and made $3,140. In July 1925, he bought a Case threshing outfit and a 20x40 tractor, paying $1,500 for it. He made $6.50 per hour and ran it all alone, using 1,100 gallons of gas threshing 66 hours.

In March 1926, Ingvald traded the tractor for a Case steam engine (25x75) and paid $385. Selmer helped to run it home. It took two days. In the fall of 1926, Ingvald threshed only two days on account of having poor crops. In the summer of 1927, Ingvald sold the threshing outfit for $1,000 and received $300 down. On November 12, 1927, Ingvald foreclosed on Conrad Lien and took the rig back. In 1928, he bought sheep from his father, Iver, and in 1929, Iver sold land to Ingvald so that he could start farming on his own.

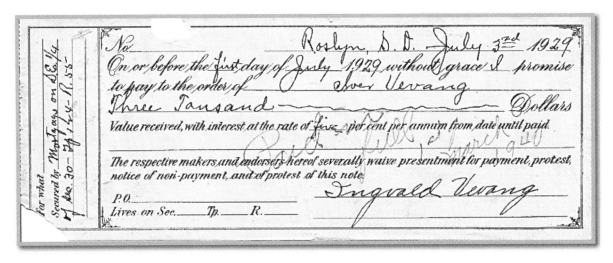

On July 3, 1929, Ingvald Vevang wrote a promissory note to the order of Iver Vevang for $3,000.00 with interest of 5% per annum from date until paid. The promissory note was paid in full on March 1, 1940.

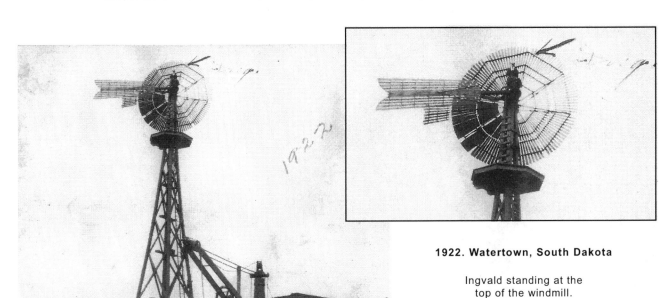

1922. Watertown, South Dakota

Ingvald standing at the
top of the windmill.

1922. Ingvald sitting in the train cab at the train yards of Watertown, South Dakota

1923. Ingvald (on the right) with friends

1922. Ingvald bought his first car.
It was a second-hand Overland for $225.

Ingvald sold the Overland and bought a new
Ford Model T on July 3, 1923 for $628.

November 21, 1938
Ingvald traded for a new 1939 Plymouth Coupe for $400.

The Fifteenth United States Federal Census taken in 1930
Nutley Township, Day County, South Dakota

Vevang	Iver J	Head	O		R	Yes	M	W	64
—	Serina	Wife				×	F	W	58
—	Ingvald	Son				×	M	W	27
—	Laura M	Daughter				×	F	W	22
—	Ella	Daughter				×	F	W	20
—	Alida	Daughter				×	F	W	19
—	Myrtle H	Daughter				×	F	W	15
—	Lawrence G	Son				×	M	W	14

Selmer & Ingvald

Ingvald

Ingvald in the 1930s taken along the countryside near Roslyn

Ingvald Vevang arrived Wednesday evening by car from Minneapolis where he has been employed the past several months. He left Minneapolis last Friday but his car stalled in a snowdrift between Willmar and Montevideo and he took refuge in a nearby farm house. By Sunday, so much snow had fallen and drifted that his car was completely buried. When the roads were opened, he succeeded in getting it out and continued on his journey. He is visiting at the home of his sister, Mrs. Henry Hanson in Webster, until the road is opened to Roslyn when he will go on to the home of his parents, Mr. and Mrs. Iver Vevang.

Reporter and Farmer Webster, SD

Ingvald liked to roam, too. In 1936, he drove over 8,500 miles. This was mentioned in between the lines of his ledger book, which he started writing in 1926. He wanted to see what the world had to offer him outside of where he grew up. On July 18, 1936, Ingvald left for New York, New York. He was gone for three weeks. On October 18, 1936, he left for Los Angeles, California, and was gone for three weeks. He was in 21 states.

Ingvald worked in Minneapolis for a few months in 1936 as an engineer for three heating plant boilers at a hotel. On the way back to South Dakota his car stalled in a snow drift, and he took refuge in a farmhouse. His travels were noted in the local newspaper. In the summer of 1938, Ingvald started to work for Jahnig and Davis doing road construction. The first job was building a road through Big Stone, South Dakota. When not working elsewhere, he helped his father with the farm, and he also had a little piece of land for himself.

In 1939, the winter was about average, Ingvald writes. "Had lots of snow and about two inches of rain in January. Very good crop. Some wheat went $25 a bushel an acre, oats $60 a bushel." He finished his spring work and started to work again for Jahnig and Davis Construction Company as a Letourneau operator at $1 per hour. In the spring of 1940 on April 4th, he bought Waddle's farm from Day County for $3,300. Ted Hosseth was his tenant, and Lawrence Vevang had the other quarter free. The farm Ingvald purchased was directly north of the Iver Vevang family farm. Ingvald had no income from the land that year.

In the Sixteenth Census of the United States of 1940, taken in April, Ingvald lived in Hayfield Township, Dodge County in Minnesota as part of a Jahnig and Davis road construction crew. He was classified as a Blade Operator. Ingvald started on April 20th and finished on November 9th making $935. He was also considered part of Iver Vevang's household.

The Sixteenth United States Federal Census taken in 1940
Hayfield Township, Dodge County, Minnesota

ALBERTA KATHERINE SYVERSON

Born
December 21, 1920
Waubay, Day County, SD

Died
August 3, 1982
Lewistown, Fergus County, MT
Laid to rest in Webster Cemetery, Webster, SD

Ingvald and Alberta were married at the home of Albert Syverson. Ingvald Vevang and Alberta Syverson were united in marriage at 2:00 p.m. Friday, December 6th, 1940. The bride wore a grape wine dress trimmed with a white collar and cuffs. The bridesmaid was Elvira Peterson. The best man was Lawrence Vevang. Catherine Rider sang "I Love You Truly" and Mary Norris sang "I Love You" by Grieg. Luncheon was served to 40 guests with Maxine Brehm, Blanche Hawkinson, and Orvilla Syverson assisting.

INGVALD & ALBERTA VEVANG

Married December 6, 1940
Webster, Day County, South Dakota

RECORD OF MARRIAGE

South Dakota State Board of Health

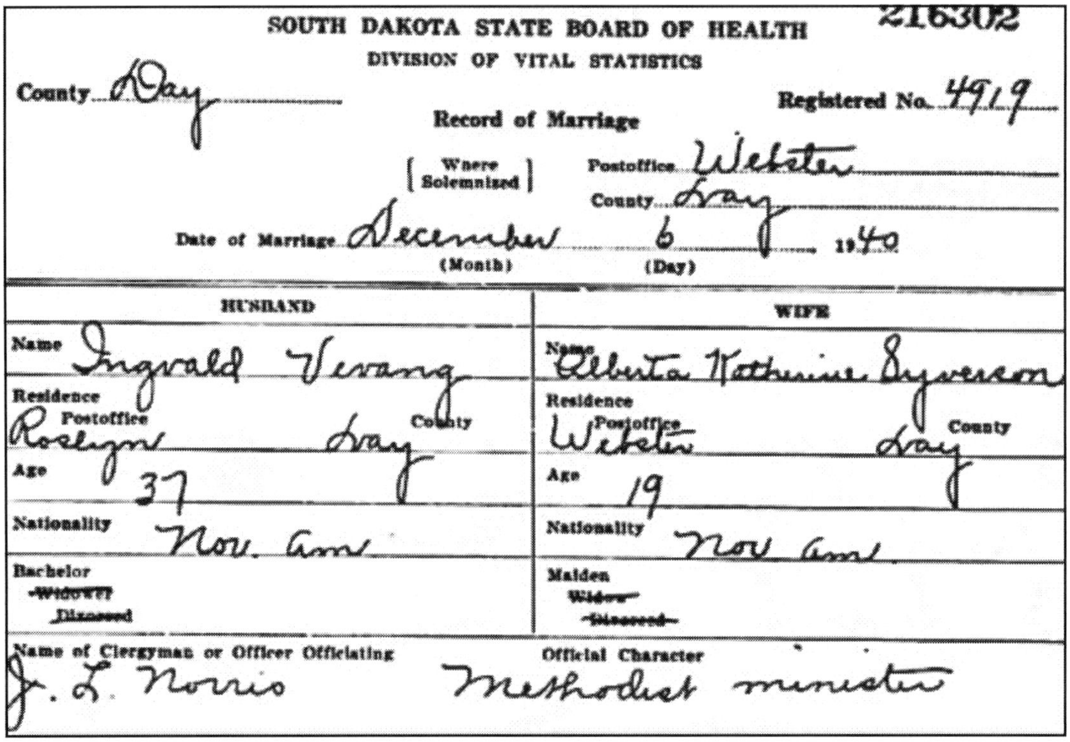

SOUTH DAKOTA STATE BOARD OF HEALTH

DIVISION OF VITAL STATISTICS

216302

County _Day_

Record of Marriage

Registered No. _4919_

[Where Solemnized]

Postoffice _Webster_

County _Day_

Date of Marriage _December_ 6 19_40_

(Month) (Day)

HUSBAND	WIFE
Name _Ingvald Vevang_	Name _Alberta Katherine Syverson_
Residence Postoffice _Roslyn_ County _Day_	Residence Postoffice _Webster_ County _Day_
Age _37_	Age _19_
Nationality _Nov. Am._	Nationality _Nov. Am._
Bachelor Widow?? Divorced	Maiden Widow Divorced

Name of Clergyman or Officer Officiating _J. L. Norris_

Official Character _Methodist minister_

HUSBAND	WIFE
INGVALD VEVANG	ALBERTA KATHERINE SYVERSON
ROSLYN, DAY COUNTY, SD	WEBSTER, DAY COUNTY, SD
AGE 37	AGE 19
NORWEGIAN AMERICAN	NORWEGIAN AMERICAN
BACHELOR	MAIDEN

Transcript of Audio Recorded by Ingvald Vevang

Now we'll jump ahead to about the time that Alberta and I started out. As you know we got married in December of 1940 and took off for California that fall. We thought we'd probably get a job, but we stayed in California about two and a half or three months.

Ingvald and Alberta on the road to California

December 14, 1940
Ingvald and Alberta made their home in a Los Angeles, California Villa at 903 South Burlington.

Ocean Beach, Santa Monica, California, Dec. 12, 1940

> Mr. and Mrs. Ingvald Vevang arrived Tuesday from Los Angeles, Calif., where they have spent the past two and a half months. At present they are at the Iver Vevang farm home. 2-25-1941

Published in *Reporter and Farmer* in Webster, SD

newbrightonhistory.com

It was impossible to find anything to do, so we came back in the spring, I think it was in March of 1941. We bought ourselves a little white trailer house and I went to work for Jahnig and Davis again and moved to Britton.

After we got done there we moved up to Little Falls, Minnesota, and worked on Highway #10 up there. Then in the fall we went up to New Brighton, Minnesota and started to help build a new defense plant. It was quite a project. I was a Letourneau operator at the Twin City Ordinance Plant. I worked there until February 1942.

Alberta was pregnant with our first little girl, our first baby. So, I sent her home and she stayed with Laura, my sister in Webster. But unfortunately, we lost our first girl and that was quite a blow to both of us.

Alberta gave me a lot of encouragement. We lost our little girl on December 29, 1941. It was quite a shock to both of us, a little black-haired girl. She was stillborn.

We named her Sandra Kae Vevang. Sandra was buried in the Roslyn cemetery. A graveside service was held. Reverend. O. M. Simundson oversaw the burial ceremony.

The Ingvald Vevang farm is directly north of Iver Vevang's farm.

I'll jump ahead now to about the time when Alberta and I started to farm on my farm. We came from New Brighton, Minnesota, in about March I guess to settle on the farm. We had an awful good crop the first year, a big crop. One thing I remember that was kind of comical—we had a rooster that always chased Alberta around, and our sheep buck. We had sheep the first couple of years and it got so bad that she had to take the car to go down and get a pail of water. Even to go get the eggs from the chicken coop, she had to take the car because the rooster was always standing on a corner looking to see if he could see Alberta. Then he'd come running and chase her back up to the house.

We enjoyed the three years we lived on the farm… three and a half, I guess. We had a good radio in wintertime. A battery radio as we didn't have electric lights yet… and we did chores and milked a few cows. It didn't matter what the problems were, Alberta never complained. In those days we farmed with a McCormick gearing tractor. During harvest time I got my nephew, Spencer Olson from Minneapolis to help. I taught him to drive a tractor. He got so he was pretty good and I rode the binder. Alberta always brought lunch out for us. We sure enjoyed seeing that coffee coming.

And I was still restless. I had a chance to apply for a job outside of the United States. Tremendous salary for that time. $500 a month and free board and room. But we didn't know where the location was, so I left St. Paul on a special train. It was August 7, 1942, and as we traveled, I found out we were going up towards Winnipeg. The following day we got an idea we were going up to Hudson Bay. We weren't sure, none of us on the train. We probably had 150 men on the train. But we found out we were going up to Fort Churchill, on the Hudson Bay and when we got up there, we found out that we were supposed to go up to South Hampton Island up in the northern part of the Hudson Bay, up in the Arctic Circle to build an airport.

We stayed in Fort Churchill for about ten days. I slept on an old boat that they were fixing up to take up to South Hampton Island. An old timer in Fort Churchill said he wouldn't go up to the Arctic Circle for all the money in the country, plus you'd probably freeze your lungs. There would be no mail, no letters or anything. So, I kind of got cold feet. A lot of other guys did, too. So, a lot of them wanted to head back home. I wanted to do the same thing.

My boss, he started to suspect that I might go home. So, he tried to keep me busy. He gave me a big bulldozer. And when the tide was down in the Hudson Bay, I would go out and push the sand up to make kind of a beach area. I was doing that for quite a bit. The boss was keeping me busy, I guess. I had to work, I don't know about six or seven hours I guess until the change of the tide. Then when the tide came in we had ten feet of water there. Then we'd have to shut down and wait until the tide went out. Then after the tide went out and the water disappeared, I was out in the bay again, dozing sand up.

Still, I thought the best deal was to get back home to good old South Dakota again. Alberta was supposed to go to California because Harvey and Orvilla were out there at that time. It would have been quite a change in our marriage life. Me up in the Arctic Circle and South Hampton Island and she out in California. Too much of a change I guess, a year after getting married. I couldn't take it. I was going to head back home.

Of course, we weren't supposed to take much money up there, so I didn't have enough money to head back home. I wired my brother Julius in Watertown to send some money up and send it to the next station down south pass, about 400 miles south of Fort Churchill. I got on a train and sure enough when I got to the pass the money was there. I was safe and sound and on my way home. I arrived home on August 22nd. I was sure glad to get back to good old South Dakota and to the farm again. I decided I'd keep on farming.

As I reported before, I farmed for three and a half or four years. But the old caterpillar and road construction work was in my system. So, I made a decision… It was quite a hard one to make, to quit farming and try and get into the road construction work. But in them days you couldn't buy road equipment on account of the war still on. That had priority for everything. I sent the priority in, but it was a year before I could get an outfit. The second year we were on the farm, that's when Linda Ann came to us, born in 1943. She was a very easy baby to take care of and we didn't have a bit of trouble. Alberta was just wonderful.

Ingvald was born in 1902 and would have been about 40 years old when he received these Selective Service Classification Notices.

July 23, 1942

Ingvald was deferred due to dependency reasons.

January 1, 1943

Ingvald was deferred in war production.

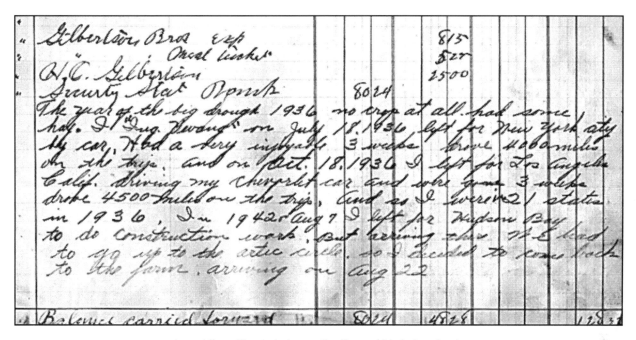

Ingvald's writing in between the lines of his ledger book.

Alberta and Ingvald with their daughter, Linda Ann Vevang

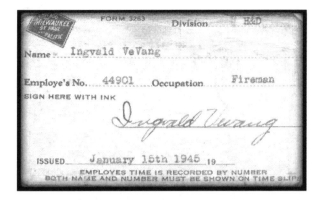

Dennis Ingvald Vevang was born in May of 1945. He is pictured with his older sister, Linda.

In the meantime, in the winter of 1944, I went to Aberdeen and got a job as a fireman and fired on the Milwaukee for three or four months. I fired between Aberdeen and Mobridge most of the time. We had some great big steam locomotives which burnt 25 or 30 tons of coal in a trip. I sat behind a bunch of valves and controlled the coal going in the fire box. Anyway, my first trip out, I had to make three student trips. The first trip out we ran 17 cars off the track, and it took all night to get back to Mobridge. Then there were times when we had two great big locomotives on one train. We pulled about 125 cars of freight, then going through the night with snow coming down across the track in front of the headlight. You can't imagine the thrill of it. I would have stayed by the railroad, for the simple reason it was interesting and a challenge. But I had the roadwork in my system and that's what I wanted to get into. So, I resigned from firing and stuck to the roadwork. The first year I worked for Nick Martin while waiting to get my own outfit. I worked twelve hours a day and was getting 80 cents an hour. That wasn't very much in them days. It was the average price of wages.

INGVALD VEVANG ROAD CONSTRUCTION COMPANY

Webster, South Dakota

Ben Anderson, my regular, worked with me for 15 years, Elwood Monson about twelve years, and Flip Sorrel about eight years. They were my three regulars, and my son, Dennis, worked during the summers running the bulldozer while he was going to college. I was fortunate to have real good men all those 20 years I built roads. I built mostly township roads. From anywhere east of Lake City, down south of Clark to Willow Lake. A lot of times we drove 50 miles to get to work in the mornings. Drove like heck. With five of us in a car sometimes. We used to try and put in 12 hours a day. That's quite a job especially after driving 50 miles to work and 50 miles back.

Of course, coming back we took things a little easier. Especially during the summertime when it was real hot. We always had to go buy a couple cans of beer, so we were drinking beer all the way home. It sure tasted good. Especially during the hot weather in summertime. We drank too much water during the daytime of course so we were sick of water.

Well, that's about all I can think of. I'm recording this in January of 1978, and I intend on having someone type this and then have it put in my safety deposit box at the Security Bank. It will probably lay there for 45 years and then probably my grandchildren will read it someday and know what kind of life their grandfather, Ingvald Vevang, had back in the early 1900s. That should be quite interesting.

Ingvald started his own road construction company in Webster, South Dakota

1947. Alberta Syverson Vevang, Dennis Vevang, Linda Vevang, and Ingvald Vevang.

Linda & Dennis

1948. Ingvald & Alberta's house at 220 W 6th Ave in Webster, SD. Dennis is standing in the driveway.

Linda, Alberta, Ingvald, Pamela, Dennis

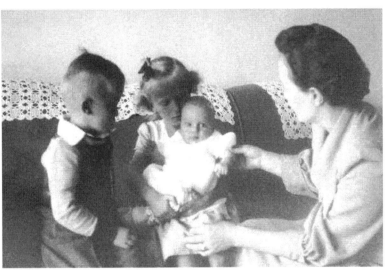

1949. Pamela Jean Vevang was born in the summer. Linda is holding her with Dennis and Alberta.

Pamela, Alberta & Linda

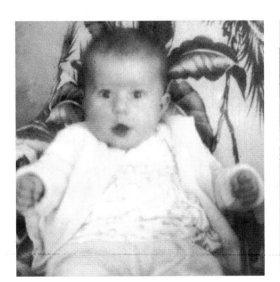

1954. Debra Diane Vevang was born.

Ingvald, Pamela, Dennis, Linda & Alberta holding Debra.

228

Easter Sunday 1957. Linda, Dennis, Pamela, Debra

Christmas 1964. Ingvald, Alberta, Linda, Dennis, Pamela, Debra

1966. Debra, Dennis, Pamela, Linda, Alberta, Ingvald

INGVALD & ALBERTA VEVANG

History of Day County, pg. 923
Day County Historical Research Committee

Ingvald Vevang was born to Serina and Iver Vevang northeast of Roslyn. He helped his parents run the home farm for some years. He later bought a steam threshing outfit, which he ran for about ten years. In 1940, he bought the Fred Waddle farm and married Alberta Syverson of Webster.

Ingvald worked for Jahnig and Davis of Britton for several years. In 1942, the Vevangs started to farm. They farmed for three years, and then in 1945 Ingvald bought his own road grading outfit, and formed the Ingvald Vevang Construction Company of Webster, a business Ingvald ran for 20 years.

Ingvald and Alberta had four children: Linda, Mrs. Gerald Forslund, Apple Valley, Minnesota; Dennis, Triangle, Virginia; Pamela, Mrs. Tim Schneider, Great Falls, Montana; and Debra, Mrs. William Menzel, Aberdeen, South Dakota.

1969
Dennis, Linda, Pamela, Debra
Alberta and Ingvald

OBITUARY

Alberta Syverson Vevang

Mrs. Ingvald (Alberta) Vevang, 61, of Webster, South Dakota was dead on arrival at a hospital in Lewistown, Montana, Tuesday August 3, 1982, as a result of a two-car accident on US Highway 87 west of Lewistown. She was passenger in a car driven by her husband. Their son, Dennis, was also a passenger. The Vevangs were westbound when the accident occurred about 2:30 PM.

Funeral services were held Monday at 10 AM at St. John's Lutheran Church in Webster with the Rev. Harald Palm officiating. Interment was in the Webster Cemetery. Mrs. David Prieb was organist and James Dedrickson, soloist. Casket bearers were Richard Syverson, Allen Vevang, Kim Dedrickson, Karry Syverson, Larry Vevang and Lyle Guderian. Alberta Katherine Syverson was born December 21, 1920 to Albert and Tacy Syverson at Waubay, South Dakota. She graduated from Webster High School and for the past several years had been employed as a nurse's aide. She married Ingvald Vevang December 6, 1940 at Webster. Mrs. Vevang was active in the Day County Hospital Auxiliary, was a member of the Gray Ladies, Bridge Club, Thursday Club and Birthday Club. She was a member of St. John's Lutheran Church.

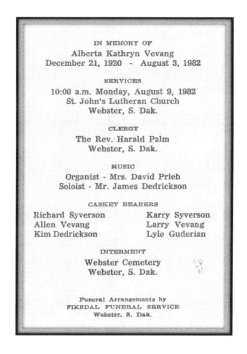

IN MEMORY OF
Alberta Kathryn Vevang
December 21, 1920 - August 3, 1982

SERVICES
10:00 a.m. Monday, August 9, 1982
St. John's Lutheran Church
Webster, S. Dak.

CLERGY
The Rev. Harald Palm
Webster, S. Dak.

MUSIC
Organist - Mrs. David Prieb
Soloist - Mr. James Dedrickson

CASKET BEARERS
Richard Syverson   Karry Syverson
Allen Vevang   Larry Vevang
Kim Dedrickson   Lyle Guderian

INTERMENT
Webster Cemetery
Webster, S. Dak.

Funeral Arrangements by
FIKSDAL FUNERAL SERVICE
Webster, S. Dak.

Survivors include her husband, Webster; one son, Dennis, Triangle, Virgina; three daughters, Mrs. Gerald (Linda) Forslund, Apple Valley, Minnesota; Mrs. Tim (Pamela) Schneider, Great Falls, Montana; and Mrs. William (Debra) Menzel, Aberdeen, South Dakota; Two brothers, Colonel Douglas Syverson, San Antonio, Texas; and Gordon Syverson, Stewart, Minnesota; two sisters, Mrs. Ruth McGuire, Jacksonville, Florida; and Mrs. Robert (Maxine) Moore, Fort Collins. Colorado; and five grandchildren, Kristin Kae Forslund, Eric Gerald Forslund, Amy Jo Forslund, Clinton Timothy Schneider, and Kelly James Menzel. She was preceded in death by her parents, one brother and one infant daughter.

Grandma's Touch

Written by Kristin Kae Forslund (Alberta's Granddaughter) at age 16

The telephone rang at eight o'clock that hot, summer night. It was long distance from Montana. Uncle Tim stood shaking in the hospital lobby trying to force the words out. "Grandma, Grandpa, and Dennis were in an accident on their way here—Grandma's dead." I will never forget that night (or those words) because the tragic death of my grandma forced me to face emotions I had never before experienced.

I was very close to my grandma, and I never had someone close to me die before. This, and the fact that her death was so tragic and sudden, had quite an emotional impact on me. My emotions went wild and I didn't understand what was happening. I cried myself to sleep the night she died, and when I awoke I couldn't remember if I had had a nightmare or if it was reality. I saw that my eyes were swollen half shut and I felt very confused. But when I saw the pastor sitting at our kitchen table, I realized what was happening. Sitting down and talking with him and my parents was very hard, but it helped me to accept and absorb everything that was happening. I didn't realize until much later that this was only the beginning of the different emotions I would experience.

Understanding Grandma's death was very difficult for me because she was still so young and healthy. I blamed everyone and everything for her death. I felt life was unfair and cruel to take her the way it did. I kept asking myself, "Why her? Why did she have to die?" She was such a wonderful person and everyone loved her. I also couldn't stop saying, "What if?" I could make a list of hundreds of these questions that tormented me until my mind was spinning. I found out, though, that blaming others and asking impossible, never-ending questions did not help. I realized that I was better off not actually understanding, but simply accepting what happened.

Grandma's premature death made me think much more about life. It is sad that it took something as drastic as death to make me think more deeply about living. I realized until Grandma was gone just how much I took her for granted. I think I more or less assumed that she would always be around. Whenever I thought about my life in the future, I always pictured her there with me and with the rest of my family. I thought she would be at my high school graduation and I always thought she would be there when I got married. After Grandma's death, I realized that life was not to be taken for granted. It is very important to appreciate what you have while it is still there to appreciate. I never knew (until it was too late) just how important and irreplaceable Grandma was in my life.

I would have given anything for that car accident to never have taken place. I have learned a great deal from this life-changing experience. I can only hope that Grandma knows just how much I loved and appreciated her— and I still do.

OBITUARY

Ingvald Vevang

Ingvald Vevang, 82, Webster, died Friday, May 17, 1985, at Apple Valley Medical Care Center, Apple Valley, Minnesota. Services were Tuesday, at 10:30 AM in St. John's Lutheran Church, with the Rev. Vernon Severson and the Rev. Thomas Hagen officiating. Burial was in Webster Cemetery. Mrs. Donald Waldowski was organist, Mrs. Douglas Olawsky was soloist. Casket bearers were Kenneth Baukol, Harold Hoven, Clint Schneider, Ben Anderson, James Dedrickson, and Eric Forslund.

Ingvald Vevang was born December 30, 1902, to Iver and Serina Vevang near Roslyn. He grew up and attended rural school in the Roslyn area. He worked for the railroad and farmed in the area for a short time. He married Alberta Syverson on December 6, 1940, in Webster. He owned and operated a road construction company for about 20 years before retiring in 1964. He had lived in Webster for the last 35 years.

IN MEMORY OF
Ingvald Vevang
December 30, 1902 - May 17, 1985

SERVICES
10:30 a.m. Tuesday, May 21, 1985
St. John's Lutheran Church
Webster, S. Dak.

CLERGY
Rev. Vernon Severson
Rev. Thomas Hagen

MUSIC
Organist - Mrs. Donald Waldowski
Soloist - Mrs. Douglas Olawsky

CASKET BEARERS
Kenneth Baukol   Ben Anderson
Harold Hoven   James Dedrickson
Clint Schneider   Eric Forslund

INTERMENT
Webster Cemetery
Webster, S. Dak.

Funeral Arrangements by
FIKSDAL FUNERAL SERVICE
Webster, S. Dak.
LISTOE & WOLD FUNERAL HOME
St. Paul, Minn.

Survivors include one son, Dennis, Triangle, Virginia; three daughters, Mrs. Gerald (Linda) Forslund, Apple Valley, Minnesota; Mrs. Tim (Pamela) Schneider, Great Falls, Montana; and Mrs. William (Debra) Menzel, Aberdeen, South Dakota; three brothers, Julius Vevang, Webster, South Dakota; and Elmer Vevang and Lawrence Vevang, both of Roslyn, South Dakota; and four sisters, Mrs. Hilda Olson, Minneapolis, Minnesota; Mrs. Laura Hanson, Webster, South Dakota; Mrs. Charles (Myrtle) Watkins, Osceola, Florida; and Mrs. Ella Montgomery, Rocky Mount, Virginia. He was preceded in death by his parents, his wife on August 3, 1982, an infant daughter, three brothers, and one sister.

Age at the Time of Death

Alberta was 61

Ingvald was 82

FAMILY

Ingvald Vevang b: 30 Dec 1902, Nutley Township, Day County, South Dakota; d: 17 May 1985, Apple Valley, Dakota County, Minnesota; buried: Webster Cemetery, Webster, Day County, South Dakota

Ingvald married Alberta Katherine Syverson b: 21 Dec 1920, Waubay, Day County, South Dakota; m: 06 Dec 1940, Webster, Day County, South Dakota; d: 03 Aug 1982, Lewistown, Fergus County, Montana; buried: Webster Cemetery, Webster, Day County, South Dakota

CHILDREN
of Ingvald Vevang and Alberta Katherine Syverson Vevang

Sandra Kae Vevang b: 29 Dec 1941, Webster, Day County, South Dakota; d: 29 Dec 1941, Webster, Day County, South Dakota; buried: Roslyn Cemetery, Roslyn, Day County, South Dakota

Linda Ann Vevang b: 11 Jun 1943, Peabody Hospital, Webster, Day County, South Dakota; d: 06 Mar 2013, Burnsville, Dakota County, Minnesota; buried: Fort Snelling National Cemetery, Minneapolis, Minnesota

Dennis Ingvald Vevang b: 12 May 1945, Peabody Hospital, Webster, Day County, South Dakota

Pamela Jean Vevang b: 01 Jul 1949, Peabody Hospital, Webster, Day County, South Dakota; d: 02 Dec 2022, Missoula, Missoula County, Montana

Debra Diane Vevang b: 10 Nov 1954, Peabody Hospital, Webster, Day County, South Dakota

LINDA ANN VEVANG

Born

June 11, 1943

Webster, Day County, SD

Died

March 6, 2013

Burnsville, Dakota County, MN

Laid to rest in Fort Snelling National Cemetery, Minneapolis, MN

Mr. and Mrs. Ingvald Vevang
request the honour of your presence
at the marriage of their daughter
Linda Ann
to
Gerald L. Forslund
on Saturday, the fifth of September
Nineteen hundred and sixty-four
at seven-thirty o'clock in the evening
St. John's Lutheran Church
Webster, South Dakota

Reception
following ceremony

Wedding party. From left: Nancy Forslund, Pamela Vevang, Sharon Martin, Linda Vevang Forslund, Jerry Forslund, Duane Forslund, Lee Ross, Dennis Vevang

Linda and Jerry with their children: Kristin Kae, Eric Gerald, and Amy Jo

November 1984
The Ingvald Vevang family in Webster, South Dakota

From left: William Menzel holding Kelly Menzel, Debra Vevang Menzel holding Jenny Menzel, Pamela Vevang Schneider, Clinton Schneider, Timothy Schneider, Dennis Vevang, Amy Forslund, Linda Vevang Forslund, Kristin Forslund, Eric Forslund and Gerald Forslund. Seated in front is Ingvald Vevang.

To Linda
Written by Jenny Menzel (Linda's Niece)

Dear Aunt Linda,

This gift was meant to be a Christmas present. I suppose it is still a Christmas present, except it didn't get delivered to you by Christmas. I wanted to get something for you, and I asked myself, "What would Linda want the most—for herself?" We all know you would wish for a whole lot of great things for all of those you love. But, for you, I guess that you would love to simply feel loved and supported through your struggle with this illness. I know that being sick can get lonely, mostly because you don't want to burden or worry your loved ones with what you are going through. Being ill for so long takes its toll, not only on the body, but your mind, heart, and soul.

I'm not sure of the reasons for this rough journey you've been on for so many years, but I think everyone can see that you still have a purpose and that you are so deserving of love, hugs, thoughts, and prayers. I pray for you often, that you find healing, contentment, and peace, and that you feel loved, not only by your family, but by yourself.

Even though I don't think pink is at the top of the list when people think of what color blanket they would want, I picked this color specifically for you for a few reasons. Pink is the color of happiness, relationships, and our hearts. It is soft, nurturing, caring, renewing, and compassionate. It builds a comforting confidence, dissolving any thoughts or feelings of low worth. Pink opens the heart to receive true healing and, above all—it is the color of LOVE. All of this I wish for you but cannot wrap them in a box with a bow. I hope that while this blanket will keep you warm, it will also remind you of all you deserve.

Remember, even though we are not around, and we don't speak every day, we think of you, pray for you, and religiously admire your courage to face illness—day in, and day out. Some of us are just terrible at expressing feelings in person! Writing helps. We have no doubts you are still with us for a reason, Linda! And we couldn't be happier that you are such a fighter. You are a brave and stubborn soul (in a great way). You go through so much, and you do it all so quietly. I wanted to make it a point this year to make sure you know that this is how we feel about you, even if it's not expressed so clearly.

"A heart of gold stopped beating.
Two shining eyes at rest.
God broke our hearts to prove
he only takes the best."

A Heart of Gold was a phrase
Jerry used to describe Linda.
Jenny, Linda's niece, created
this image for Jerry in 2013
after her passing.

Dancing in the Sky
Written by Jenny Menzel

Six years ago, my aunt Linda passed after a long battle with cancer. For as long as I have been alive, she was always a bit sickly and stationary, but she never complained. I could always count on her to be home when I traveled through the cities as an adult. It didn't matter the day or the time—she would be there.

A couple of days after Linda's funeral, I dreamed of her. I was so happy to see her in my dream and I could feel how much I missed her. In the dream, though, she was not the same aunt I had known. She was so exuberant! She sported short, fluffy hair like in the pictures I'd seen her in photo albums from before I was born, and she was all dressed up. She didn't have time to talk to me because she just *had* to leave right then to go dancing!

Dancing? I felt miffed, left behind, and sad. I'd never seen her dance a day in my life.

I told my younger brother, Brian, about the dream. "What day was that?" I told him it was Thursday. "Hmm," he contemplated. "I had a dream of her that same night." She looked the same as I had described her. Months or years later, I told my cousin Eric about the dream. He couldn't believe it. "You *have* to tell this to my dad," Eric emphasized excitedly as he rushed out of the room to go get Jerry.

I repeated the dream to Jerry in full detail and included how Brian shared a similar dream. He quietly listened the entire time, never interrupting. I'll never forget the look in my Uncle Jerry's eyes when I got to the end of the dream. I can still see his expression now.

His eyes lit up, sparkling with tears, and a warmth beamed from his smiling face. He told me that before I was born, he and Linda would often go out dancing together. I never knew.

Fast forward to now, as I write this, Jerry has had a major stroke, and it cannot be recovered from. I have every bit of faith that he will soon be reunited with his bride, and they'll be dancing in the sky forever.

FAMILY

Linda Ann Vevang b: 11 Jun 1943, Peabody Hospital, Webster, Day County, South Dakota; d: 06 Mar 2013, Burnsville, Dakota County, Minnesota; buried: Fort Snelling National Cemetery, Minneapolis, Minnesota

Linda married Gerald (Jerry) Leroy Forslund b: 16 Mar 1937, Union County, South Dakota; m: 05 Sep 1964, St. John's Lutheran Church, Webster, Day County, South Dakota; d: 07 Oct 2019, Apple Valley, Dakota County, Minnesota; buried: Fort Snelling National Cemetery, Minneapolis, Minnesota

    Linda and Jerry's children:
Kristin Kae Forslund b: 06 Feb 1967, St. Paul, Ramsey County, Minnesota
Eric Gerald Forslund b: 21 Oct 1969, Farmington, Dakota County, Minnesota
Amy Jo Forslund b: 20 Feb 1974, Farmington, Dakota County, Minnesota

CHILDREN AND GRANDCHILDREN
of Linda Ann Vevang and Gerald Leroy Forslund

Kristin Kae Forslund married Donald Walter Henrichs Jr. b: 28 Apr 1967, Jamestown, Stutsman County, North Dakota; m: 27 Sep 1996, Las Vegas, Clark County, Nevada: div.

    Kristi and Donnie's children:
Jacob Alexander Henrichs b: 06 Aug 1997, Edina, Hennepin County, Minnesota
Kaelee Ann Henrichs b: 08 May 2002, Edina, Hennepin County, Minnesota

Eric Gerald Forslund

Amy Jo Forslund

Kristin Kae Forslund Henrichs   Jacob Alexander Henrichs   Kaelee Ann Henrichs   Eric Gerald Forslund   Amy Jo Forslund

DENNIS INGVALD VEVANG

Born

May 12, 1945

Webster, Day County, SD

Dennis Vevang, Elwood Monson, and Ben Anderson working on the county roads

Dennis worked the summers of 1960-1962 on his father's road crew.

Dennis Vevang

Vevang given space grant

Dennis Vevang, son of Mr. and Mrs. Ingvald Vevang of Webster, has been informed that he has been awarded a scholarship for participation in a summer institute in space science and engineering to be held July 5-Aug. 12 at Columbia University in New York.

Vevang, a junior at South Dakota State University, Brookings, is one of only 30 college students in the country selected for the institute.

The grant will defray tuition, and fees, and provide a subsistence allowance, along with providing travel expenses for the 30 students.

The first five weeks of the course will be devoted to daily lectures on space science and engineering dealing with aerodynamics-heat transfer, introduction to orbital mechanics, and materials and structures.

The final week will consist of a field trip to national centers of space research. These will include the Manned Spacecraft Center in Houston, Texas to view space flight projects and astronaut training facilities; the Marshall Space Flight Center in Huntsville, Ala. for a tour of projects in propulsion, rocket and spacecraft guidance and control and spacecraft development; Launch Operations Center at Cape Kennedy, Fla.; and the Goddard Space Flight Center at Greenbelt, Md. to examine experimental work in progress on scientific satellites.

Vevang graduated from Webster High School in 1963.

In the summer of 1966, Dennis was awarded a scholarship to participate in a summer institute in space science and engineering at Columbia University in New York.

Dennis attended South Dakota State University in Brookings, South Dakota, and graduated with a Mechanical Engineering degree in 1967.

The Vevang family accompanied Dennis to New York and visited Ella Vevang Montgomery's family in Virginia. Time was spent in Washington D.C. as well.

Standing on the steps of the United States Capitol Building in Washington D.C.
From Left: Dennis, Debra, Alberta, Pamela

1968. Dennis's Seattle apartment
Dennis, Debra, and Alberta Syverson Vevang

Dennis's first job out of college was working for Boeing. He moved to Seattle, Washington in June of 1967. In 1969, Dennis moved to Cincinnati, Ohio to work with General Electric. In 1976, Dennis studied accounting in Minneapolis, Minnesota for one year. In 1977, he moved to Triangle, Virginia where he worked on the Quantico Marine Base.

In 1986, Dennis worked in Frankfurt, Germany for three years. His sister Debra and her husband William Menzel visited him in 1988. In 1989, Dennis chose where he would like to live—Hood River County in the state of Oregon, and built a house where he would later retire.

He went back to Triangle, Virginia, until his move to California in 1999. He lived in and worked in Sacramento in an engineering position for the Army Center Public Works. For three years, his position moved to San Francisco. Dennis commuted to San Francisco from Sacramento due to the high cost of living in San Francisco. He retired in 2005 and moved to Oregon.

Germany in 1988
Dennis Vevang, Debra Vevang Menzel, William Menzel

Mt. Hood, Oregon in 2016
From Left: Dennis Vevang, Brian Menzel, Eric Forslund (with dog, Rufus), and Kristin Forslund Henrichs

Dennis's view of Mt. Hood from his home in Mt. Hood Parkdale, Oregon

The Ingvald Vevang farm, just north of the Iver Vevang farm and northeast of Roslyn, is still in the family. Dennis now owns the farm that Ingvald purchased in the early 1940s. Today, the land is mostly part of Hazelden Lake. The farmhouse is on an island and the other buildings are at the bottom of the lake. Dennis rents out the remaining land to the Hanson Brothers, who grow corn, soybeans, and wheat.

Ingvald Vevang farmland now shared with Hazelden Lake

Ingvald and Alberta's house still remains on an island

Ingvald Vevang farm in 1966

PAMELA JEAN VEVANG

Born

July 1, 1949

Webster, Day County, SD

Died

December 2, 2022

Missoula, Missoula County, MT

Mr. and Mrs. Ingvald Vevang
request the honour of your presence
at the marriage of their daughter
Pamela Jean
to
Mr. Timothy S. Schneider
on Saturday, the twenty-fourth of August
Nineteen hundred and sixty-eight
at seven-thirty o'clock in the evening
St. John's Lutheran Church
Webster, South Dakota

Reception
in Church Parlors

Wedding party. From left: Debra Vevang, Judy Schneider, Linda Vevang Forslund, Pamela Vevang Schneider, Timothy Schneider, Daniel Schneider, Dennis Vevang and Larry Phillips

1969. Clinton Timothy was born.

Mischievous cousins, Clint & Eric

1967. Pam & Tim were high school sweethearts.

1967. Clinton, Kristin, and Eric

1972. Clinton's 3rd birthday with parents Pam & Tim

1974. Clinton's 5th birthday with Grandma Alberta

Clint hunting for gophers on the Ingvald Vevang family farm.

Clinton, Pamela, and Tim Schneider

Sisters Linda, Pam, and Debra with their mother, Alberta

FAMILY

Pamela Jean Vevang b: 01 Jul 1949, Peabody Hospital, Webster, Day County, South Dakota; d: 02 Dec 2022, Missoula, Missoula County, Montana

Pamela married **Timothy Sheldon Schneider** b: 18 Aug 1949, Webster, Day County, South Dakota; m: 24 Aug 1968, St. John's Lutheran Church, Webster, Day County, South Dakota

    Pamela and Timothy's son:
Clinton Timothy Schneider b: 19 Nov 1969, Aberdeen, Brown County, South Dakota

CHILDREN
of Pamela Jean Vevang and Timothy Sheldon Schneider

Clinton Timothy Schneider married **Marie Georgette Christine Denis** b: 27 May 1974, Quebec, Canada; m: 12 May 2012, King County, Washington

DEBRA DIANE VEVANG

Born

November 10, 1954

Webster, Day County, SD

Debra Diane Vevang
and
William Theodore Menzel
together with their parents
Mr. and Mrs. Ingvald Vevang
and
Mr. and Mrs. Clarence Menzel
invite you to share in the joy
of the beginning of their new life together
when they exchange marriage vows
on Saturday, the twenty-fourth of September
Nineteen hundred and seventy-seven
at seven-thirty o'clock in the evening
St. John's Lutheran Church
Webster, South Dakota

Reception following
in Church Parlors

Wedding party. From left: Cathy Ruckdaschel, Mary Kehrwald, Pamela Vevang Schneider, Linda Vevang Forslund, Debra Vevang Menzel, William (Bill) Menzel, Marlin Zahn, Richard Menzel, Keith Andreason, and Kevin Andreason. Michael Menzel as ring bearer, and Melissa Menzel as flower girl.

Christmas 1976 at the Ingvald Vevang home in Webster. From left: Debra Vevang, Gerald Forslund holding Amy Forslund, Linda Vevang Forslund, Dennis Vevang, Alberta Syverson Vevang, Ingvald Vevang, and Pamela Vevang Schneider. In front: Kristin Forslund and Clinton Schneider.

Bill & Debra

Kelly James was born in 1981.

Jenny Lynn was born in 1984.

Bill & Debra

Brian Joseph was born in 1987.

FAMILY

Debra Diane Vevang b: 10 Nov 1954, Peabody Hospital, Webster, Day County, South Dakota

Debra married **William Theodore Menzel** b: 04 Mar 1954, Appleton, Swift County, Minnesota; m: 24 Sep 1977, St. John's Lutheran Church, Webster, Day County, South Dakota

Debra and William's children:
Kelly James Menzel b: 11 Oct 1981, St. Luke's Hospital, Aberdeen, Brown County, South Dakota
Jenny Lynn Menzel b: 05 Jul 1984, St. Luke's Hospital, Aberdeen, Brown County, South Dakota
Brian Joseph Menzel b: 16 Feb 1987, St. Luke's Hospital, Aberdeen, Brown County, South Dakota

2016
Jenny coordinated a photo shoot at the Iver Vevang family farm, and edited it to make it look like an old photo.
From left: Brian Menzel, Debra Vevang Menzel, William Menzel, Jenny Menzel, and Kelly Menzel

CHAPTER VII

SELMER

Born

August 12, 1904

Vevang Family Farm

Nutley Township, Day County, SD

Died

September 29, 1972

Seattle, King County, WA

Laid to rest in Greenwood Memorial Park, Renton, WA

Selmer (Sam) was baptized in the Lutheran Christian faith on September 11, 1904

Sponsors: Andrew and Louise Anderson, Pedar Stavig, and Anne Vinaas

1904	Døbte,					Døbte.	
No.	Barnets Navn.	Fødselsdatum.	Daabsdatum.	Formldrenes Navne.		Fadderne Navne.	
	Selmer	12 August	11 September	Iver & Serina Vevang		Andrew & Louise Anderson, Pedar Stavig, Anne Vinaas	

Selmer in 1908

Laura, Iver, Selmer, Serina holding Alida, Ella, and Hilda in 1911.

The Thirteenth United States Federal Census taken in 1910
Nutley Township, Day County, South Dakota

Vevang Iver A.	Head	M	W	44
Serina	Wife	F	W	38
Julius	Son	M	W	12
Hilda	Daughter	F	W	11
Elmer	Son	M	W	9
Ingvald	Son	M	W	7
Selmer	Son	M	W	5
Laura	Daughter	F	W	2
Ella	Daughter	F	W	6/12
Gaara Halvor	Lodger	M	W	36

Selmer was confirmed in the Lutheran Christian faith in the Roslyn Lutheran Church in 1919

Selmer in 1919

—1919—
Josie Marie Hatle-Sathre
Kristense Glosimodt-Nelson
Otilie Haagenson-Nelson
Belvira Mathilde Olson-Schable
Myrtle Viola Hagen-Hartman
Alf Hammer
Robert Bernhard Hemmah
John Clarence Peterson
Selmer Vevang
Sigurd Theodore Hagen

1919 Confirmation Class

The Fourteenth United States Federal Census taken in 1920
Nutley Township, Day County, South Dakota

	Relation	O	M	Sex	Color	Age
Vevang drew A.	Head	O	M	m	w	54
—, Serina	Wife			F	w	47
—, Julius S.	Son			m	w	23
—, Elmer L.	Son			m	w	18
—, Engvald	Son			m	w	17
—, Selmer	Son			m	w	15
—, Jama M.	Daughter			F	w	11
—, Ella H.	Daughter			F	w	10
—, Alida	Daughter			F	w	9
—, Myrtle H.	Daughter			F	w	5
—, Lawrence A.	Son			m	w	4 2/12

Selmer Vevang was part of the Roslyn Baseball Team of 1923

BASEBALL

In 1915, the first independent baseball team was organized in Roslyn School. In 1928, a team league called the Lake Region Baseball league was organized with Roslyn, Sisseton, Bristol, Eden, Summit and Peever as members. Roslyn won the first league championship and repeated in 1929.

Baseball team of 1923
From left: Selmer Vevang, Elmer Skaaden, Clement Hammer, Ted Gilbertson, George Nado, Floyd Jacobs, Ted Johnson. **Sitting:** Art Gilbertson, Julius Stavig

Selmer graduated from Roslyn High School in 1924

Selmer E. Vevang

Class of 1924
Marie Christianson Jandle, Francis Granstrom Peterson, Ted Haaseth*, Clement Hammer*, Floyd Jacobs*, Ted Johnson*, Henry Opsahl, Selmer Vevang*.

SELMER

attended Northern State Teacher's College in Aberdeen, SD, and taught school for two years, then went to Augustana College in Sioux Falls, SD.

Vevang Ella student Augustana Coll r do
Vevang Selmer E student Augustana Coll r do

From the Sioux Falls, SD City 1929 Directory
Sister and brother, Ella and Selmer, were students at Augustana College in Sioux Falls, South Dakota.

Augustana College Demosthenian Literary Society

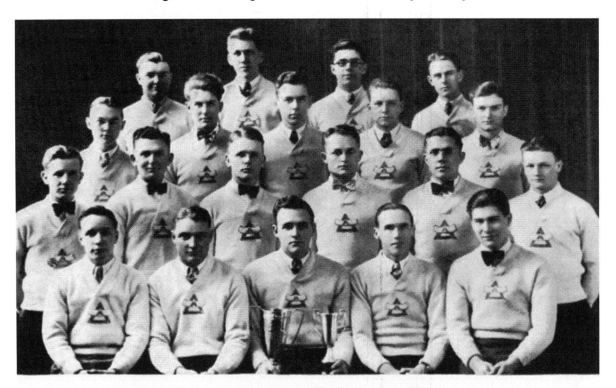

Fourth row: A. Myklebust, Enstrom, Hawley, Turmo
Third row: Rogness, Anderson, Larson, Borst, H. Myklebust.
Second row: Lewis, Holland, Nelsen, Hanson, Halverson, Sonstegaard
Front row: Spence, Mosby, Vevang, Burke, Ronshaugen

DEMOSTHENIAN

The members of the Demosthenian Literary Society have always displayed a particular interest in debate and oratory. The aim of the group is to cultivate the art of speech in both practice and theory.

In 1929 the Demosthenians were winners of the annual intersociety oratorical and play contests, and they tied with the Websterian Society for first place in the debate contest. Melvin Nelsen, Arthur Larson, Helmer Myklebust, Harold Burke, Carl Turmo, and Richard Hanson were the participants of the debate contests while Arthur Larson and Ralph Enstrom were the representatives as society orators. The members chosen as the extemporaneous speakers weer Arthur Larson and Melvin Nelsen.

The Demosthenians have permanent possession of one intersociety cup having been winners of the intersociety contests three successive years. As winners of the contests last year they were also awarded a second cup. It is the hope of every loyal Demosthenian to make that cup also a permanent possession of the society.

Iota Chi Sigma, a national honorary journalistic fraternity, Augustana College

Back Row: Koller, Lokken, Vevang, Miss Dahl, Rogness, S. Monserud
Front row: G. Monserud, Halverson, Ronshaugen, Engen

IOTA CHI SIGMA

Iota Chi Sigma, installed at Augustana College in 1928, is a national honorary journalistic fraternity. Augustana, having the South Dakota Alpha chapter, has the first and only chapter in the state. It was begun here with five members. Membership is limited to those who have served with distinction for a specified term on the college newspaper staff.

The purpose of the organization is to stimulate interest in, and uphold the standards of college journalism. This is accomplished by promoting closer fellowship between the students operating publications in American colleges and by conferring honors upon candidates who have served with distinction in that capacity. The fraternity motto is, "Ideas Conquer the World."

The Alpha chapter now has a membership of twelve. The present officers are Clifford Halverson, President; Raydon Ronshaugen, Vice-President; Gloria Monserud, Secretary; and Evelyn Engen, Treasurer. Hiss Borghild M. Dahl is the faculty member and the adviser of the group. E. Fred Koller served as president of the fraternity when it was first organized.

257

VEVANG
Guard

SELMER E. VEVANG
ROSLYN

*"When you can, use discretion;
When you can't, use a club."*

Demosthenian 1, 2, 3, 4; Football 1, 2,
3, 4; "A" Club 2, 3, 4; Business Manager Mirror 4; Demosthenian President
4; Mission Union President 2; "B"
Choir 4; Luther League Vice-President
1; Bible Class President 3; Iota Chi
Sigma 4; Thucydian Society 4; Circula-
tion Manager of Mirror 3; Delegate to
L. S. U. 3.

Sam was a guard for the Augustana Vikings.
He is in the second row, third from the right.

Selmer graduated from

Augustana College in 1930

Here are some of the groups Sam belonged to
and the positions he held: A Club, Business
Manager Mirror, Mission Union President,
B Choir, Luther League Vice President, Bible
Class President, Thucydian Society, and Cir-
culation Manager of Mirror.

258

The Timeline of Selmer (Sam) Vevang

August 12, 1904	Born in Nutley Township, Day County, South Dakota
September 11, 1904	Baptized in the Lutheran Christian faith
1919	Confirmed in the Roslyn Lutheran Church
1924	Graduated from Roslyn High School
1925	Attended Normal State Teachers' College in Aberdeen, South Dakota
1926-1927	Taught public school and worked two summers with Home Missions, MT
1930	Graduated from Augustana College in Sioux Falls, South Dakota
1933	Graduated from Luther Theological Seminary, St. Paul, MN in 1933, and accepted a Letter of Call to serve his first congregation
1933	Sam married Bea on September 1st, and they moved to New Jersey
1933-1945	Ministered at Bethlehem Norwegian Lutheran Church in Elizabeth, NJ
1935	Daughter Beverley Joan Vevang was born
1936	Daughter Shirley Elaine Vevang was born
1942	Son Paul Sholl Vevang was born
1943	Son Timothy Iver Vevang was born
1945	Son James Sholl Vevang was born
1945-1953	Ministered at Zion Lutheran and Hardies Creek Congregations in Galesville, WI
1953-1960	Organized and ministered St. Timothy's Lutheran Church, a Home Mission congregation in Seattle, WA
1960-1969	Ministered at First English Lutheran Church (currently named Gloria Dei Lutheran Church) in Redwood Falls, MN
1969	Retired and moved to Seattle, WA, but remained active in the ministry
	Visitation pastor at Bethlehem Lutheran in Seattle, WA; interim pastor at First Lutheran Church in Bothell, WA; Kent Lutheran Church in Kent, WA; and Our Savior's Lutheran Church in Issaquah, WA
1972	Passed away September 29

BERNICE MARCEL SHOLL

Born
September 9, 1911
Minneapolis, Hennepin County, MN

Died
July 12, 2009
Issaquah, King County, WA
Laid to rest in Greenwood Memorial Park, Renton, WA

SELMER & BERNICE VEVANG

Married September 1, 1933
Minneapolis, Hennepin County, Minnesota

Wedding Party
From left: Henry Hanson Sr., Ingvald Vevang, Selmer and Bernice Sholl Vevang, Ella Vevang, Marie Hamm,
John Rienertson as the ring bearer, and Dorothy Jeanne Storvick as the flower girl.

Bernice Marcel Sholl and Selmer Edwin Vevang Marry

Wearing the white satin wedding gown which had been worn previously by two of her sisters, Miss Bernice Sholl, youngest daughter of Mrs. Christine Sholl, 2540 Pierce Street N. E., Minneapolis, became the bride of Mr. Selmer E. Vevang of Roslyn, South Dakota, at a ceremony which took place at the Concordia Lutheran Church, corner of 22nd Avenue and Filmore St. N. E., Minneapolis, on Friday evening, September 1, 1933, at 8:30 o'clock.

The bride was attended by Miss Ella Vevang, a sister of the groom as maid of honor and Miss Marie Hamm as bridesmaid. They were attired in ankle length gowns of blue and green georgette. Little Dorothy Jeanne Storvick of Mitchell, a niece of the bride acted as flower girl. The groom was attended by his brother, Ingvald Vevang of Roslyn and Henry M. Hanson, a brother-in-law of Webster.

Three pastors took part in the impressive double ring service, the Rev. Walter L. Wang, pastor of Concordia Lutheran Church, the Rev. Elmer O. Reinertson of Amherst, Wisconsin and the Rev. Alfred O. Storvick of Mitchell, S. D., the last two named being brothers-in-law of the bride. Music for the service was furnished by Mrs. Erick Furuholmen who presided at the organ and Mrs. L. M. Stavig of Northfield who sang several vocal numbers. About 80 guests, mostly relatives and close friends of the family were entertained at an informal reception given at the home of the bride's mother following the ceremony. The Rev. L.M. Stavig of Northfield, Minnesota acted as toastmaster at the reception.

The groom is a graduate of the Roslyn High School; Augustana College at Sioux Falls, South Dakota and Luther Theological Seminary in St. Paul, Minnesota and has been called to serve as pastor at Elizabeth, New Jersey, which is close to New York City. After a brief honeymoon trip to Chicago and other points of interest in the east, the young couple will make their home at Elizabeth, New Jersey.

Guests from out of the city who were in attendance included; Mr. and Mrs. Iver Vevang, Mrs. Edwin Olson, Ingvald Vevang, Ella Vevang and Alida Vevang, all of Roslyn, South Dakota, Mr. and Mrs. Julius Vevang of Watertown, South Dakota, Mr. and Mrs. Henry M. Hanson of Webster, South Dakota, Rev. and Mrs. E. C. Reinertson, Amherst, Wisconsin, Rev. and Mrs. Alfred O. Storvick, Mitchell, South Dakota, Rev. and Mrs. Lawrence M. Stavig, Northfield, Minnesota, and Rev. and Mrs. Stephen Dale, St. James, Minnesota.

Leaves for New Jersey in September of 1933

Published in *Reporter and Farmer* in Webster, SD

Mr. and Mrs. Iver Vevang, Ingvald and Alida, Mrs. Edwin Olson and Mr. and Mrs. Henry Hanson left for Minneapolis last Friday morning to be present at the wedding of Selmer Vevang and Miss Bernice Sholl of Minneapolis which took place Friday evening.

Selmer Vevang recently graduated from the Seminary of Minneapolis and on Sunday was ordained. Rev. Vevang has accepted a call from the state of New Jersey and with his bride will leave at once to take up his new field of work.

Rev. Vevang was formerly a lad from this vicinity being reared here and is a graduate of the Roslyn High School with the class of 1924. Upon finishing high school he took a normal course at Aberdeen, South Dakota and a four year course at the Augustana College at Sioux Falls, South Dakota after which he taught for a few years in rural schools. He then took the call to ministry.

We extend to Rev. and Mrs. Selmer Vevang congratulations and the very best of luck and success in their new undertaking.

Bethlehem Norwegian Lutheran Church
Elizabeth, New Jersey

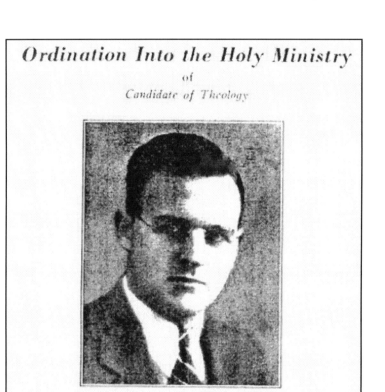

Ordination Into the Holy Ministry
of
Candidate of Theology

SELMER E. VEVANG

Called to Elizabeth, New Jersey
Who Will Receive the
Ordination of the
Church

TWENTY-FOURTH SUNDAY AFTER TRINITY
November 26, 1933

Bethlehem Norwegian Lutheran Church
Elizabeth, New Jersey
3:00 P. M.

Bethlehem Lutheran Church

Elizabeth, New Jersey

THE REV. SELMER E. VEVANG
ORDAINED AND INSTALLED
NOVEMBER 26, 1933.

FAREWELL SERVICES—DECEMBER 2, 1945

Christmas Day 1933

Parish Growing.

The present minister, Rev. Mr. Vevang, came to Elizabeth in September, 1933, and his pastorate has been attended with much success. There has been an all-round development of the work, and activities are provided for all ages. Because most of the members now enrolled speak only the English language, the Norwegian services are held only once a month. There is a progressive Sunday school, the young people have a live Luther League, the Men's Club is active, and the two women's organizations—the Ladies' Aid Society and the Willing Workers—contribute time and money to the church.

Beverley (Bev) Joan Vevang, Selmer and Bea's first child was born in 1935.
From left: Serina Hustad Vevang, Bernice Sholl Vevang, Selmer Vevang holding Beverley, Iver Vevang

From left: Christine Sholl (Selmer's mother-in-law),
Myrtle Vevang, Beverley, and Selmer in 1937

Shirley Elaine Vevang, born in 1936, standing
in front of her father's church in 1938.

Beverley, Bernice, Selmer, and Shirley

Bernice and Shirley Vevang are on the left, Selmer
is in the center, Myrtle Vevang is on the front of the
sled with a church group member, and Beverley is
to their left watching them slide down the hill.

The Sixteenth United States Federal Census taken in 1940
Elizabeth, Union County, New Jersey

Vevang	Selmer Ⓧ	Head	M	W	34	M	No	C-5	South Dakota
—	Bernice	Wife	F	W	27	M	No	C-v	Minnesota
—	Beverley	Daughter	F	W	5	S	Yes	O	New York
—	Shirley	Daughter	F	W	3	S	No	O	New York
—	Myrtle	Sister	F	W	25	S	No	C-1	South Dakota
Morrison, Ralph		roomer	M	W	3v	S	No	C-4	Maine

Those in the Selmer and Bernice Vevang's household were Beverley Vevang (5) and Shirley Vevang (3).
Selmer's sister, Myrtle Vevang (25), was considered part of their household.
They also had a boarder named Ralph Morrison.

Bethlehem Lutheran Church Elizabeth, New Jersey
54th Anniversary

SUNDAY SCHOOL TEACHERS
"Feed My Lambs"

CHILDREN'S CHOIR
Organized 1943

MISS HELEN KJELDSEN, *Director*

NORMA TONNESEN   SOLVIG OLSEN

SIGNE KJELDSEN   HELEN KJELDSEN

BERTHA THERKILDSEN   EMMA ORSINI

KAREN TOBIASSEN   GERTIE KJELDGREN

DOLORES HJORTH   ANNA TOBIASSEN

DOROTHY VANDYKE   BEATRICE WILFRID

INGEBORG HJORTH   KENNETH NELSON

S. E. VEVANG

Front Row—JOYCE THERKILDSEN, ELEANOR WILFRID, SHIRLEY VEVANG, BARBARA CHALMERS, NORMA PEDERSEN, CAROLINE WILFRID. *Second Row*—MISS HELEN KJELDSEN, BEVERLY VEVANG, SHIRLEY WATKINS, JO ANN COYLER, JOYCE WIRTH, ALBERT FISCHER.

Sunday School Teachers: Selmer Vevang
Children's Choir: Shirley Vevang and Beverley Vevang

Paul Sholl Vevang was born in 1942.
From left: Selmer, Shirley, Beverley, Bea holding Paul

Father and son, Selmer and Paul, sitting on
the lawn of Selmer's church.

Shirley, Paul, and Beverley

Selmer

Timothy Iver Vevang was born in 1943.
From left: Selmer, Paul, Beverley, Bernice
holding Timothy, and Shirley

James Sholl Vevang was born in 1945.
Standing: Shirley, Selmer, Bernice, Beverley
Sitting: Paul, James, Timothy

Zion Lutheran and Hardies Creek Congregations
Galesville, Wisconsin
1945 - 1953

Rev. S.E. Vevang in his duster
in the spring of 1952.

Back: Shirley and Beverley
Front: Bernice, James, Paul, Timothy, and Rev. Selmer Vevang

The Galesville Wisconsin Congregation

269

Rev. Selmer Vevang of Galesville, Wisconsin, formerly of Roslyn, has been called by the Pacific District of the Home Missions field to attempt to organize a congregation and build an Evangelical Lutheran Church in the southwest corner of Seattle. There is no church there at present.

Rev. Vevang is the son of Iver Vevang of Roslyn. He graduated from Roslyn High School in 1924 and then attended Northern State Teachers College in Aberdeen, South Dakota for one year. Following that he taught in a rural school for two years and then attended Augustana College in Sioux Falls, South Dakota for four years. Selmer was ordained as a minister in the spring of 1933 after he had attended a seminary in Minneapolis. He married the former Bernice Sholl of Minneapolis, and they now have five children. He has been serving a Lutheran church in Galesville, Wisconsin for the past seven years and previously was a minister at a church in Elizabeth, New Jersey for twelve years.

Rev. and Mrs. Vevang and four of their children left recently for their new home, which was built by the people in the community in which he will serve, after visiting with relatives in this vicinity. One daughter is attending St. Olaf's College at Northfield, Minnesota where she is studying to become a nurse. While Rev. Vevang was here he conducted communion services in the Roslyn and Fron Lutheran churches.

The Congregation of
St. Timothy Lutheran Church
requests the pleasure of your company at the
Silver Wedding Anniversary
and 25th year in the Ministry of
Pastor and Mrs. S. E. Vevang
on Sunday, the twelfth of October
Nineteen hundred and fifty-eight
At 10056 Renton Avenue
Seattle, Washington

Open House
3 to 5 p.m.

Former Roslyn Man Going to Seattle

(Roslyn News)

Rev. Selmer Vevang of Galesville, Wis., formerly of Roslyn, has been called by the Pacific District of the Home Missions field to attempt to organize a congregation and build an Evangelical Lutheran Church in the southwest corner of Seattle. There is no church there at the present time.

Rev. Vevang is the son of Iver Vevang of Roslyn. He graduated from Roslyn High School in 1924 and then attended N. S. T. C. in Aberdeen for one year. Following that he taught in a rural school for two years and then attended Augustana College for four years. He was ordained as a minister in the spring of 1933 after he had attended a seminary in Minneapolis. He married the former Bernice Scholl of Minneapolis and they now have five children. He has been serving a Lutheran church in Galesville, Wis. for the past seven years and previously was a minister at a church in Elizabeth, N. J. for 12 years.

Rev. and Mrs. Vevang and four of their children left recently for their new home, which was built by the people in the community in which he will serve, after visiting with relatives in this vicinity. One daughter is attending St. Olaf's College at Northfield, Minn. where she is studying to become a nurse. While Rev. Vevang was here he conducted communion services in the Roslyn and Fron Lutheran churches.

Reporter and Farmer Webster, SD

270

St. Timothy Lutheran Church
Seattle, Washington
1953 - 1960

1955
From left: Beverley Vevang, Shirley Vevang,
Paul Vevang, Timothy Vevang, and James Vevang.

1954
Ingvald Vevang and his son, Dennis, took a
train to Seattle to visit his brother, Sam, and
his family. James Vevang is on the left.

S. E. VEVANG
Lutheran Pastor
6304 Ryan St.
Seattle 88, Wash.

The Rev. Vevang family home at 6304 Ryan Street in Seattle, Washington.

The Only Son of Our Congregation
Roslyn Lutheran Church 75th Anniversary's Booklet

The only son of our congregation, Pastor Vevang was born and reared near Roslyn, graduating from Roslyn High School in 1924. He attended Augustana College and completed his work at Luther Seminary in 1933. The same year he was ordained at Elizabeth, New Jersey, his first parish, and served there until 1945. From then until 1952 he served at Galesville, Wisconsin. At present, he is pastor of St. Timothy Lutheran, Seattle, Washington, and his address is 6304 Ryan Street.

Pastor Vevang has submitted the following statement for this occasion as he will be unable to attend.

Through the Grace of God, we have been given a precious heritage by the pioneers of this community. Today, the 75th Anniversary of our church, should remind us of their love and concern for us. May God give us a larger portion of His Spirit so that we may stand firm in the faith given us through the ministry of this church.

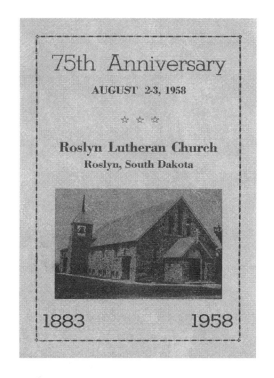

75th Anniversary
AUGUST 2-3, 1958

☆ ☆ ☆

Roslyn Lutheran Church
Roslyn, South Dakota

1883   1958

SUFFERS HEART ATTACK
(Roslyn News)

Rev. Selmer Vevang, 53, suffered a heart attack at his home in Seattle Saturday evening and was placed on the critical list at a Seattle hospital. In a phone call to relatives here Monday evening, Mrs. Vevang stated he has now been removed from an oxygen tent. For the past five years, Rev. Vevang has served as pastor of the Timothy Lutheran Church, a home mission congregation in Seattle. He is a son of the Roslyn Lutheran congregation and is scheduled to give the main address at the 75th anniversary of the church Aug. 2 and 3.

Reporter and Farmer Webster, SD

The Ingvald Vevang family drove to Seattle from Webster in 1959 to spend Christmas with his brother, Sam, and his family.

Back: Dennis Vevang, Alberta Syverson Vevang, Linda Vevang, Beverley Vevang, Selmer Vevang, Timothy Vevang, Bernice Sholl Vevang and Paul Vevang.

Front: Pamela Vevang, Debra Vevang, and James Vevang.

The Ingvald Vevang Family
From left: Linda, Pamela, Dennis, Ingvald, Alberta, and Debra

First English Lutheran Church
(Currently named Gloria Dei Lutheran Church)
Redwood Falls, Minnesota
1960 - 1969

Service of Installation

The Rev. S. E. Vevang

INSTALLER
The Rev. Dr. E. C. Reinertson, President of the Southern Minnesota District of the Evangelical Lutheran Church

First English Lutheran Church

REDWOOD FALLS, MINNESOTA

Sunday, June 26, 1960

Bernice Vevang
408 Veda Drive
Redwood Falls, Minn. 56283

In 1960 Selmer was called to serve at the First English Lutheran Church in Redwood Falls, Minnesota.

Reverend Selmer Edwin Vevang Service of Installation on June 26, 1960.

The Rev. S. E. Vevang, son of the late Mr. and Mrs. Iver Vevang, was reared in Roslyn, South Dakota.

He is a graduate from Augustana College, Sioux Falls. After teaching public schools for two years and working with Home Missions in Montana for two summers he enrolled at Luther Seminary in St. Paul.

Following graduation from the Seminary he accepted a Letter of Call to serve Bethlehem Lutheran congregation at Elizabeth, New Jersey.

His second parish was at Galesville, Wisconsin where he served Zion Lutheran and the Hardies Creek congregations. In 1953 he accepted a call to start a home mission's congregation in Seattle.

Mrs. Vevang (Bernice Sholl) is from Minneapolis where she was a member of Concordia Lutheran. Mr. and Mrs. Vevang have five children, Beverley, an instructor in the School of Nursing at the University of Washington, Shirley (Mrs. James Gillard) living at Hopkins, Minnesota, Paul, Timothy and James.

Retiring Pastor Has Faith in Youngsters

Communicating the gospel to the young is getting more difficult but Rev. S. E. Vevang, retiring pastor of First English Lutheran church of Redwood Falls, has confidence in today's young people.

"They're going to cause us some heartbreaks but give them time," said Rev. Vevang, who announced his impending retirement at the recessed session of the church's annual meeting Wednesday night. "I have great confidence in youth; their abilities are way beyond what ours were at their age."

A minister since his ordination in 1933 at Elizabeth, N. J., Rev. Vevang has noted a change in inter-church relationships in those 36 years. "Churches used to be very provincial, every church for itself," he said. "Now there is a spirit of cooperation and a respect for each other as a true church. The change has been for the good." The 36 years also have produced a better-informed laity, Rev. Vevang believes. "The caliber of lay leadership has improved greatly," he said.

Rev. Vevang came to the Redwood Falls congregation in 1960 after serving as a pastor twelve years at Elizabeth New Jersey, eight years at Galesville, Wisconsin, and eight years at Seattle, Washington, where he established a new church which had 450 members when he left.

During his nine years here, the First English congregation has grown from 1,000 to 1,400 members with an increase of 100 communing members. The congregation bought property east of the church for parking and purchased a second parsonage during Rev. Vevang's tenure. Indicating the constantly changing makeup of a church congregation, Rev. Vevang noted that about 900 new members have been admitted at First English since 1960 but the overall gain was cut by 550 through transfers and deaths. "People really move around these days," he observed.

Rev. Vevang also will do some moving. When his retirement as pastor becomes effective at the end of September, he and his wife will move to Seattle, where he will do visitation work for Bethlehem Lutheran church. Coincidentally, his first congregation in Elizabeth also was a Bethlehem church. A native of Roslyn, South Dakota, he graduated from Augustana College in Sioux Falls, South Dakota and Luther seminary in St. Paul, Minnesota. Three of the Vevang's children are living in Seattle, Mrs. D. Wayne (Beverley) Price, a teacher at Seattle University; James, graduate student at University of Washington; and Paul employed in Seattle. Other children are Mrs. Jules (Shirley) Gillard and Tim both of Minneapolis.

To the Holy Land

Reporter and Farmer Webster, SD

S. E. Vevang, retired pastor who was born and raised in the Roslyn area and now lives in Seattle, Wash., visited friends and relatives in the area this week after returning from a European and Middle East tour.

Vevang spent 15 days on an educational tour which took him to such places as Switzerland, Rome, Egypt, Jerusalem, Lebanon, Beirut and Athens with 14 other persons from points in the U. S.

The group toured most of the cities by bus and saw indications of war in Cairo, Egypt and Jerusalem with barricaded bridges and public buildings. "We were not allowed to take pictures in those areas," he explained.

The traveler attended Ascension Day services in Rome last Friday and saw the Pope at St. Peter's Church. He also indicated he saw improved methods of farming and crops by the Jews, consisting mainly of oranges, bananas and olives at the Sea of Galilee. He added that the area was probably the "most beautiful" he saw on the trip.

Vevang noted that it took only six hours to fly from New York to Switzerland on the trip over and just seven hours to fly from Lisbon, Portugal to New York on the return trip. He will leave for Seattle Friday.

S.E. Vevang spent 15 days on an educational tour which took him to such places as Switzerland, Rome, Egypt, Jerusalem, Lebanon, Beirut and Athens with 14 other persons from points in the United States. The group toured most of the cities by bus and saw indications of war in Cairo, Egypt and Jerusalem with barricaded bridges and public buildings.

The traveler attended Ascension Day services in Rome last Friday and saw the Pope at St. Peter's Church. He also indicated he saw improved methods of farming and crops by the Jews, consisting mainly of oranges, bananas and olives at the Sea of Galilee.

He added that the area was probably the "most beautiful" he saw on the trip.

The Great Invitation
Written by Rev. Selmer E. Vevang

This was Sam's last sermon written before his death, but not delivered.
In 1980 around Christmas time, Bea read Sam's sermon in the chapel where she lived.

Come to me, all who labor and are heavyladen,
and I will give you rest.

There is a strange magic about these words. They cast a spell upon us, even before we know who said them or know just what they mean, they do something to us. First, I suppose, because they are addressed to the weary, the tired and the worn, not tired by hard work so much, as by the tensions of life. We notice the wonder and beauty of the words because they begin with an invitation. An invitation is a happy event and it makes us happy.

We Are Remembered

An invitation makes up happy because we realize we are remembered and our company is wanted, other times we are needed; someone needs our help or company. It is an indication that someone wants us to be with them. In the case of our text the invitation comes from Jesus. It has all the warmth of his love and concern for us. It has the authority of His wonderful confidence.

Coming from Him, it means even more than this because in a way that is beyond our understanding. Jesus is the love of God in person. Therefore, this invitation comes to us not only from a young Jesus in Nazareth, but from the very heart of God.

The Bitterness of Man's Indifference

At the very time when Jesus was experiencing the bitterness of man's indifference and opposition he turns in praise to the Father and says, "I thank you O Father that Thou hast hidden these things from the wise and understanding and revealed them to babes."

The great and deep yet simple truths of the gospel are often hidden from the worldly wise. I Corinthians, tells us, "The world by wisdom knew not God." The invitation is that we may come to wisdom.

276

The Invitation is Accepted

You remember that Paul, the learned Pharisee knew much about God, but not the God Jesus came to reveal. It was after his experience on the Damascus Road when he became a babe and was willing to let the Holy Spirit reveal to him his need.

Paul accepted the invitation and followed Christ and fed on the Word and by God's grace lived a life that was obedient to His will and he grew in grace, wisdom and usefulness.

Come to Me All You That Labor

"Come to me, all you that labor and are heavy laden and I will give you rest." God's word from cover to cover is our urgent invitation to sinners to come to God for salvation. This invitation has been accepted by you and through that acceptance you have experienced the lifting power of God, forgiveness and through an inner peace and rest.

Take the Water of Life Freely

As we read in Revelations 22: "And the spirit and the bride say: Come. And he that heareth let him say: Come. And he that thirsteth let him come: and he that will, let him take the water of life, freely."

Before we can experience rest, we must know distress. Before we can be healed, we must be torn. Before we can rest, we must know the anguish of sin.

There is no rest apart from Jesus. True there may be false rests not based on God's truth. Jesus Christ is our Noah, a name which means 'rest'. Resting in Jesus we are free from the terror and power of sin.

We Are at Peace in His Love

We are at peace in His Love. When we have this rest, we are released from the drudgery of sin and receive not a crown for our head, but also a yoke for our neck.

277

To take Christ's yoke is to discover that sin's heavy burden is removed and that subjection to Christ is rest indeed. His yoke is lined with love and we find that we are one with Him who is the lover of our souls.

Take My Yoke Upon You

Our invitation in our text says, "Take my yoke upon you and learn of me." It's as though He is saying I cannot take your burdens away from you. We expect burdens in life. Jesus says I cannot carry them for you but I can show how to carry them.

I can teach you the secret of burden-bearing if you watch me, learn of me. When Paul learned this he says his sufferings are called "light afflictions". Jesus says, "My burden is light." He helps us, gives us strength. We share in the God-Given love. Love makes the burden light and joyful.

The Ship in the harbor carries heavy cargo. The Ship says I brought it for you. The Sea says I bore you up. Come unto Me. I come just as I am.

```
CHRISTMAS GREETINGS       1980

          From Bea




    Sam's sermon notes in preparation
    for Sunday September 17, 1972, but
    not delivered ..... until now!
```

OBITUARY
Rev. Selmer Edwin Vevang

Selmer E. Vevang, the son of Serina and Iver Vevang, was born in Nutley Township, Day County, South Dakota, August 12, 1904.

He attended Roslyn Consolidated School; Northern State College, Aberdeen; taught school for two years; graduated from Augustana College in 1930; graduated from Luther Seminary, St. Paul, Minnesota in 1933.

He was married to Bernice Sholl, Minneapolis, in 1933 at Concordia Lutheran Church, Minneapolis. They made their first home at Elizabeth, New Jersey, where he was ordained into the ministry and served Bethlehem Lutheran Church from 1933 to 1945.

To this union were born two daughters, Mrs. Beverley Price, Issaquah, Washington, Mrs. Shirley Gillard, Minneapolis, Minnesota, and three sons Paul, Seattle, Washington; Timothy, Minneapolis, Minnesota; James, Bellevue, Washington.

Opening Prayer

"Our Father, we think of that

inner room of a family's sorrow

into which only you can enter.

Though all our sympathies

go out to these, our friends, we

know that sympathy cannot bind

up the broken heart. Only you

can do that. We ask you now

to perform that gracious and

healing ministry." Amen.

— words of Peter Marshall —

He died early Friday morning, September 29, 1972, from a heart attack and services were held at Bethlehem Lutheran Church, Seattle, Washington, October 2.

To folks at Bethlehem Lutheran Church in Elizabeth, NJ; Zion Lutheran and Hardies Creek Congregations in Galesville, WI; St. Timothy's Lutheran Church in Seattle, WA (organized this congregation); Gloria Dei Lutheran Church in Redwood Falls, MN; he was pastor. To those at Bethlehem Lutheran Church in Seattle WA; First Lutheran Church in Bothell WA; Kent Lutheran Church, Kent, WA; and Our Savior Lutheran Church in Issaquah, WA; he had special titles of "Pastor", "Visitation Pastor" and "Interim Pastor."

The Gospel text for the last Sunday he was in the pulpit included the words "come unto me all you who are tired from carrying heavy loads and I will give you rest."

Selmer was a son, a brother, a husband,
a father, a father-in-law, a grandfather, and a pastor

He was husband to you, Bernice. More than 39 years were shared with each other.

To you: Beverley, Shirley, Paul, Timothy, and James, he was a father.

To you: Julius, Elmer, Ingvald, Lawrence, Hilda, Laura, Ella, and Myrtle he was a brother.

To five of you: He was father-in-law. To seven he was a grandfather.

To his congregations, he was pastor.

To Iver and Serina, he was son, born August 12, 1904. And to God, he was a son, a son who heard his Father's words, "Go, work today in my vineyard" — a son who responded to those words and went — a son who worked in that vineyard through the heat of the day — he was still in the vineyard when he was stricken early in the morning of September 29.

There was a sermon almost ready to be preached at Our Savior's, Issaquah, that was never preached. The Gospel text for the last Sunday he was in the pulpit included the words, "Come unto me, all who are tired from carrying heavy loads and I will give rest."

He had planned to spend the Sabbath a week ago with the people of God at Issaquah, circumstances forbade — but now he is enjoying the Sabbath rest with people of God — the rest referred to by the writer of the letter to the Hebrews: "A Sabbath rest awaits the people of God: for anyone who enters God's rest, rests from his own work as God did from His."

One of Selmer's children commented, not many hours after his father had been ushered into that rest early Friday morning, September 29, "What a fantastic experience it must have been for dad this morning."

With these notes: confidence, hope, thanksgiving and praise, we begin our service of Praise to God in Memory of Selmer E. Vevang.

Vevang Memories
By Arthur F. Giere

We will remember Selmer E. Vevang who came with his family from Elizabeth, New Jersey, to Zion Congregation, here in Galesville, Wisconsin to be our pastor. That happened in the year 1945. He had been a clergyman for a dozen years at that time and he was 41 years old. It was not long before the old Trinity Church building, seemed to be too small, for the congregation and that was one of the reasons why the new pastor had suggested that the congregation appoint a planning committee for the parish. His written advice to the new committee was, "Except the Lord build the temple, they labor in vain who build thereon."

Shortly thereafter the planning group reported that the immediate needs of the church were classrooms for the Sunday School pupils. Later this new pastor published an 18-page pamphlet about the real necessity for a larger church facility. In that brochure he quoted, "This is not an assignment for a few, every person must be prepared to do." "For the sake of our children," he said, "and our children's children, we shall give ourselves that in the days to come they will rise and say this our fathers did for us in the name of the Lord". Then came the erection of a parish hall which was dedicated in the year 1952. The erection of the present edifice, years later, was the result of the preparatory doing of Pastor Vevang.

When Pastor Vevang left Galesville he said, "I go with a book in my hand and a faith in my heart to carry out the commands of my Lord Jesus Christ". Then, the faithful soldier of Christ, with his dear ones, started out on the long trek across the western plains and mountains to the Pacific Coast to make another start there. It was a sad day for Zion Church. Pastor Vevang was a good preacher, because he always had a message. Pastor Vevang was a good shepherd, because he always wanted to be helpful. Pastor Vevang was a good neighbor because he was always friendly. He was missed by all who knew him.

This preacher also had a hobby, which was hunting, and his other hobby was a way of winning friends and admirers and many of his friends in Galesville shall never forget, a newspaper item, which appeared, in a leading daily publication, in this area, and which it is hoped, no one who reads these lines will take offense of this mention of it. After he had entered into a deer hunting area near Pray, Wisconsin, and the newspaper printed in bold letters, "A PREACHER, NAMED SAM, WENT AWAY TO PRAY, AND POP HE CAME HOME WITH A BUCK." The records of his ministry in Galesville disclose that he had performed many baptismal ceremonies and confirmation rites and that he had married many couples and that he had escorted many of his friends to their final resting places. Pastor Selmer E. Vevang and his wife visited here in Galesville at the tenth anniversary of Zion Church building, in 1966, when he also preached a sermon he entitled, "The Missions of the Church."

Rev. and Mrs. Vevang had two daughters and three sons. God bless his fine family and God bless the memory of this kind gentleman who had dedicated his whole life, in and to the service of Jesus, the Redeemer.

Bea wrote a letter to Ingvald and Alberta Vevang about a month after Selmer's death. She wrote about the same to Sam's siblings as well, stating that as time goes on, she misses Sam more and more. She notes that Sam always cherished a close relationship with his brothers and sisters.

Bernice Vevang

Thursday
Oct 26, 1972

Dear Alberta and Ing:

As time goes on I miss Sam more and more.

Sam always cherished a close relationship with his brothers and sisters. It shows in the Christian love you all have that this is possible.

I'm sorry I didn't have the opportunity to visit with you more, but it was a difficult time for all of us.

From all of Sam's Children and myself, thank you.

This is a hard letter for me to write so I'm more or less saying the same to all. — Love

Bea

OBITUARY

Bernice S. Vevang

Seattle Times, July 2009

Bernice S. Vevang - A loving mother and grandmother was born on September 9, 1911, in Minneapolis, Minnesota to Julius and Christine Sholl. She passed away peacefully in her sleep July 12, 2009. Bernice grew up in Minneapolis and married Pastor S. E. Vevang in 1933. They lived in New Jersey, Wisconsin, Minnesota and Washington where he served many Lutheran Churches.

Preceding her in death were her husband in 1972, her son, Timothy Vevang (Judy), in Auburn, Washington, in 2005, Timothy and Judy's daughter, Lesley in 2000, and her son, Paul Vevang (Teri) in Burien, Washington, in 2006. Surviving are her daughters Beverley (Wayne) Price in Issaquah, Washington, and Shirley (Jules) Gillard in Hopkins, Minnesota, and son James Vevang (Jeanne) in Renton, Washington, along with six grandchildren, twelve great-grandchildren and one great-great-grandson.

Memorial to Our Savior Lutheran Church, 745 Front St. So, Issaquah, Washington, 98027. Memorial service is at Our Savior Lutheran Church, same address on July 19th at 1:00 p.m.

Pastor S.E. and Bernice S. Vevang are buried at Greenwood Memorial Park in Renton, Washington

FAMILY

Selmer (Sam) Edwin Vevang b: 12 Aug 1904, Nutley Township, Day County, South Dakota; d: 29 Sep 1972, Seattle, King County, Washington; buried: Greenwood Memorial Park, Renton, King County, Washington

Sam married **Bernice (Bea) Marcel Sholl** b: 09 Sep 1911, Minneapolis, Hennepin County, Minnesota; m: 01 Sep 1933, Concordia Lutheran Church, Minneapolis, Hennepin County, Minnesota; d: 12 Jul 2009, Issaquah, King County, Washington; buried: Greenwood Memorial Park, Renton, Washington

CHILDREN
of Selmer Edwin Vevang and Bernice Marcel Sholl

Beverley Joan Vevang b: 22 Feb 1935, Brooklyn, Kings County, New York

Shirley Elaine Vevang b: 07 May 1936, Brooklyn, Kings County, New York; d: 10 May 2018, Minnetonka, Hennepin County, Minnesota; buried: Fort Snelling National Cemetery, Minneapolis, Hennepin County, Minnesota

Paul Sholl Vevang b: 09 Jun 1942, Brooklyn, Kings County, New York; d: 19 Oct 2006, Burien, King County, Washington

Timothy Iver Vevang b: 09 May 1943, Elizabeth, Union County, New Jersey; d: 09 Jun 2005, Auburn, King County, Washington; buried: Hillcrest Burial Park, Kent, King County, Washington

James Sholl Vevang b: 14 Jul 1945, Brooklyn, Kings County, New York

BEVERLEY JOAN VEVANG

Born
February 22, 1935
Brooklyn, Kings County, NY

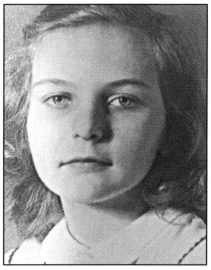

Births Reported in 1935, in the Borough of Brooklyn, New York, New York

Beverley J. Vevang February 22

NAME	DATE OF BIRTH.	No. of Certificate.	NAME	DATE OF BIRTH.	No. of Certificate.
——————, Patricia M	Oct. 15	33427	Villalobos, Ismael	Feb. 21	5923
Vetrigian, Lorraine A	Aug. 15	26715	Villani, Arlene	Dec. 5	38521
Vevang, Beverly J	Feb. 22	6726	——————, Vincenzino	Apr. 1	10887
Vey, Petley C	Mar. 17	8991	Villano, Antoinetti	Sep. 16	30236
Vezzi, Milchiora	June 20	19586	——————, Jennie	Sep. 15	29321
Viale, Walter F	June 6	18441	——————, Robert P	Mar. 30	11512

BIRTHS REPORTED IN 1935—BOROUGH OF BROOKLYN   V

Beverley Joan Vevang

The Virginia Mason Division of the
University of Washington
School of Nursing
invites you to be present at the
Pinning Exercises
Friday evening, December the ninth
nineteen hundred and fifty-five
at eight o'clock
Trinity Parish Hall
609 Eighth Avenue
Seattle, Washington

286

Miss Vevang, D.W. Price Are Married

Beverley Joan Vevang and Darold Wayne Price were married January 1, 1967, in First English Lutheran Church, Redwood Falls, Minnesota, where the bride's father is pastor.

The bride is the daughter of the Rev. and Mrs. Selmer E. Vevang, Redwood Falls. The groom is the son of Mrs. Irvin M. Price, Salina, Kansas, and the late Mr. Price.

After a honeymoon trip to California, the couple will be at home in Mercer Island, Washington.

Rev. Selmer E. Vevang, Ray Price (brother of the groom), D. Wayne Price, Beverley Vevang Price, and Shirley Vevang Gillard (sister of the bride).

The bride attended St. Olaf College and graduated from the University of Washington, where she completed graduate work and was on the faculty in the School of Nursing. She was assistant professor of nursing at Seattle University and assistant professor at California State College.

The groom graduated from Kansas State University and served in the Navy as an aviator. He is employed as a sales engineer with Aluminum Company of America, Seattle.

From left: Julius Vevang, Elmer Vevang, Selmer Vevang, Hilda Vevang Olson, Ingvald Vevang, Laura Vevang Hanson, Alida Vevang, Beverley Vevang Price, and Darold Wayne Price

Christine (Tia) Anne Price, Wayne and Beverley's daughter, was born and baptized in 1972.

Grandchildren, Serena and Alanna

Wayne and Beverley Price

Wayne and Tia

Beverley and Serena

OBITUARY

D. Wayne Price

Darold Wayne Price (Wayne) passed away Saturday, December 11, 2021, at Overlake Hospital (Bellevue, WA). Wayne was a true leader, kind, and generous to everyone he came in contact with. He was a wonderful and loving husband, father, father-in-law, grandfather, and friend. We are all better people for having Wayne in our lives. He will be greatly missed.

Wayne was born July 12, 1933, in Salina, Kansas, the son of Irvin Merril and Bertha Olive Price. He was raised in Salina and graduated from Salina High School. He attended Kansas State University and received a BA degree in Business Administration and Labor Economics. Upon graduation in 1955 Wayne joined the United States Navy and was accepted into the prestigious Naval Flight School in Pensacola, Florida. After pre-flight basic training, he did a half year of advanced flight training in Corpus Christi, Texas where he received his "Wings of Gold" as a Naval Aviator. He was stationed in Guantanamo Bay, Cuba from 1957-1959 where he flew single and multi-engine aircraft.

Wayne left the Navy in 1959 and traveled Europe with two fellow aviators for six months. When he returned to the States, he accepted a position with ALCOA as an Industrial Sales Engineer. He worked in Oklahoma City, Wichita, Kansas, and finally settled in Seattle, WA in 1965. In 1966 he met the love of his life Beverley Vevang while living next door to her on Mercer Island. Bev's father, a Lutheran minister, married them in January 1967.

In 1973, Wayne decided to take a risk that would change his life path forever. He left the safety of the corporate world, and formed Western House Contractors, which later became Western House Properties. He started purchasing and rehabbing single and multi-family homes around the greater Seattle area. Over the years the business moved more towards property management with properties in Issaquah, Sammamish, Maui, and California.

Relationships were important to Wayne. His vibrant personality was captivating. He loved spending time with his granddaughters, listening to music and dancing with them. His daughter Tia and her dad had a special bond and talked on the phone multiple times a day when they were not spending time together.

Wayne also had a heart for serving his community and a love of Jesus Christ. He was a significant part of the building committee for Our Savior Lutheran Church in Issaquah. He served many years as the President of the Issaquah Kiwanis Club and was always willing to help those in need.

Wayne is survived by his wife Beverley, his daughter Tia Town and son-in-law John Erik Town, and his two granddaughters Alanna and Serena Town of Sammamish, WA. Wayne's niece summed him up well, "We thought of him as our own James Bond, he lived a mysterious, sophisticated existence."

FAMILY

Beverley Joan Vevang b: 22 Feb 1935, Brooklyn, Kings County, New York

Beverley married **Darold Wayne Price** b: 12 Jul 1933, Salina, Salina County, Kansas; m: 01 Jan 1967, Redwood Falls, Redwood County, Minnesota; d: 11 Dec 2021, Bellevue, King County, Washington; buried: Tahoma National Cemetery, Kent, King County, Washington

Beverley and Wayne's child:
Christine (Tia) Anne Price b: 10 Aug 1972, Seattle, King County, Washington, adopted

CHILDREN AND GRANDCHILDREN
of Beverley Joan Vevang and Darold Wayne Price

Christine (Tia) Anne Price married **John Erik Town** b: 06 Nov 1970, Seattle, King County, Washington; m: 16 Aug 1998, Issaquah, King County, Washington

Tia and Erik's children:
Alanna Christine Town b: 20 Nov 2003, Bellevue, King County, Washington
Serena Anne Town b: 05 Jul 2005, Bellevue, King County, Washington

Tia and Erik

Serena   Alanna

SHIRLEY ELAINE VEVANG

Born
May 7, 1936
Brooklyn, Kings County, NY

Died
May 10, 2018
Minnetonka, Hennepin County, MN
Laid to rest in Fort Snelling National Cemetery, Minneapolis, MN

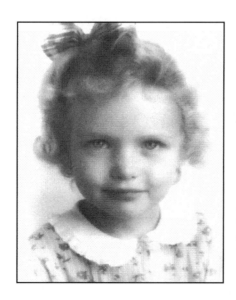

The Reverend and Mrs. Selmer Edwin Vevang
request the honour of your presence
at the marriage of their daughter
Shirley Elaine
to
Mr. Jules James Gillard
on Sunday, the twenty-second of June
nineteen hundred and fifty-eight
at half after four o'clock
Shepherd of the Hills Lutheran Church
Maloney and Blake Road, Edina
Minneapolis, Minnesota

Shirley Elaine Vevang

married

Jules James Gillard

June 22, 1958

Edina,
Hennepin County,
Minnesota

The Selmer Vevang Family
From left: Beverley Vevang, Selmer Vevang, Timothy Vevang, Bernice Sholl Vevang,
Shirley Vevang Gillard, Jules Gillard, James Vevang, and Paul Vevang

V	BIRTHS REPORTED IN 1936—BOROUGH OF BROOKLYN						
NAME		DATE OF BIRTH	No. of Certificate	NAME		DATE OF BIRTH	No. of Cert.
Vevang	Shirley E.	May 7	15069	Villacres	female	Mar. 14	
Viall	Carolyn M.	Nov. 3	15246	Villafane	Julio	June 9	
Viano	Frederick	Feb. 6	4954	Villalba	Estelle	Aug. 20	
Vicario	Frank, Jr.	Feb. 23	6482	Villalovos	Diane	Aug. 30	
	Grace M	Aug. 23	27181	Villani	Richard	Feb. 19	
	Salvatore	Feb. 23	6463	Villano	Agnes P.	Aug. 10	

Births Reported in 1936, in the Borough of Brooklyn, New York, New York   Shirley with her family in 1975

Shirley Elaine Vevang Gillard

Shirley was born in the city of New York, New York to a Lutheran minister and his wife. She was one of five bouncing babies. The family moved from New Jersey when little Shirley was in the fourth grade. The family headed off to the Midwest when her father was called to a church in Galesville, Wisconsin, outside of LaCrosse.

Shirley was destined to move once more with the family when her father was called to Seattle, Washington during Shirley's Jr. year in high school. Shirley graduated and moved back to the Midwest to attend school at Luther College, a liberal arts college in Decorah, Iowa. This became a monumental decision in young Shirley's life because she was destined to never leave the Midwest again. Her family remains in Seattle and Shirley married a man from Minneapolis, Minnesota and has been here ever since.

Shirley and Big Jim settled into a house in Eden Prairie, Minnesota and raised two children. Bruce James was born in 1959 and Suzanne Marie was born in 1963. In 1971, Shirley decided it was time to go to work and landed a plum job as a teacher's aide and Xerox lady in the brand-new school, still under construction, called Forest Hills Elementary. Little did she know when she started her new job in temporary quarters in what is now the administration building, that it would be the beginning of 27 years working in a district that was ALWAYS under construction.

In 1973, Shirley received a promotion and became the switchboard operator at the high school. She had this job for five years before she became a secretary in the principal's office of Eden Prairie High School. Her bosses at this job, which spanned nine years, included: David Flannery, Head Principal; Curt Connaughty, Assistant Principal; Arne Johnson, Head Principal; Paula Tezloff, Annette Bell, and Vickie Petzko, all Assistant Principals who came and went while Shirley held down the fort.

In 1987, change was in the wind once again and Carol Parker, who was in the guidance office and Shirley, in the principal's office decided to switch jobs. Shirley then became the constant, steady force that kept her ever-increasing guidance staff organized, on task and happy. Needless to say, our office will miss her terribly, but her organization skills and attention to detail over the years will keep us immeasurably to cope with our new jobs and the loss of one of our most valuable assets. Here is a brief one-word list of Shirley's loves and dos: Birthdays, especially her own, grandkids and kids, Lucky Inn, a long story, her colors, mauves and purples, her diet, how can she stand anymore Slim Fast? Mrs. Fixit and Mrs. Findit.

OBITUARY

Jules James Gillard

Gillard, Jules J. Age 79, of Minnetonka, passed away peacefully with family by his side on Mon, September 16, 2013. Preceded in death by parents, George and Martha, also brother, George. Jules grew up in Hopkins, Minnesota and raised his family in Eden Prairie, Minnesota. He retired as a salesman in the food brokerage industry and later enjoyed working part-time at Menards. An avid outdoorsman, he enjoyed duck hunting with friends, as well as fishing trips to Canada and big game in Colorado into his seventies. Most memorable were family vacations to his cabin in Webb Lake, Wisconsin.

He was a wonderful husband, father, grandfather, great-grandfather, and friend. His spirit lives on in the hearts of those who knew him.

Survived by his loving wife of 55 years, Shirley; two children, Bruce (Kanitta) Gillard and Suzanne (James III) Williams; grandchildren, Christine (Mike) Rostvold, Netra Gillard and Nick Gillard; Sam Williams, James Williams IV, and Ben Williams; three great-grandchildren, Noah Rostvold, Gage Rostvold and Knox Rostvold; many other relatives, as well as friends and those from Immanuel Lutheran Church.

A special thank you to Fairview Hospice staff. Visitation is on Thursday, September 26, 2013, at 10am, Immanuel Lutheran Church, 16515 Luther Way, Eden Prairie, Minnesota. Immediately followed by a memorial service at 11 am.

At their great-grandfather's grave site from left: Knox Rostvold, Noah Rostvold, and Gage Rostvold

In Loving Memory of

Shirley E. Gillard

Born
May 7, 1936
New Jersey, New York

Died
May 10, 2018
Minnetonka, Minnesota

Visitation
Immanuel Lutheran Church
16515 Luther Way
Eden Prairie, Minnesota 55346
9-11 a.m. Saturday, June 9, 2018

Interment
Fort Snelling National Cemetery

For Those I Love
For Those Who Love Me

When I am gone release me, please just let me go.
I have so many things to do, I leave you now and so;
You must not suffer for my loss or bother with the tears
Just be grateful we shared all these many years;
I gave you my love, and you can only guess
How in return you gave me so much happiness;
I thank you for the love each of you have shown
But now it's time I traveled went on ahead alone;
So grieve awhile for me, if grieve you must
But know that I am now with the Lord I trust;

It's only for a while that we must be apart
I am there in the memories encased within your heart;
I won't be far, for life will go on some.
When you need me, call me, and I will come;
You won't see me nor touch me, but I'll be near.
Never too far to comfort your hurt or a tear
Listen to your heart...my whispers you'll hear.
All my love around you soft and near.

When your time has come to make your way alone
I'll greet you, smile, and whisper..."Welcome Home."

Remembrances of Shirley Vevang Gillard

Written by Netra Gillard (Shirley's Granddaughter)

For those of you who may not know me, my name is Netra and Shirley was my grandmother. I believe it would suffice to say that she was one of the best things in my life. We shared a very close bond and as I see everyone here today, it is clear she was loved by many.

As many of you know, for the last few years, Grandma Shirley suffered from Alzheimer's, which subsequently in her later days caused her to be a shadow of her former self. Fortunately for me, I got a lot of time with my grandma, more than most do and the good memories, the meaningful memories that I have of her will go on with me for the rest of my life.

When I was younger, my fondest memories were of her at every birthday, school event, and in day-to-day life. She was a constant figure in our lives, and she made it a point to be there for all of us all the time.

While the most meaningful memories of Grandma are those from days long past, the most accurate memories, the ones that reveal her true character, are the most recent ones. You see Alzheimer's has a way of revealing the true essence of a person. It strips away the layers of etiquette and social pretense that most of us have learned to operate with. What you see is what you get. There is no filter. Who Grandma Shirley was in her final years is who she really was at the core. A loving, joyful, witty little spitfire who would give you the occasional eye roll without a second's hesitation.

295

In Loving Memory

And while there are many things that stand out to me as part of her enduring legacy, there are a few important ones I will take with me.

The First Cheerfulness

"A cheerful heart has a continual feast" (Proverbs 15:15). No matter what she was struggling with internally that none of us can imagine as you begin to lose your memory, it never stopped her from having a smile on her face and a joyous laugh that accompanied it. She could have been having an awful day, but she'd still say she was great and go on to ask me questions about my life. She took so much pride in knowing and holding on to what details she could. She kept her cheerful spirit in the good days, the bad days, and every day between.

Pride

A sanctified pride in her family. If one of the grandkids got a job or a new car, you heard about it for the next year or two. Whether we excelled in school or one of us was struggling she'd tell us and anyone willing to listen how proud of us she was, to her we were the VIP players at every sporting game. As the family gathered at times like Thanksgiving and Christmas, both she and my Grandpa Jules made it a point to let everyone know how proud of us they were. They also made a point to spoil all of us rotten in every way they could. Nothing came before family. Growing up as a small child with that kind of a grandmother, it had a way of bestowing confidence, self worth, and a sense of rootedness.

Happiness is a Choice

Let me be very clear, it didn't take much to make her happy, a turtle ice cream sundae or the occasional Snickers bar would do it. The entire bag if you really wanted to spoil her. But above all else, a phone call, a card, or a simple visit made her day. Let her play the piano for you, tell you a few stories, and sit with her as you listened. It wasn't about what she had or didn't have, where she was versus where she wanted to be. She chose to remain steadfast in her joy each day. The world has very few people who have so much hope and optimism, even fewer who are willing to share it with others. I will always feel blessed that one of them was my grandma.

In Closing

I love my grandma very much and will miss her dearly. Her lifetime of dedication, love for others, and selflessness serve as a monument to the exemplary woman she was. Although she is physically gone, I know she will continue to inspire those who knew her.

As she rests, finally free of any pain, I pray she knows how proud she made all of us and how much she will be sorely missed. While my family and I stand here today deeply grieved by the loss of one of the pillars in our family, we are also thankful for the chance to have had her. As we eagerly wait for that day, when we see her again, we will keep her in our minds and hearts, where her memory will live on for as long as we do.

FAMILY

Jim and Shirley

Shirley Elaine Vevang b: 07 May 1936, Brooklyn, Kings County, New York; d: 10 May 2018, Minnetonka, Hennepin County, Minnesota; buried: Fort Snelling National Cemetery, Minneapolis, Hennepin County, Minnesota

Shirley Elaine Vevang married **Jules James Gillard** b: 02 Jul 1934, Minneapolis, Hennepin County, Minnesota; m: 22 June 1958, Shepherd of the Hills, Edina, Hennepin County, Minnesota; d: 16 Sep 2013, Minneapolis, Hennepin County, Minnesota; buried: Fort Snelling National Cemetery, Minneapolis, Hennepin County, Minnesota

Shirley and James' children:
Bruce James Gillard b: 21 Mar 1959,
Methodist Hospital, St. Louis Park, Hennepin County, Minnesota
Suzanne Marie Gillard b: 16 Oct 1963,
Methodist Hospital, St. Louis Park, Hennepin County, Minnesota

CHILDREN AND GRANDCHILDREN
of Shirley Elaine Vevang and Jules James (Jim) Gillard

Kanitta and Bruce

Bruce James Gillard married **Kanitta Rainbow** b: 12 May 1961, Sattahip, Thailand; m: 01 Nov 1980, Eden Prairie, Hennepin County, Minnesota

Bruce and Kanitta's children:
Christine Marie Gillard b: 24 Oct 1984,
St. Louis Park, Hennepin County, Minnesota;
Netra Kathryn Gillard b: 14 Feb 1987,
St. Louis Park, Hennepin County, Minnesota
Nicholas James Gillard b: 31 Jul 1991,
Robbinsdale, Hennepin County, Minnesota

Noah, Bruce holding Ella, Knox,
Kanitta holding Colt, and Gage

Christine and Michael

Christine Marie Gillard married **Michael David Rostvold** b: 10 Feb 1986, Rochester, Olmsted County, Minnesota; m: 15 Aug 2009, Prior Lake, Scott County, Minnesota

Christine and Michael's children:
Noah James Rostvold b: 25 Aug 2005,
Burnsville, Dakota County, Minnesota
Gage Michael Rostvold b: 28 Dec 2010,
Burnsville, Dakota County, Minnesota
Knox Bennett Rostvold b: 23 Mar 2013,
Burnsville, Dakota County, Minnesota
Ella Jules Rostvold b: 10 Apr 2017, Katy, Texas
Colt Lane Rostvold b: 18 Oct 2019, Katy, Texas

Gage, Colt, Knox, Noah, Ella

Netra Kathryn Gillard

Netra's son:
Hudson James Ruzicka b:15 Aug 2019, Cypress, Harris County, Texas

Nicholas James Gillard is partnered with **Kaylee Elizabeth Pogue** b: 20 Sept 1992, Faribault, Rice County, Minnesota

Kaylee's son:
Raiden James Gunnells b: 23 May 2012,
Clearwater, Pinellas County, Florida

Nicholas and Kaylee's children:
Charlotte Jean Gillard and **Harlow Noel Gillard**
b: 07 May 2020, Burnsville, Dakota County, Minnesota

Suzanne Marie Gillard married **James Sherman Williams III** b: 12 Jul 1964, St. Louis Park, Hennepin County, Minnesota; m: 18 Aug 1990, Eden Prairie, Hennepin County, Minnesota

Suzanne and James' children:
Samantha Marie Williams b: 22 Jan 1994,
St. Louis Park, Hennepin County, Minnesota
James Sherman Williams IV b: 12 Sep 1996,
St. Louis Park, Hennepin County, Minnesota
Benjamin James Williams b:10 May 2001,
St. Louis Park, Hennepin County, Minnesota

Samantha Marie Williams married **Charles Austin Stauber** b: 20 Mar 1994, St. Louis Park, Hennepin County, Minnesota; m: 30 May 2023, Minnetonka, Hennepin County, Minnesota

James Sherman Williams IV

Benjamin James Williams

PAUL SHOLL VEVANG

Born
June 9, 1942
Brooklyn, Kings County, NY

Died
October 19, 2006
Burien, King County, WA

Paul served four years in the United States Marine Corp from June 1960 to June 1964.
Upon his discharge he was ranked as a corporal.

Paul in his lemon-yellow English sports car in 1965.

Paul

Paul (center) with his fellow Marines

Selmer Vevang Family
From left: Timothy Vevang, James Vevang, Shirley Vevang Gillard, Bernice Sholl Vevang,
Rev. Selmer E. Vevang, Beverley Vevang Price, and Paul Vevang

Paul Sholl Vevang

married

Theresa (Teri) McHugh Shaw

April 28, 1998

Seattle,
King County,
Washington

Paul visited his uncle, Lawrence Vevang, on the Vevang family farm in 2003.

Reminiscing of Years Gone By
Shirley Vevang Gillard, Lawrence Vevang, Larry Vevang, Allen Vevang, and Paul Vevang

OBITUARY

Paul Sholl Vevang

Paul was born in Brooklyn, New York on June 9, 1942. He died October 19, 2006, in Burien, Washington. Paul spent his early childhood in Galesville, Wisconsin, before coming to Seattle in 1952. He has been a resident of Burien for the last 15 years.

He graduated from Franklin High School in 1960 and entered the Marine Corps the same year. He served in the Far East for most of his four year enlistment.

After leaving the Marine Corps, he worked as a Longshoreman, did home remodeling and finally retired from the General Services Administration in 1998 after over 20 years.

Paul enjoyed watching mystery movies, cooking, traveling and spending time with his family, especially his Boston terrier, Tricks, who preceded him in death. Paul, you will be missed; your memory will be with us forever. He was a devoted husband and although he never had children of his own, he was a loving father to many. His love to his extended family was always a priority. Paul remained a proud Marine all of his life.

Paul is survived by his wife Teri, his mother Bea Vevang of Issaquah, Washington; his stepdaughter, Anne Shaw of Burien, Washington; his stepson, Bill Shaw of Denver, Colorado; his sisters, Bev and Wayne Price of Sammamish, Washington; Shirley and Jules Gillard of Minnetonka, Minnesota and his brother, Jim and Jeanne Vevang of Renton, Washington. He was preceded in death by his father, Rev. Sam Vevang and his brother, Tim Vevang. He also left behind many nieces and nephews. He will be missed by all.

Memorials may be made to the Washington Lung Association.
2625 3rd Ave., Seattle, WA 98121. Please sign the online memorial at
www.bonneywatson.com

FAMILY

Paul and Teri

Ann and Bill

Paul Sholl Vevang b: 09 Jun 1942, Brooklyn, Kings County, New York; d: 19 Oct 2006, Burien, King County, Washington

Paul Sholl Vevang married **Theresa (Teri) McHugh Shaw** b: 10 Mar 1951, Seattle, King County, Washington; m: 28 Apr 1998, Seattle, King County, Washington

Teri's children/Paul's stepchildren:
Ann Elizabeth Shaw b: 03 Mar 1975, Seattle, King County, Washington
William (Bill) Charles Shaw b: 28 Jan 1977, Seattle, King County, Washington

TIMOTHY IVER VEVANG

Born

May 9, 1943

Elizabeth, Union County, NJ

Died

June 9, 2005

Auburn, King County, WA

Laid to rest in Hillcrest Burial Park, Kent, WA

Timothy (Tim) Iver Vevang

married

Judith (Judy) Anne Boelter

August 7, 1971

Seattle,
King County,
Washington

Back row: Bev Vevang Price, Bea Sholl Vevang, Sam Vevang, and Shirley Vevang Gillard
Front row: James Vevang, Timothy Vevang, and Paul Vevang

Judy and Tim with Lesley and Matthew

From left: Judy Boelter Vevang, Matthew Vevang,
Lesley Vevang, and Timothy Vevang

OBITUARY

Lesley Vevang

Lesley Anne Vevang, 19, of Auburn, Washington formerly of Eagan, Minnesota, died in a car accident in Stevens Pass, Washington, July 23, 2000.

She was born March 17, 1981, in Winona, Minnesota. She lived in Owatonna for a short time and spent several years as a child in Eagan. While there, she attended William Byrne Elementary through the first grade and was a member of Mary, Mother of the Church in Burnsville until moving to Atlanta for two years and then the Seattle area. She was active in dance and volleyball and lettered in swimming.

Lesley is survived by her parents, Tim and Judy (Boelter) Vevang, of Auburn, Washington; brother, Matt Vevang, of Renton, Washington; relatives in the Seattle area, Iowa and Minnesota, including Jules and Shirley (Vevang) Gillard of St. Louis Park, Minnesota, Bruce and Kanitta Gillard of Burnsville, Minnesota, James and Suzanne (Gillard) Williams of Hopkins, Minnesota, Richard and Pat (Boelter) Huber of Apple Valley, Minnesota, Charlie Huber of Minneapolis, Minnesota, Tre, and Gretchen (Huber) Critelli of Des Moines, Iowa and friend Megan Levake of Lakeville, Minnesota.

A funeral mass was held at St. John the Baptist Catholic Church in Covington, Washington. Interment was at Hillcrest Burial Park in Kent, Washington.

A day of friends and tragedy

By Andrew DeMillo, Benjamin Shors, Lisa Rivera
July 25, 2000 *Seattle Times staff reporters*

In one car were three best friends from high school whose bonds remained strong even as they set off last fall for different colleges. In the other vehicle was a retired couple from Spokane who had just finished celebrating high-school friendships dating back six decades.

Tomeo and Namiko Mukai were returning from a North Kitsap High School 60th reunion in Poulsbo as they headed across the Cascades on state Highway 2 early Sunday afternoon. Just west of Stevens Pass, the 1992 Acura driven by Mya Thompson, 19, of Auburn, veered across the centerline and struck the Mukais' van head-on, according to the State Patrol. It was not known where Thompson and her passengers, who were westbound, were coming from.

Thompson; her friends Meredith Diegel, 18, and Lesley Vevang, 19; and Namiko Mukai, 74, were killed in the crash. Tomeo Mukai, 78, was in serious condition at Harborview Medical Center in Seattle with back and hand injuries.

State Patrol officials said the Acura may have been going nearly 80 mph on the winding mountain road. They don't believe alcohol was a factor in the crash. The accident has left friends and family members to reflect on one life full of memories and three young lives that had just begun.

Namiko Mukai had deep and prominent family ties in the Seattle area. Her brother is King County Superior Court Judge Richard Ishikawa. She had attended high school in the Minidoka Internment Camp in Idaho before going to college in Minnesota and becoming a nurse. Her husband, Tomeo, whose high-school reunion the couple was attending, is a retired carpenter who had earned two Purple Hearts in World War II.

Beloved Daughter & Sister
LESLEY ANNE VEVANG
March 17, 1981 – July 23, 2000

Your memory is our keepsake, with which we'll never part; God has you in His keeping, and we have you in our hearts.

High school also bound the three friends in Thompson's car

They all were members of Kentlake High School's 1999 graduating class — the first for the new Auburn school and seemed inseparable even beyond the day they walked out with diplomas in hand, according to friends and former teachers.

Thompson was the social butterfly of the group, the one always counted on for a party or shopping excursion. Diegel was a virtuoso at tennis and hoped to be a pediatrician. Vevang was a determined student who planned to become a teacher.

Lesley Vevang

Drew Terry, a volleyball coach and teacher at Cedar Heights Junior High School, may not remember Lesley as one of the best volleyball players in junior high or high school, but she was one of his favorite players. "Win or lose, she always had a smile on her face and was willing to put herself into the game," Terry said. "She was die-hard."

A regular attendee at St. John the Baptist Catholic Church in Covington, Vevang was considered a quiet leader by her teachers and classmates. She was going to start her sophomore year at Green River Community College in Auburn and hoped to transfer to Central Washington University in Ellensburg, where she could pursue her goal of becoming a teacher. "She was pretty quiet, but once you got her to open up you saw how much of a sweetheart she was," said Jamie Raczka, who graduated from Kentlake with Vevang.

OBITUARY

Timothy Iver "Tim" Vevang

June 12, 2005 *Seattle Times*

Timothy I. Vevang, 62, passed away June 9, 2005, at his home in Auburn, Washington. He is survived by his loving wife, Judy, of 33 years; son, Matt; brothers, Jim and Paul; sisters, Beverley and Shirley and his mother, Bernice.

Tim is preceded in death by his daughter, Lesley in 2000, and father, Pastor Selmer Vevang in 1972.

Funeral Mass 1:00 p.m. Mon., June 13th, at St. John the Baptist Catholic Church in Covington, Washington; Inurnment at Hillcrest Cemetery.

FAMILY

Tim and Judy

Timothy Iver Vevang b: 09 May 1943, Elizabeth, Union County, New Jersey; d: 09 Jun 2005, Auburn, King County, Washington; buried: Hillcrest Burial Park, Kent, King County, Washington

Timothy Iver Vevang married **Judith Anne Boelter** b: 14 Oct 1947, Sioux Falls, Minnehaha County, South Dakota; m: 07 Aug 1971, Seattle, King County, Washington

Timothy and Judy's adopted children:
Matthew Timothy Vevang b: 07 Feb 1978, Minneapolis, Hennepin County, Minnesota,
Lesley Anne Vevang b: 17 Mar 1981, Winona, Winona County, Minnesota;
d: 23 Jul 2000, Stevens Pass, Washington;
buried: Hillcrest Burial Park, Kent, King County, Washington

CHILDREN AND GRANDCHILDREN
of Timothy Iver Vevang and Judith Anne Boelter

Matthew, Liam, Michelle

Matthew Timothy Vevang significant other **Michelle Ann Corder** b: 8 Feb 1978, Wenatchee, Chelan County, Washington

Matthew and Michelle's child:
Liam Matthew Vevang b: 05 Aug 2011, Renton, King County, Washington

Lesley Anne Vevang

JAMES SHOLL VEVANG

Born

July 14, 1945

Brooklyn, Kings County, NY

James Sholl Vevang

married

Jeanne Elizabeth Lussenhop

December 19, 1964

Redwood Falls,
Redwood County,
Minnesota

The James Vevang Family
Jeanne Lussenhop Vevang, James Vevang, Jason Vevang, and Elizabeth (Lisa) Vevang in 1993.

Jim and Jeanne Vevang traveled to Vevang Norway in 2002

Jakob Jonsen Vevang, born in 1820 and died in 1912, is buried in the Vevang Norway Cemetery

FAMILY

James Sholl Vevang b: 14 Jul 1945, Brooklyn, Kings County, New York

James Sholl Vevang married **Jeanne Elizabeth Lussenhop** b: 06 Sep 1945, Redwood Falls, Redwood County, Minnesota; m: 19 Dec 1964, Redwood Falls, Redwood County, Minnesota

James and Jeanne's children:
Elizabeth (Lisa) Jean Vevang b: 19 May 1965, Mankato, Mankato County, Minnesota
Jason Sholl Vevang b: 15 Feb 1972, Seattle, King County, Washington

CHILDREN AND GRANDCHILDREN
of James Sholl Vevang and Jeanne Elizabeth Lussenhop

Elizabeth (Lisa) Jean Vevang married **Mark VanderPol** b: 29 Sep 1964, Seattle, King County, Washington; m: 15 Jun 1993, Bellevue, King County, Washington: div.

Lisa and Mark's children:
Kasey Elizabeth VanderPol b: 12 Apr 1994, Bellingham, Whatcom County, Washington
Brent Charles VanderPol b: 10 Sep 1997,Bellingham, Whatcom County, Washington
Blake Steven VanderPol b: 10 Sep 1997, Bellingham, Whatcom County, Washington

Kasey Elizabeth VanderPol

Brent Charles VanderPol

Blake Steven VanderPol married **Caitlin Ann Cox** b: 05 Nov 1997, Bellingham, Whatcom County, Washington; m: 11 Sep 2021, Bellingham, Whatcom County, Washington

From left: Chris Delaney, Kasey VanderPol, Blake VanderPol,
Caitlin Cox VanderPol, Lisa Vevang VanderPol and Brent VanderPol

Jason Sholl Vevang married **Casey Claire Welch** b: 25 May 1975, Renton, King County, Washington; m: 19 May 2002, Bellevue, King County, Washington

Jason and Casey's child:
Jordan Sholl Vevang b: 01 Nov 2005, Bellevue, King County, Washington

Back row: Jordan Vevang, Jason Vevang, and Casey Welch Vevang
Middle row: Jeanne Lussenhop Vevang, James Vevang, and Lisa Vevang VanderPol
Front row: Blake VanderPol, Kasey VanderPol, and Brent VanderPol

The Rev. Selmer Vevang family pictured in 2001
Standing: Paul Vevang, James Vevang and Timothy Vevang
Sitting: Shirley Vevang Gillard, Bernice Sholl Vevang and Beverley Vevang Price

CHAPTER VIII

LAURA

Born
March 18, 1908
Vevang Family Farm
Nutley Township, Day County, SD

Died
April 24, 1991
Webster, Day County, SD
Laid to rest in Webster Cemetery, Webster, SD

The Thirteenth United States Federal Census taken in 1910
Nutley Township, Day County, South Dakota

Vevang	Iver A.	Head of		M	W	44
	Serina	Wife		F	W	38
	Julius	Son		M	W	12
	Hilda	Daughter		F	W	11
	Elmer	Son		M	W	9
	Ingvald	Son		M	W	7
	Selmer	Son		M	W	5
	Laura	Daughter		F	W	2
	Ella	Daughter		F	W	6/12
Gaara	Halvor	Lodger		M	W	36

1908. Laura as a baby

1915. Laura at age 7

1919. Laura at age 11

The Fourteenth United States Federal Census taken in 1920
Nutley Township, Day County, South Dakota

Vevang	Iver A.	Head	O	M	m	w	54
	Serina	Wife			F	w	47
	Julius S.	Son			m	w	23
	Elmer L.	Son			m	w	18
	Engvald	Son			m	w	17
	Selmer	Son			m	w	15
	Laura M.	Daughter			F	w	11
	Ella H.	Daughter			F	w	10
	Alida	Daughter			F	w	9
	Myrtle H.	Daughter			F	w	5
	Lawrence G.	Son			m	w	4 3/12

LAURA was confirmed in 1922 at age 14 in the Lutheran Christian faith at the Roslyn Lutheran Church. Laura's sister, Ella, was confirmed in 1923.

—1922—
George Melvin Gilbertson
Arthur Miller
Josie Marie Aspen-Ronshaugen
Hazel Mathilda Stavig-Kallstrom
Thelma Malinda Gilbertson-Nerland
Laila Borghild Steffenson-Arenson
Laura Mathilda Vevang-Hanson
Esther Lensegrav-Farness
Myrtle Elizabeth Rood-Berglund
Alice Clara Teigen-Gjerde
Olga Josephine Lange
Ole Haaseth
Carl Nerland
Albert Danielson
George Stavik
Julius Monshaugen
Bardon Julius Skaaden

U.S. Evangelical Lutheran Church in America Church Records

Roslyn High School — Class of 1926

Laura Mathilda Vevang

Melvin Dokken, Myrtle Floren Locken, Martin Floren*, Arthur Gilbertson*, George Gilbertson, Elsie Jacobs Stavig, Bennie Opsahl*, Clara Ronshaugen Stavig, Paul Steffenson, Laura Vevang Hanson.

Class of Nineteen Hundred Twenty-six

Roslyn High School

requests your presence at its

Commencement Exercises

Thursday Evening, May Twenty-seventh

Gymnasium

Normal State Teachers' College — Class of 1927

Laura graduated in 1927 in Aberdeen, South Dakota from a one-year teachers' program.

Laura (top center) with her teacher and graduating class

Laura is kneeling in front with students and fellow teacher.

A schoolroom teacher

Laura taught in rural schools in South Dakota.
A few of them: Langford, Holmquist, Grenville.

Laura with her students and another teacher

The Fifteenth United States Federal Census taken in 1930
Nutley Township, Day County, South Dakota

Laura was considered part of the Iver Vevang family household in 1930. She was 22 years old.

Vevang	Iver J	Head	O		R	Yes		M	W	64
—	Serina	Wife					x	F	W	58
—	Ingvald	Son					x	M	W	27
—	Laura M	Daughter					x	F	W	22
—	Ella	Daughter					x	F	W	20
—	Alida	Daughter					x	F	W	19
—	Myrtle H	Daughter					x	F	W	15
—	Lawrence G	Son					x	M	W	14

Right. Laura making fudge at the home of the Torness cousins, descendants of Maren Hustad Stavig in Sisseton, SD. Maren is Serina Hustad Vevang's oldest sister. Maren and Beret were born in Hustad, Norway, and they, too, came to America for a better life.

Above. Laura with Agnes Sophia Holm, Laura's first cousin. Agnes' mother is Beret Hustad Holm, one of Serina Hustad Vevang's sisters.

HENRY MARK HANSON

Born

July 29, 1897

Grenville Township, Day County, SD

Died

May 2, 1984

Roslyn, Day County, SD

Laid to rest in Webster Cemetery, Webster, SD

HENRY & LAURA HANSON

Married June 14, 1932
Vevang Farm, Nutley Township, Day County, South Dakota

RECORD OF MARRIAGE

South Dakota State Board of Health

HUSBAND	WIFE
HENRY MARK HANSON	LAURA MATHILDA VEVANG
WEBSTER, DAY COUNTY, SD	ROSLYN, DAY COUNTY, SD
AGE 34	AGE 24
NORWEGIAN AMERICAN	NORWEGIAN AMERICAN
BACHELOR	MAIDEN

Iver Vevang walked his daughter, Laura, down the aisle.

Iver and Serina Vevang seated front and center.

Wedding Party
From left: Carl Hanson (Henry's brother), Henry Hanson,Sr.,
Laura Vevang Hanson, and Alida Vevang (Laura's sister)

326

Happily Married

Reporter and Farmer
Webster, SD

HAPPILY MARRIED

CO. TREAS. HENRY HANSEN WED TO LAURA VEVANG

Four Day County Couples Join in Life's Matrimonial Journey

(Roslyn Correspondence)

A beautiful wedding was solemnized at the Vevang home Tuesday morning at 11 o'clock when Miss Laura Vevang, daughter of Mr. and Mrs. Iver Vevang became the bride of Henry Hansen of Webster.

The home was decorated in a profusion of the seasons flowers. Rev. Stephen Dale performed the ceremony in the presence of about forty friends and relatives.

The bride was attractively attired in a full length gown of pale blue satin. She carried a bouquet of snow white peonies. Miss Alida Vevang was her sister's bridesmaid. She wore a gown of a soft shade of rose. The groom and his brother, Carl as attendant, both wore conventional blue.

Following the ceremony the guests partook of a bounteous two course dinner.

Mrs. Hansen is a young lady of pleasing personality. She has been a successful teacher in the rural schools of Day county the past three years. She is a graduate of Roslyn high school and of the Normal course of the teachers college at Aberdeen. Mr. Hansen is a native of Nutley township but at present is a resident of Webster serving as county treasurer. They left immediately after dinner for a trip to the Black Hills. Upon their return home they will make their home at Webster.

Guests from a distance who attended the wedding were Mr. and Mrs. Iver Holm and daughter Agnes, Mrs. Engebret Stetten of Sisseton, Mr. and Mrs. Arnt Hloues of Langford, Mr. and Mrs. Henry Bendickson and son, and Mr. and Mrs. Melvin Hansen of Nutley.

Mr. and Mrs. H.M. Hanson rented apartments in the Security Bank building.

HANSON-VEVANG

Miss Laura Mathilda Vevang of Roslyn and Mr. Henry Marcus Hanson of Webster were united in marriage at the home of the bride near Roslyn at 11 o'clock Tuesday morning, June 14. Rev. S. Dale, pastor of the Roslyn Lutheran Church, officiated.

The bride, wearing a dress of blue satin and carrying a bouquet of flowers, was given in marriage by her father. Her sister, Miss Alida Vevang, was her bridesmaid and wore rose crepe. The groom wore blue. His attendant was Mr. Carl Hanson, his brother.

Before the ceremony, a duet, "Oh Promise Me" was sung by Mrs. S. Dale and Miss Myrtle Vevang, a sister of the bride.

Following the ceremony, a wedding dinner was served to about 45 guests at the Vevang home. Those present included in addition to the bridal couple and their attendants, Mr. and Mrs. August Hanson of Roslyn, Mr. and Mrs. Iver Vevang, Mr. and Mrs. Melvin Hanson, and Mr. and Mrs. Iver Holm, Agnes and Henry Holm, all of Sisseton; Mr. and Mrs. Art Holnes of Langford; Mr. and Mrs. Herman Moen and family, Mr. and Mrs. Henry Bendickson and family, Mr. and Mrs. Ed Olson and family, Rev. and Mrs. S. Dale and family and Mr. and Mrs. Elmer Vevang.

The bride is the daughter of Mr. and Mrs. Iver Vevang of Roslyn vicinity. She is a graduate of Roslyn high school and later attended Northern Normal at Aberdeen. For the past five years, she has taught with marked success in the Day County rural schools.

The groom is the son of Mr. and Mrs. August Hanson of Nutley township. After completing his education in the Day County schools, he took a commercial course at Mankato Commercial College at Mankato, Minn. He was elected county treasurer of Day County in 1928 and is now completing his second, successful term in the office.

Mr. and Mrs. Hanson left for the Black Hills on a honeymoon trip. They will make their home in Webster. The Reporter and Farmer joins with the many friends of Mr. and Mrs. Hanson in extending congratulations and best wishes.

Silver Gray Satin Wedding Gown

displayed in the Day County Museum
in Webster, SD

worn by
Laura Vevang

of Nutley Township
at her wedding to
Henry M. Hanson
of Nutley Township
June 14, 1932

Laura served as Webster City Finance Officer 1970-1979.
Henry was City Finance Officer 1960-1969.
They lived in Webster.

Laura and Henry honeymooned in Sylvan Lake, Black Hills, South Dakota

Henry and Laura at their family home in Webster, South Dakota

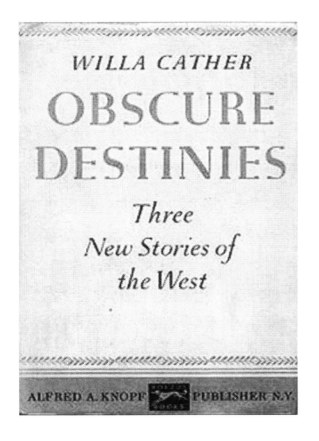

Laura presented a lesson for the Websterian Study Club in 1933.

As reported in the local newspaper, the *Reporter and Farmer*, in Webster, South Dakota, *Obscure Destinies* is a collection of three short stories by Willa Cather, published in 1932.

Each story deals with the death of a central character and asks how the ordinary lives of these characters can be valued.

"Beauty was found or created in seemingly ordinary circumstances."

WEBSTERIAN STUDY CLUB

The Websterian Study Club met at the home of Mrs. Edith French on Nov. 16, 1933.

The club being one lesson behind schedule two lessons were given at this meeting.

Mrs. H. M. Hanson had charge of the first lesson. She gave a very instructive study of Willa Cather and her works with special emphasis on her latest novel, Obscure Destinies. In her early novel Miss Cather has written intimately and feelingly of the old pioneer West, with its ceaseless struggle for food and clothing. She has drawn on material which she knows first hand, for the early days of her girlhood helped her to see into the lives of the foreigners who settled around her home. These people were very near and dear to her heart and she has written of them with love and understanding. Later Miss Cather abandoned the pioneer West as the setting for her novels and laid the scenes elsewhere, but in Obscure Destinies, she turns once more to the great American West as the background for her characters.

Mrs. R. M. Jones, in charge of the second lesson, presented an interesting review of Bright Skin by Julia Peterkin. She took up in detail the career of Cricket, the girl with the bright skin.

Laura and Henry's first child, Lorraine Harriet Hanson, was born in 1933.

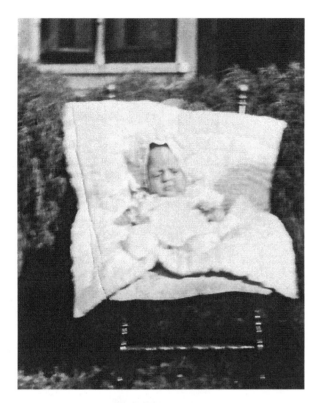

Laura and Lorraine

Lorraine sitting on the steps of the Hanson home

Laura and Henry's second child, Henry Mark Hanson Jr., was born in 1935.

The Sixteenth United States Federal Census taken in 1940
Huron, Beadle County, South Dakota

At the time of the 1940 U.S. Federal Census, Henry Hanson rented a house in Huron, SD
with his wife, Laura, and their two oldest children, Lorraine and Henry Jr.
Henry Sr. was employed as a bookkeeper for a grain elevator.

Twins, David August Hanson and Douglas Iver Hanson, were born in 1942

Mr. and Mrs. Iver Vevang of Roslyn received word of the birth of twin boys to Mr. and Mrs. H.M. Hanson on Friday, December 18, 1942, at the Swedish Hospital in Minneapolis, Minnesota. Mrs. Hanson is a daughter of Mr. and Mrs. Iver Vevang

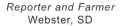

Mr. and Mrs. Iver Vevang of Roslyn received word of the birth of twin boys to Mr. and Mrs. H. M. Hanson on Friday, Dec. 18 at the Swedish Hospital in Minneapolis. Mrs. Hanson is a daughter of Mr. and Mrs. Vevang.

Sympathy is extended to Mr. and Mrs. Henry Hanson of Minneapolis in the loss of their twin baby boy. Burial was made in the Saron cemetery on Saturday.

Reporter and Farmer
Webster, SD

Swedish Hospital in Minneapolis, Minnesota

Douglas Iver Hanson's baptismal day

Parents Henry & Laura

David August Hanson

Born: December 18, 1942
Died: December 22, 1942

Twin brother of Douglas Iver Hanson

Douglas Hanson and his cousin, Linda Vevang, in 1947. The Laura Vevang Hanson family
and the Ingvald Vevang family lived next to each other for a short time.
Brothers, Douglas and Henry Hanson Jr. at the Hanson home in Webster, South Dakota.

Douglas and Linda

Douglas and Henry Jr.

Mrs. Henry Hanson and sons
and Mrs. Elmer Vevang of Roslyn returned home Thursday
from a five weeks vacation trip
spent visiting a sister, Mrs. Ed
Olson at Minneapolis, another
sister, Mrs. Charles Watkins at
Chicago, a brother, Rev. S. E.
Vevang at Dalesville, Wisc., and
a sister, Mrs. John Montgomery
at Rocky Mt., Va. They were
joined in Minneapolis Sunday by
Mr. Hanson who returned home
with them.
1947

Mrs. Henry Hanson entertain-
ed at a coffee party Monday af-
ternoon for Mrs. M. L. Hanse,
Mrs. Theresa Boyd, Mrs. Tom
Lensegrav, Mrs. Iver Vevang of
Roslyn, Mrs. Warneking and Mrs.
E. P. Ludtke.

Reporter and Farmer
Webster, SD

Henry Hanson Jr. on the Vevang family farm

Laura and Henry's home in Webster in 1962
420 West Eighth Avenue.

Laura, her sons, and sister-in-law Elna Vevang,
returned home Thursday from a five-week vacation
trip spent visiting a sister, Mrs. Ed Olson in
Minneapolis, another sister, Mrs. Charles Watkins
in Chicago, a brother, Rev. S.E. Vevang in Galesville,
Wisconsin, and a sister, Mrs. John Ed Montgomery
in Rocky Mount, Virginia. They were joined in
Minneapolis Sunday by Mr. Hanson who returned
home with them.

Your Vote Appreciated

LAURA M. HANSON

Democratic Candidate for

County Auditor

General Election, Nov. 7, 1950

Eight years teaching experience   Native of Day County

Laura was Day County Auditor from 1951 to 1955, and Deputy City Auditor for Webster. She was appointed Webster City Finance Officer in 1970 and retired in 1979.

Henry was the Day County Treasurer and Auditor, as well as Webster City Auditor. He was also self-employed as an accountant.

Day County Board of Commissioners

As 1953 gets underway, the board of county commissioners has two new faces, although four out of five begin new elective terms. The board is pictured here as they met for their annual meeting this month.

Seated: Chairman Edwin C. Lee, third district; Mrs. Laura Hanson, county auditor

Standing, left to right: Albert Prieb, second district; Ed Tracy, first district; Archie Fossum, fifth district; Ed Raap, fourth district

Fossum and Raap are new members of the board; Prieb and Tracy previously served by appointment. Lee was elected to office in November 1950.

VOLUME LXXI   OFFICIAL COUNTY & CITY NEWSPAPER

Two New Faces On County Board

As 1953 gets underway, the board of county commissioners has two new faces, although four out of five begin new elective terms. The board is pictured above as they met for their annual meeting this month.

Seated: Chairman Edwin C. Lee, third district; Mrs. Laura Hanson, county auditor.

Standing, left to right: Albert Prieb, second district; Ed Tracy, first district; Archie Fossum, fifth district; Ed Raap, fourth district.

Fossum and Raap are new members of the board; Prieb and Tracy previously served by appointment. Lee was elected to office in November 1950.

1957

Christmas with the Ingvald Vevang family

From left: Dennis Vevang, Henry Hanson Sr., Douglas Hanson, Ingvald Vevang with Debra Vevang in front, Alberta Syverson Vevang, Linda Vevang, Laura Vevang Hanson, and Pamela Vevang

1960

Christmas at the home of Ingvald Vevang in Webster, SD

Standing from left: Douglas Hanson and Henry Hanson Jr.

Sitting: Henry Hanson Sr. and Laura Vevang Hanson

At the home of Laura and Henry Sr. Hanson, in the mid 1960s

From left: Dennis Vevang, Pamela Vevang, Douglas Hanson, Henry Hanson Jr., Debbie Vevang, Jerry Forslund, and Linda Vevang Forslund

OBITUARY

Henry Mark Hanson Sr.

Reporter and Farmer
Webster, SD

Henry Hanson, 86, Webster, South Dakota, died Wednesday, May 2, 1984, at the Strand-Kjorsvig Nursing Home, Roslyn, South Dakota.

The funeral will be at 2 p.m. Saturday at St. John's Lutheran Church, Webster, with the Rev. Vernon Severson officiating. Burial will be in Webster City Cemetery. Mohs Funeral Home, Webster, is in charge of the arrangements.

Visitation will be from 7:00 p.m. to 9:00 p.m. Thursday, all day Friday and from 10:00 a.m. to 11:30 a.m. Saturday at the funeral home and prior to the service at the church.

Casketbearers will be Alden Hanson, Richard Hanson, Mark Hanson, Allen Vevang, Steven Hanson and Larry Vevang. Mrs. Don Waldowski, Webster, will be the organist.

Henry Mark Hanson was born July 29, 1897, in Grenville Township, Day County.

He married Laura Mathilda Vevang on June 14, 1932, on the Iver Vevang family farm near Roslyn, South Dakota. Henry was a former Day County treasurer and auditor and was Webster City Auditor for many years. He was also self-employed as an accountant. Henry was a member of the men's group at St. John's Lutheran Church.

Survivors include his widow, Laura Hanson; two sons, Henry Hanson, Jr., Minneapolis, Minnesota; and Douglas Hanson, Santa Fe, New Mexico; one brother, Melvin Hanson, Sisseton, South Dakota; and four grandchildren. He was preceded in death by one daughter, Lorraine Harriet, in 1947 and one son David August, in 1942, two brothers and one sister.

The sun shines - - -
   The tree flourishes,
Just as God's love shines,
   And we flourish.

But - - - as the sun's warmth
   Passes away into autumn,
The tree fades into slumber - - -
   So must we.

How wonderful though,
   When spring comes - - -
Life comes to the tree again.
   God's love shines and - - -
Unto everlasting life we pass.

The trees and God's children - - -
   All born again.

IN MEMORY OF
Henry Mark Hanson
Webster, S. Dak.
July 29, 1897 - May 2, 1984

SERVICES
2:00 p.m. Saturday, May 5, 1984
St. John's Lutheran Church
Webster, S. Dak.

CLERGY
Rev. Vernon Severson
Webster, S. Dak.

ORGANIST
Mrs. Donald (Lenny) Waldowski

MUSIC
Congregational Singing

CASKET BEARERS
Alden Hanson   Richard Hanson
Mark Hanson   Allen Vevang
Steven Hanson   Larry Vevang

INTERMENT
Webster City Cemetery
Webster, S. Dak.

MOHS FUNERAL HOME
Webster, South Dakota

Henry and Laura Hanson are buried in the Webster Cemetery, Webster, South Dakota.

OBITUARY

Laura M. Hanson

Reporter and Farmer
Webster, SD

Laura M. Vevang was born March 18, 1908, to Iver and Serina (Hustad) Vevang in Nutley Township, rural Roslyn, South Dakota. She graduated from Roslyn High School. She attended Northern State Teachers' College in Aberdeen, South Dakota.

She married Henry M. Hanson on June 14, 1932 on the Iver Vevang family farm near Roslyn. She taught in various rural schools in South Dakota.

Laura was Day County Auditor from 1951 to 1955 and was Deputy City Auditor for Webster, South Dakota. She was appointed Webster City Finance Officer in 1970 and retired in 1979.

Laura was a member of St. John's Lutheran Church in Webster. Survivors include two sons, Henry Mark Hanson Jr. of East Dubuque, Illinois and Douglas Iver Hanson of Montgomery, Alabama; two brothers, Elmer Vevang and Lawrence Vevang, both of Roslyn, South Dakota; three sisters, Hilda Olson of Minneapolis, Minnesota, Ella Montgomery of Rocky Mount, Virginia and Myrtle Watkins of Ocala, Florida; four grandchildren, David, Jennifer, Michelle, Joshua; and one great-grandson, Kyle.

Laura was preceded in death by her husband Henry Mark Hanson Sr. in 1984, one daughter, Lorraine Harriet Hanson, one son, David August Hanson, five brothers, Julius Vevang, Ingvald Vevang, Selmer Vevang, Edvin Vevang, Jacob Vevang, and one sister, Alida Vevang.

He is not here; for he has risen, as he said.
Matthew 28:6

Laura M. Hanson

Funeral services for Laura M. Hanson, 83, of Webster were April 27 at St. John's Lutheran Church in Webster. The Rev. Vernon Severson officiated.

Burial was in the Webster City Cemetery.

She died Wednesday, April 24, 1991, at Lake Area Hospital in Webster.

Casket bearers were David Hanson, Alden Hanson, Jerry Forslund, Jim Dedrickson, Todd Bullera and Atty. James Delaney.

Organist was Suzanne Olawsky and soloist was David Prieb.

Laura M. Vevang was born March 18, 1908, to Iver and Serina (Hustad) Vevang in Nutley Township, rural Roslyn. She graduated from Roslyn High School. She attended Northern State Teachers College in Aberdeen.

She married Henry M. Hanson June 14, 1932, at Roslyn. She taught in various rural schools in South Dakota, and was Day County auditor from 1951 to 1955. She was deputy city auditor for Webster and was appointed Webster city finance officer in 1970, retiring in 1979.

She was a member of St. John's Lutheran Church in Webster.

Survivors include two sons, Henry Hanson of East Dubuque, Iowa, and Douglas Iver Hanson of Montgomery, Ala.; two brothers, Elmer Vevang and Lawrence Vevang, both of Roslyn; three sisters, Hilda Olson of Minneapolis, Ella Montgomery of Rocky Mount, Va., and Mrs. Charles (Myrtle) Watkins of Ocala, Fla.; four grandchildren; and one great-grandson.

She was preceded in death by her husband in 1984, one daughter, four brothers and one sister.

Reporter and Farmer
Webster, SD

IN MEMORY OF
Laura M. Hanson
Webster, South Dakota
March 18, 1908 – April 24, 1991

SERVICES
2:00 p.m. Saturday, April 27, 1991
St. John's Lutheran Church
Webster, South Dakota

CLERGY
Rev. Vernon Severson
Webster, S.D.

ORGANIST
Mrs. Douglas (Suzanne) Olawsky
Webster, S.D.

SOLOIST
Mr. David Prieb
Webster, S.D.

CASKET BEARERS
David Hanson   Alden Hanson
Jerry Forslund   Jim Dedrickson
Todd Bullera   Atty. James Delaney

INTERMENT
Webster City Cemetery
Webster, S.D.

Funeral Arrangements By
MOHS FUNERAL HOME
Webster, S.D.

Henry M. Hanson
1897 – 1984

Laura M. Vevang Hanson
1908 - 1991

FAMILY

Laura Mathilda Vevang b: 18 Mar 1908, Nutley Township, Day County, South Dakota; d: 24 Apr 1991, Webster, Day County, South Dakota; buried: Webster Cemetery, Webster, Day County, South Dakota

Laura married **Henry Mark Hanson** b: 29 Jul 1897, Grenville Township, Day County, South Dakota; m: 14 Jun 1932, Iver Vevang family farm, Nutley Township, Day County, South Dakota; d: 02 May 1984, Strand-Kjorsvig Nursing Home, Roslyn, Day County, South Dakota; buried: Webster Cemetery, Webster, Day County, South Dakota

CHILDREN
of Laura Mathilda Vevang and Henry Mark Hanson Sr.

Lorraine Harriet Hanson b: 21 Apr 1933, Peabody Hospital, Webster, Day County, South Dakota; d: 10 May 1947, Webster, Day County, South Dakota; buried: Webster Cemetery, Webster, Day County, South Dakota

Henry Mark Hanson Jr. b: 06 Aug 1935, Peabody Hospital, Webster, Day County, South Dakota

David August Hanson b: 18 Dec 1942, Minneapolis, Hennepin County, Minnesota; d: 22 Dec 1942, Minneapolis, Hennepin County, Minnesota; buried: Saron Lutheran Cemetery, Roslyn, Day County, South Dakota

Douglas Iver Hanson b: 18 Dec 1942, Minneapolis, Hennepin County, Minnesota

LORRAINE HARRIET HANSON

Born
April 21, 1933
Webster, Day County, SD

Died
May 10, 1947
Webster, Day County, SD
Laid to rest in Webster Cemetery, Webster, SD

Girl of 14 Dies; Funeral Wednesday

Reporter and Farmer
Webster, SD

Lorraine Harriet Hanson, 14-year-old daughter of Mr. and Mrs. Henry M. Hanson of Webster passed away Saturday morning, May 10, 1947 at her home. Funeral services were held Wednesday afternoon at 2 o'clock at St. John's Lutheran Church with Rev. R. A. Wangberg in charge. Interment was made at the Webster cemetery with six uncles acting as pall bearers.

She was born April 21, 1933 in Webster and was baptized in the Roslyn Lutheran Church. Although she never enjoyed a strong and healthy life, she was dearly loved by all who knew her.

Surviving her besides her parents, are two brothers, Henry Jr., and Douglas; her maternal grandparents, Mr. and Mrs. Iver Vevang of Roslyn, in addition to other relatives. One brother, David preceded her in death. Attending the funeral from a distance were Rev. and Mrs. Selmer Vevang, Paul and Timothy, Galesville, Wisconsin; Mrs. Charles Watkins, Chicago, Illinois; Mr. and Mrs. J. S. Vevang, Watertown, South Dakota; Mrs. Ed Olson, Mrs. Don Danielson, Minneapolis, Minnesota; Mr. and Mrs. Melvin Hanson, Mr. and Mrs. Carl Hanson, Mrs. Martin Olson, Mrs. Ed Berg, Sisseton, South Dakota; Mrs. Henry Bendickson and George, Grenville, South Dakota; Mr. and Mrs. Iver Vevang and Alida, Mr. and Mrs. Elmer Vevang and children, Mr. and Mrs. Lawrence Vevang, Mr. and Mrs. Albert Hanson, Mr. and Mrs. Oscar Johnson and Mr. and Mrs. George Moen, all of Roslyn, South Dakota

Girl Of 14 Dies; Funeral Wednesday

Lorraine Harriet Hanson, 14 year old daughter of Mr. and Mrs. Henry M. Hanson of Webster passed away Saturday morning, May 10, at her home.

Funeral services were held Wednesday afternoon at 2 o'clock at St. John's Lutheran Church, with Rev. R. A. Wangberg in charge. Interment was made at the Webster cemetery with six uncle acting as pall bearers.

She was born April 21, 1933 in Webster and was baptized in the Roslyn Lutheran Church. Although she never enjoyed a strong and healthy life, she was dearly loved by all who knew her.

Surviving her besides her parents, are two brothers, Henry Jr., and Douglas; her maternal grandparents, Mr. and Mrs. Iver Vevang of Roslyn, in addition to other relatives. One brother, David preceded her in death.

Attendng the funeral from a distance were Rev. and Mrs. Selmer Vevang, Paul and Timothy, Galesville, Wis.; Mrs. Chas Watkins, Chicago; Mr. and Mrs. J. S. Vevang, Watertown; Mrs. Ed Olson, Mrs. Don Danielson, Minneapolis; Mr. and Mrs. Melvin Hanson, Mr. and Mrs. Carl Hanson, Mrs. Martin Olson, Mrs. Ed Berg, Sisseton; Mrs. Henry Bendickson and George, Grenville; Mr. and Mrs. Iver Vevang and Alida, Mr. and Mrs. Elmer Vevang and children, Mr. and Mrs. Lawrence Vevang, Mr. and Mrs. Albert Hanson, Mr. and Mrs. Oscar Johnson and Mr. and Mrs. George Moen, all of Roslyn.

HENRY MARK HANSON JR.

Born

August 6, 1935

Webster, Day County, SD

Henry graduated from the University of South Dakota
in Vermillion, South Dakota in 1957

Henry Mark Hanson Jr.

married

Janet Mary Ann Lind

June 10, 1967

Minneapolis,
Hennepin County,
Minnesota

FAMILY

Henry Mark Hanson Jr. b: 06 Aug 1935, Peabody Hospital, Webster, Day County, South Dakota

Henry married **Janet Mary Ann Lind** b: 20 Mar 1946, Town, Sherborne County, Dorset, England; m: 10 Jun 1967, Minneapolis, Hennepin County, Minnesota: div.

> Henry and Janet's adopted children:
> **Jennifer Susan Hanson** b: 08 May 1971, St. Paul, Ramsey County, Minnesota
> **Joshua Mark Hanson** b: 16 Dec 1974, Minneapolis, Hennepin County, Minnesota

CHILDREN AND GRANDCHILDREN
of Henry Mark Hanson Jr. and Janet Mary Ann Lind

Jennifer

Jennifer Susan Hanson

Jennifer's son with **Todd Mathew Bulera** b: 01 Jan 1969, Ramsey County, Minnesota:
Kyle Mathew Hanson-Bulera b: 20 Mar 1990, Edina, Hennepin County, Minnesota

Kyle married **Amy Lynn Foster** b: 17 Oct 1979, St. Paul, Ramsey County, Minnesota; m: 07 Oct 2017, Inver Grove Heights, Dakota County, Minnesota

Amy and Kyle

Joshua and Daralene

Joshua Mark Hanson

Joshua's children with **Amanda Marion Bays** b: 19 Feb 1978, Fort Worth, Tarrant County, Texas:
Samantha Marie Hanson b: 29 Sept 1995, Iowa City, Johnson County, Iowa
Joshua Mark Hanson Jr. b: 07 Nov 1999, Dubuque, Dubuque County, Iowa
Maryanna Lynn Hanson b: 23 Mar 2002, Dubuque, Dubuque County, Iowa

From left: Samantha, Joshua, and Maryanna

Joshua married **Daralene Archer Leighton** b: 11 Jan 1962, South Portland, Cumberland County, Maine; m: 01 Sep 2019, Pequot Lakes, Crow Wing County, Minnesota

DOUGLAS IVER HANSON

Born

December 18, 1942

Minneapolis, Hennepin County, MN

Douglas Iver Hanson

married

Bonita Louise Beck

March 19, 1966

Herreid,
Campbell County,
South Dakota

Wedding Guests. In back: Julius Vevang with Hazel Gilbertson Vevang in front of him, Alida Vevang, Allen Vevang Second Row: Jerry Forslund, Dennis Vevang, Henry Hanson Jr., Linda Vevang Forslund, Elna Olson Vevang, Laura Vevang Hanson, Elmer Vevang First row: Darlis Vevang Dedrickson, Debbie Vevang, Henry Hanson Sr., Alberta Syverson Vevang In front: Keith Dedrickson, Vicki Dedrickson and Kimberly Dedrickson

Douglas Iver Hanson, Bonita Beck Hanson, David Hanson, and Michelle Hanson

David and Michelle

Hanson Family
Standing: Tiffany Myers Hanson holding Zachary Hanson,
David Hanson and Michelle Hanson Sitting: Douglas
Hanson, Bonita Beck Hanson holding Joshua Hanson

FAMILY

Douglas Iver Hanson b: 18 Dec 1942, Minneapolis, Hennepin County, Minnesota

Douglas married **Bonita Louise Beck** b: 05 Sep 1944, Eureka, McPherson County, South Dakota; m: 19 Mar 1966, Herreid, Campbell County, South Dakota

Douglas and Bonita's adopted children:
David Scott Hanson b: 14 Jul 1969, El Paso, El Paso County, Texas
Michelle Leigh Hanson b: 25 Aug 1972, Sturgis, Meade County, South Dakota

CHILDREN AND GRANDCHILDREN
of Douglas Iver Hanson and Bonita Louise Beck

David Scott Hanson married **Tiffany Ann Myers** b: 13 Mar 1974, Pittsburgh, Allegheny County, Pennsylvania; m: 15 Nov 2002, Chandler, Maricopa County, Arizona

David and Tiffany's children:
Zachary David Hanson b: 09 Apr 2008, Anaheim, Orange County, California
Joshua Scott Hanson b: 26 Mar 2010, Madera, Madera County, California

Michelle Leigh Hanson

CHAPTER IX

ELLA

Born

October 12, 1909

Vevang Family Farm

Nutley Township, Day County, SD

Died

May 24, 1999

Rocky Mount, Franklin County, VA

Laid to rest in High Street Cemetery, Rocky Mount, VA

The Thirteenth United States Federal Census taken in 1910
Nutley Township, Day County, South Dakota

Vevang Iver A.	Head		M	W	44
Serina	Wife		F	W	38
Julius	Son		M	W	12
Hilda	Daughter		F	W	11
Elmer	Son		M	W	9
Ingvald	Son		M	W	7
Selmer	Son		M	W	5
Laura	Daughter		F	W	2
Ella	Daughter		F	W	6/12
Gaara Halvor	Lodger		M	W	36

ELLA was six months old in 1910 when Iver, Serina, Julius, Hilda, Elmer, Ingvald, Selmer, and Laura were in the Vevang home. They also had a lodger, Mr. Halvor Gaara, a country school teacher.

1915   **1919**   **1923**

The Fourteenth United States Federal Census taken in 1920
Nutley Township, Day County, South Dakota

Vevang Iver A.	Head	O	m	m	w	54
Serina	Wife			F	w	47
Julius S.	Son			m	w	23
Elmer L.	Son			m	w	18
Engvald	Son			m	w	17
Selmer	Son			m	w	15
Laura M.	Daughter			F	w	11
Ella H.	Daughter			F	w	10
Alida	Daughter			F	w	9
Myrtle H.	Daughter			F	w	5
Lawrence A.	Son			m	w	4

Iver, Serina, Julius, Elmer, Ingvald, Selmer, Laura, Ella, Alida, Myrtle, and Lawrence were in the Vevang home in 1920. Hilda was no longer in the family home as she married in 1919.

**Ella was confirmed in 1923,
at the age of 14**

Ella was confirmed in the
Lutheran Christian faith in the
Roslyn Lutheran Church.
Ella (right) is with her sister Laura
(left). Laura was confirmed in 1922.

—1923—
Albert Oliver Peterson
George Glosimodt
Andrew Oscar Sandvig
Paul Joseph Steffenson
Raymond Irving Hallem
Agnes C. Hatle
Esther Oline Hatle-Fiske
Ruth Edith Blank-Sundstrom
Gladys Leona Pederson-Sorenson
Hazel Clara Hagen-Mahlen
Ida Alvilda Aspen-Jacobs
Mabel Amanda Hendrickson-Harper
Ella Vevang-Montgomery
Lottie Elizabeth Granstrom-Guilford

U.S. Evangelical Lutheran Church in America Church Records

355

Roslyn High School — Class of 1928

Class of 1928

Bernard Farmen, George Glosimodt, Reuben Grorud, Agnes Hemmah Holm, LeRoy Jacobs, Philomena Janisch Lawton, Elizabeth Lardy Pekron, Ella Nerland Nelson, Elmer Nilson*, Albert Peterson*, Elmer Peterson*, Raydon Ronshaugen, Bardon Skaaden*, Sigmund Skaaden*, Ella Vevang Montgomery.

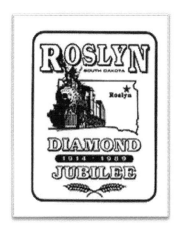

Published by
Reporter and Farmer
Webster, SD

Augustana College — Class of 1929

Ella received a diploma from Augustana College, Sioux Falls, South Dakota in 1929. She completed the One-Year Normal Course of Study.

Ella taught school in Day County after she received her diploma from Augustana College.

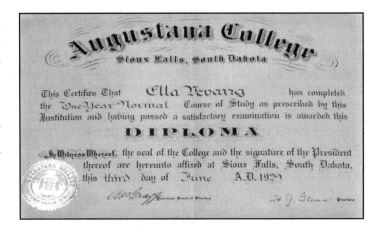

The Fifteenth United States Federal Census taken in 1930
Nutley Township, Day County, South Dakota

Vevang	Iver J	Head	O		R	Yes	M	W	64
—	Serina	Wife					×	F W	58
—	Ingvald	Son					×	M W	27
—	Laura M	Daughter					×	F W	22
—	Ella	Daughter					×	F W	20
—	Alida	Daughter					×	F W	19
—	Myrtle H	Daughter					×	F W	15
—	Lawrence G	Son					×	M W	14

Still in the Iver Vevang household: Iver and Serina, Ingvald, Laura, Ella, Alida, Myrtle, and Lawrence

The Swedish Hospital School of Nursing — Class of 1934

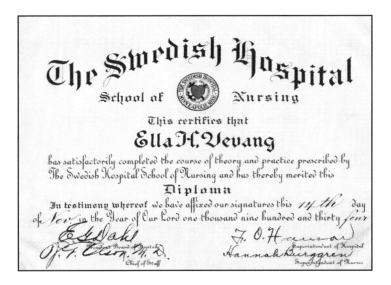

In November of 1934, Ella received a diploma from the Swedish Hospital School of Nursing in Minneapolis, Minnesota. She completed the course of theory and practice.

Ella Vevang is standing to the right on the second step.

Ella is the third from the right, standing with her classmates.

Ella on the roof of Roanoke Memorial Hospital

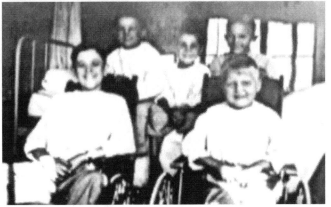

Patients from the hospital where Ella taught and worked

**In the 1935 U.S. Census,
Ella lived in Watertown, SD**

Name: Ella H Vevang

Age: 25

Birth Year: 1909

Race: White

Sex: Female

Birth Place: Roslyn, SD

Marital Status: Single

Event Place: Watertown,

Codington County , SD

Post Office: Watertown, SD

Father's Birth Place: Norway

Mother's Birth Place: Norway

FHL Film Number: 2370725

Ella soon was ready to make her place in the world. She found herself with two job offers. One was on the West Coast in San Francisco, and the other was in Roanoke, Virginia. She tossed a coin to decide in which direction she would go, and going east it was. Ella settled in Roanoke, Virginia, and was a nursing instructress at the Roanoke Hospital for two years. She worked with crippled children during a polio epidemic.

359

Winding Ridge Summit

**Allegheny Mountains
of Maryland**

*Sister and Brother
Ella and Ingvald*

1936

Left: Ella Vevang and Ingvald Vevang in Washington D.C.
Above: Sisters, Myrtle Vevang and Ella Vevang

Ella and Ingvald on the steps of the U.S. Capitol

Sisters Ella and Myrtle in Princeton, New Jersey

Ella and Bea Sholl Vevang in the big city

Ella in Brooklyn, New York

Ella in 1936 with her nieces, Beverley and Shirley Vevang, children of her brother, Selmer.

Sisters, Myrtle Vevang and Ella Vevang

Ella Vevang

Ella Vevang on a frosty winter day

JOHN EDGAR LEE MONTGOMERY
"JOHN ED"

Born
November 2, 1897
Rocky Mount, Franklin County, VA

Died
April 26, 1965
Rocky Mount, Franklin County, VA
Laid to rest in High Street Cemetery, Rocky Mount, VA

JOHN ED & ELLA MONTGOMERY

Married June 1, 1938
Elizabeth, Union County, New Jersey

Engagement photo published in
Reporter and Farmer, Webster, SD

RECORD OF MARRIAGE

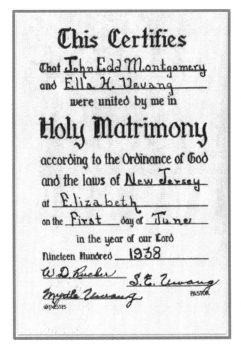

This Certifies

That _John Edd Montgomery_
and _Ella H. Vevang_
were united by me in

Holy Matrimony

according to the Ordinance of God
and the laws of _New Jersey_
at _Elizabeth_
on the _First_ day of _June_
in the year of our Lord
Nineteen Hundred _1938_

W.D. Rucker _S.E. Vevang_
Myrtle Vevang PASTOR
WITNESSES

Wedding party. From left: Pastor Selmer E. Vevang, Bernice Sholl Vevang, Witnesses: Myrtle Vevang, W.D. Rucker, Bride: Ella Vevang Montgomery, Groom: John Edgar Lee Montgomery

Ella H. Vevang and
John Edgar Lee Montgomery Marry

Reporter and Farmer, Webster, SD

Miss Ella H. Vevang of Roanoke, Virginia, originally of Roslyn, South Dakota, daughter of Mr. and Mrs. Iver Vevang of Roslyn, became the bride of John Edgar Lee Montgomery, son of Mrs. Susan Montgomery of Rocky Mount, Virginia, on the evening of June 1, 1938, at the Bethlehem Lutheran Church at Elizabeth, New Jersey. Rev. Selmer E. Vevang, a brother of the bride performed the ceremony, assisted by Rev. H.A. Oakdale of Brooklyn, N.Y. formerly of Watertown.

The bride wore a two-tone suit dress and a corsage of gardenias and lilies of the valley. She was attended by her sister, Myrtle Vevang, who wore a dusty pink dress and a corsage of tea-roses and lilies of the valley. W. Dudley Rucker of Washington, D.C., brother-in-law of the groom, was best man.

Mrs. S. E. Vevang played various selections on the organ and accompanied Mrs. J. H. Preus, of Jersey City, who sang two selections from the Lutheran church hymnal. The bride taught school in Day County for two years, after attending Augustana College in Sioux Falls. She was graduated from the school of nursing at the Swedish Hospital in Minneapolis and for the past two years has been nursing instructress at the Roanoke Hospital. The groom is a hardware merchant in Rocky Mount, his father starting the business more than 50 years ago.

Following the ceremony, a reception was held for the bridal party at the home of Rev. and Mrs. Vevang in Elizabeth. After a brief stay in New York City and Washington, D.C., the couple will go to Virginia Beach, Virginia for a month. They will make their home at Rocky Mount, Virginia. The many friends of the bride extend best wishes.

The Sixteenth United States Federal Census taken in 1940
Rocky Mount, Franklin County, Virginia

John E. Montgomery, Ella V. Montgomery and Serina Montgomery.
John E. Montgomery's occupation was a manager of a hardware store.

REGISTRATION CARD: John Edgar Lee Montgomery, age 20, from Rocky Mount, Virginia. He was a natural born citizen and was born in Rocky Mount, Franklin County, Virginia. John Edgar's occupation was that of a salesman employed by his father, Joseph Norton Montgomery.

REGISTRAR'S REPORT: John Edgar was of medium height and medium build. His eyes were blue and his hair was brown. The registration card was signed and certified by the Local Board of Franklin County in Virginia on September 12, 1918.

Early Life

Written by Johnny Montgomery Jr.
(John Ed and Ella's Son)

John Ed and Ella met through Lucy Joplin. Lucy was a nurse at Roanoke Memorial where Ella worked. Lucy's husband, Joe Joplin, was a good friend of Papa's.

John Ed had a hardware store named Montgomery Hardware in Rocky Mount, Virginia. When Mom and Papa were married, they lived in an apartment above the still-standing drug store located on the corner of Main and Floyd Avenue across from the hospital.

When sis (Serina) was born in 1939, they moved into the brick house which is still standing on the corner of Main Street and High Street. The High Street Cemetery is located behind it. From there, they moved into the Montgomery family home which they shared with Mamie, Papa's sister. Mema, Papa's mother, also lived on Mamie's side of the house and I barely remember her as this little old woman in bed. Sis and I really consider this our home place and not the New House that you all know so well. From there we moved into the New House in 1952, when Bill was born in 1953.

John Ed and Ella

Montgomery Hardware showing the front window display for the fall hunting season taken in the early 1960s on Main Street across from the Court House.

1947. Johnny in front of the store

Serina age five in about 1944   Johnny with Lodie in about 1946

John Ed was a very accomplished musician. He played piano, guitar, banjo, mandolin, clarinet, and saxophone. I have the mandolin on a shelf in our house. Papa played it in bands throughout the county.

I'm not sure when Papa actually bought the farm. It was located approximately 20 miles from our home. The farm had a cabin built next to a creek named Story Creek. There were approximately 75 acres of land, most being in pastures which Papa had cattle.

The cabin consisted of a living area including a stone fireplace and kitchen, another room in which we all slept, an outside screened shower, and a long wrap-around screened porch. There was an outside privy close to the cabin. We had a two-stall barn for our horse named Toney.

John Ed Montgomery, Lodie, and Johnny Montgomery

There was also a chicken house and at one time beehives. Along with all this, there was a large garden, where we raised snap beans, corn, tomatoes, and potatoes. The harvest was stored in a large dirt and straw mound for winter keeping.

There was no electricity, so our light source was kerosene lamps, and the kitchen stove was fueled with kerosene. The refrigerator was an ice refrigerator holding a solid piece of ice that went into a side compartment. Papa handled it with a set of ice tongs, and he bought it from an ice plant in Rocky Mount. Our water was from a spring and was piped into the cabin.

Johnny riding Toney

Mama, Papa, Serina, and I went to the farm nearly every weekend during warm weather, in those early years. During the summer we stayed there for two to three months. I have great memories of those times playing in the creek, working with the animals with Papa, and riding Toney.

Johnny and Serina playing in Story Creek

369

Ve

Written by Monty (Ella's granddaughter, Serina's daughter)

Ve, as Ella is called, told me that the Virginia doctors called her "Whizbang" because she was so good and so fast. When I was a kid, my understanding is that she worked for Community Action, an organization that helped get medical care and support for people living in poverty. Some of whom lived in the Blue Ridge, Eastern Appalachian Mountains without running water in the house.

Ve was a straight talker but not a big talker. She was extremely competent at anything she tried. Ve could bake any cake and do any type of needlework: sewing, knitting, crocheting, needlepoint, and quilting. She even made her own large spiral rugs. Her house was immaculate. She did not believe in clutter.

For us Southerners, Ve was very a Midwest Norwegian. I remember that one of her sisters came to visit and flew into Greensboro. I think it was when I was a teenager. Ve asked me to go with her on the hour's drive to pick her sister up. Ve had me drive back and the two of them just spent the whole trip critiquing my driving—too fast, too slow, etc. I was used to that from Ve, but it was funny to hear the same thing in the exact same tone from her sister.

Ella and Myrtle

Ella in the Blue Ridge Eastern Appalachian Mountains

Serina and Johnny

William

1940. Serina with Uncle Ingvald on the farm

Cousins Serina, Beverley, and Shirley

Iver & Serina's 50th Wedding Anniversary Roslyn in 1946.

From left: Iver Vevang, John Ed Montgomery, Serina Hustad Vevang, Ella Vevang Montgomery
Front: Johnny Montgomery and Serina Montgomery

Aunt alida. she visited with us. in 1942.

1944. John Ed and Ella at Myrtle and Charles Watkins' home in Cranford, NJ. They visited for a week.

Bonnie Vevang & Johnny

Paul Vevang and Johnny

Johnny, Serina, Warren Vevang and Bonnie Vevang

Shirley Vevang and Serina Montgomery at the water well on the Iver Vevang farm.

Top: Lawrence Vevang putting up hay
Bottom: Iver Vevang with his tractor in about 1944

Cousins

Bruce Watkins and Johnny Montgomery

From left: Serina Montgomery, Johnny Montgomery, Henry Hanson Jr., and Doug Hanson

From left: James Vevang, Timothy Vevang, Johnny Montgomery, and Paul Vevang

From left: Dennis Vevang, Linda Vevang, Serina Montgomery, Doug Hanson, and Johnny Montgomery

Praying at the Vevang Table. James Vevang, Paul Vevang, Serina Montgomery, Johnny Montgomery, Shirley Vevang, and Timothy Vevang

From left: Paul Vevang, Johnny Montgomery, Unknown, Timothy Vevang, Unknown, and James Vevang

373

Sister and Brother
Serina Montgomery and William Montgomery

Before Johnny's high school senior prom in 1960
From left: Johnny Montgomery, Serina Montgomery Garst,
Ella Vevang Montgomery, John Ed Montgomery, and
William Lee Montgomery in front.
It was customary for everyone to dress up for the event.

120 Church Street, Rocky Mount, Virginia

FUNERAL

John Edgar Lee Montgomery

JOHN EDGAR LEE
MONTGOMERY
NOVEMBER 2, 1897
APRIL 26, 1965

Fred and Serina Garst, Johnny Montgomery, and Ella Vevang Montgomery

John Ed died suddenly of a stroke on April 26, 1965.
Ella never remarried.

From left: Julius Vevang, Ella Montgomery, Johnny Montgomery, Serina Garst,
Fred Garst, Alberta Vevang, Ingvald Vevang, Bea Vevang, and Sam Vevang

OBITUARY

Ella Vevang Montgomery

Ella Vevang (Ve) Montgomery of Rocky Mount, Virginia died Monday, May 24, 1999.

She was the wife of John Ed Montgomery.

Survivors include daughter and son-in-law, Serina and Fred Garst of Boones Mill, Virginia; sons and daughter-in-law, John E. and Betsy Montgomery of Rocky Mount, Virginia, Bill Montgomery of London, England; grandchildren, Frederick, Serina and Carey Garst, John Ed, Ann Clark and James Montgomery; great-grandchildren, Jed Montgomery, Frederick Garst; sister, Myrtle Vevang Watkins of Florida; and brother, Lawrence Vevang of Roslyn, South Dakota.

IN MEMORY OF

ELLA "VE" VEVANG MONTGOMERY

AGE
89 Years

SERVICES
Rocky Mount Presbyterian Church
2:00 P.M. Friday
May 28, 1999

CLERGY
Dr. Murphy D. Miller

INTERMENT
High Street Cemetery

ELLA VEVANG
MONTGOMERY
OCT 12. 1909
MAY 24. 1999

FAMILY

Ella Heninga Vevang b: 12 Oct 1909, Nutley Township, Day County, South Dakota; d: 24 May 1999, Rocky Mount, Franklin County, Virginia; buried: High Street Cemetery, Rocky Mount, Virginia

Ella married John Edgar Lee (John Ed) Montgomery b: 02 Nov 1897, Rocky Mount, Franklin County, Virginia; m: 01 Jun 1938, Elizabeth, Union County, New Jersey; d: 26 Apr 1965, Rocky Mount, Franklin County, Virginia; buried: High Street Cemetery, Rocky Mount, Virginia

CHILDREN
of Ella Heninga Vevang and John Edgar Lee Montgomery

Serina Vevang Montgomery b: 06 Mar 1939, Roanoke, Roanoke County, Virginia

John Edgar Lee (Johnny) Montgomery Jr. b: 07 Jul 1942, Roanoke, Roanoke County, Virginia

William Lee Montgomery b: 10 Jul 1953, Rocky Mount, Franklin County, Virginia

SERINA VEVANG MONTGOMERY

Born
March 6, 1939
Roanoke, Roanoke County, VA

 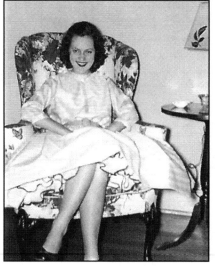

Serina Montgomery was baptized on May 19, 1939

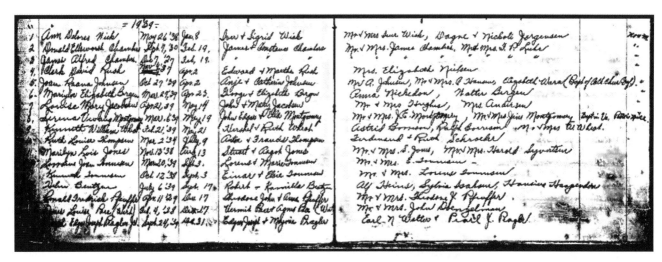

U.S. Evangelical Lutheran Church in America Church Records

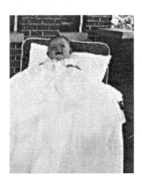

Name: Serina Vevang Montgomery

Record Type: Baptism

Birth Date: 6 Mar 1939

Baptism Date: 19 May 1939

Father: John Edgar Montgomery

Mother: Ella Montgomery

Sponsors: Mr. and Mrs. J.E. Montgomery and Mr. and Mrs. Jim Montgomery

The record shown above is of baptisms officiated at the Bethlehem Lutheran Church in Staten Island, New York by S.E. Vevang. Serina, listed as #8, was baptized in Virgina by her uncle, S.E. Vevang. Her cousin, Shirley Elaine Vevang, is listed below as #12 in the same record. Shirley's sponsors were Myrtle Vevang and Rev. and Mrs. A.O. Storvick.

U.S. Evangelical Lutheran Church in America Church Records

Christmas in the Old House

Serina and Santa

John Ed

Ve (Ella Vevang Montgomery)

Serina and Johnny

Growing Up
Written by Monty (Fred and Serina's daughter)

SERINA MONTGOMERY
Senior

We grew up in Boones Mill Virginia. My father's family had land at the base of and including most of Cahas Mountain. My grandfather, Arthur High Garst, dammed up a creek and made a small lake and we kids spent most of the summer swimming at the lake and roaming around the mountain.

My father, Fred Garst Sr., worked with his brother, Jack Garst, in his family's apple business. We had orchards, an apple packing plant, and an apple cider plant. Mom worked teaching kindergarten and then eventually as the bookkeeper for the apple business. All of us kids and most of our cousins worked on the apple farm at some point. In the 1980s, Dad started a treated lumber business with some cousins. My brothers Fred and Carey worked there, and Carey ran the lumber business until we sold it in 2012.

I practiced law in California and New Mexico, working in private practice, technology companies, and the California Department of Justice. Fred has an engineering degree and has worked as a civil engineer. Carey has a Master of Business Administration degree and ran the family lumber business. Carey and Fred have gone back to their roots and farm apples on the Garst family's land.

Fred Garst Sr.

Fred and Serina

Serina Vevang Montgomery at the Montgomery farm

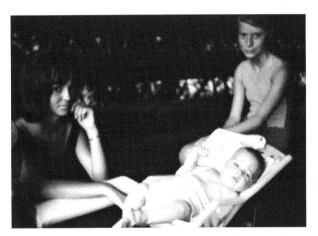

1966. Gathered at Garst's home
From left: Pamela Vevang, Carey Garst,
and Debra Vevang

1978. At Serina and Fred Garst's in Boones Mill, VA
Fred Garst Jr., Ingvald Vevang, Serina (Monty) Garst,
and Carey Garst

From left: Fred Garst Jr., Serina Montgomery Garst,
Serina (Monty) Garst and Carey Garst

OBITUARY
Frederick Garst Sr.

Frederick Garst, age 74, of Boones Mill died Friday evening, August 16, 2013. He was the son of Arthur High and Elva Alice Ferguson Garst, and was born on January 29, 1939, in Boones Mill, Franklin County, Virginia.

Frederick grew up on his family's farm which later became known as Occanneechi Orchards. Fred graduated from Franklin County High School, attended the University of Virginia and was active in the apple business for many years.

In the mid-eighties Fred became active in Rocky Top Wood Preservers, a business he and family members had founded in the mid-seventies, where he remained until his retirement.

In Fred's middle years he discovered the joys of beach saltwater fishing and later his boats; "Osprey" took him to the Atlantic Ocean and the Gulf Stream. He always fished out of Ocracoke and through the years earned many citation certificates for fish and placed one year in the Big Rock Tournament out of Morehead, NC.

Fred is survived by his wife, Serina; three children, Frederick Jr. and Joanna, Serina and Graham, Carey and Kari; eight grandchildren, Christin, Ashleigh, Frederick III, Riley, Cormac, Ambrose, Ella, Nathanael, Micah; and great-grandchild, Isla.

Memorial services will be held on Wednesday, August 21st at 1 p.m. at Trinity Episcopal Church in Rocky Mount, VA. The family will receive friends on Tuesday, August 20 at Flora Funeral Home from 5 to 7 p.m. In lieu of flowers, those who wish may make contributions to Ocracoke Working Watermen's Association (OWWA), Ocracoke, NC 27960.

Burial: Mountain View Memorial Park, Rocky Mount, Franklin County, Virginia, USA
Plot: SECTION #2 MTN VIEW Lot 82

Fred with his grandson,
Cormac, in 2007

FAMILY

Serina Vevang Montgomery b: 06 Mar 1939, Roanoke, Roanoke County, Virginia

Serina married **Frederick Garst Sr.** b: 29 Jan 1939, Boones Mill, Franklin County, Virginia; m: 06 Mar 1960, Wilson, Wilson County, North Carolina; d: 16 Aug 2013; buried: Mountain View Memorial Park, Rocky Mount, Franklin County, Virginia

Serina and Fred's children:
Frederick (Fred) Garst Jr. b: 21 Mar 1962, Roanoke, Roanoke County, Virginia
Serina (Monty) Montgomery Garst b: 18 Aug 1963, Roanoke, Roanoke County, Virginia
Carey Ferguson Garst b: 14 Apr 1966, Roanoke, Roanoke County, Virginia

CHILDREN AND GRANDCHILDREN
of Serina Vevang Montgomery and Frederick Garst Sr.

Frederick (Fred) Garst Jr. married **Joanna Woods Hurd** b: 15 Aug 1968, Martinsville, Henry County, Virginia; m: 25 Apr 1998, Boones Mill, Franklin County, Virginia

Fred and Joanna's children:
Frederick (Trey) Garst III b: 03 Jun 1999, Rocky Mount, Franklin County, Virginia
Riley Thomas Garst b: 14 Apr 2004, Roanoke, Roanoke County, Virginia

Serina (Monty) Montgomery Garst's partner is **Grahame Philip Foreman** b: 31 Jul 1973, Belfast, Northern Ireland

Grahame and Monty's children:
Cormac Cooke Foreman b: 23 Dec 2006,
San Francisco, San Francisco County, California
Ambrose Vevang Foreman b: 23 Dec 2006,
San Francisco, San Francisco County, California

Carey Ferguson Garst married **Karin (Kari) Brown** b: 25 May 1976, Waterloo, Black Hawk County, Iowa; m: 12 Jun 2002, Boones Mill, Franklin County, Virginia

Carey and Kari's children:
Ella Thomas Garst b: 11 Feb 2009, Roanoke, Roanoke County, Virginia
Nathanael Forrest Garst b: 17 Jun 2010, Roanoke, Roanoke County, Virginia
Micah Andrew Garst b: 03 Apr 2012, Roanoke, Roanoke County, Virginia

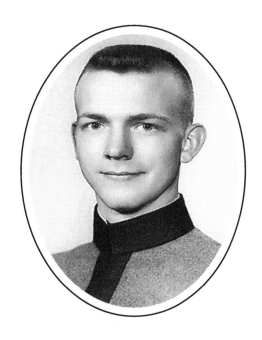

JOHN EDGAR LEE MONTGOMERY JR.
"JOHNNY"

Born

July 7, 1942

Roanoke, Roanoke County, VA

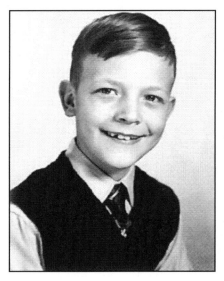 

John Edgar Lee
Montgomery Jr.

married

Betsy Clarke Whitlow

June 25, 1966

Rocky Mount,
Franklin County,
Virginia

Antioch Church of the Brethren

The bride and groom with Johnny's mother, Ella Vevang Montgomery

My Life With Johnny

Written by Betsy Clarke Whitlow Montgomery (Johnny's wife)

Johnny has really enjoyed living in the country in his retirement, as well as I, taking care of his chickens and goats. I grew up on a poultry farm and told him if he wanted chickens, he would have to take care of them because I had seen all the chickens I ever wanted to see. We have a little joke between us, "he thought he was marrying a country girl and I thought I was marrying a city boy." We've laughed a lot about it. I will have to admit it was nice having fresh eggs, and the grandchildren enjoyed helping him take care of the chickens and feeding them. Johnny is also a woodworker and has built many beautiful pieces of furniture. Now, he is always making something for the children and has retired from the chicken and goat business. He is a wonderful person and I'll never stop telling everyone that I am the luckiest girl in the world.

Johnny is board-certified in pediatrics and emergency medicine. He went to Medical College of Virginia. Me, a registered nurse from Roanoke Memorial Hospital. We met in the eighth grade and dated until we got married in 1966. I worked in Richmond, Virginia at Medical College of Virginia while Johnny was in medical school. When John Edd was born in 1969, I quit working. Ann was born in 1970.

Johnny and Betsy with Ann and John Edd in Fairbanks, Alaska

Siblings James and Ann in Vienna, West Virginia

In 1971, we flew to Fairbanks, Alaska, where Johnny spent his tour of duty in the United States Army as a pediatrician. We lived there for two and a half years and traveled all over the state in our Volkswagen Camper. John Edd and Ann Clarke were both toddlers. It was a great experience. We loved Alaska. In 1974, we moved to Vienna, West Virginia, where James was born (in Parkersburg). Johnny practiced pediatrics for about three years and then he went into emergency room medicine. At first, he only did pediatric emergency care and gradually switched to all emergency care.

We were there until 1995 when we moved back to Rocky Mount, Virginia, our home. We built a house on my family's farm.

Other hobbies of Johnny's are fruit trees: apples, sour cherries, pears, damsons, peaches, and blueberry bushes. The other was gardening, potatoes, green beans, black eye peas, zucchini and squash, tomatoes, cucumbers, green pepper, lettuce, and spinach. He also enjoyed canning tomatoes and green beans and making tomato sauce and canning it. We have all enjoyed the fruits of his hobbies, which have been shared with family and friends.

Johnny picking sour cherries to make jam and pie.

Jack Horton is feeding the chickens

2008. Kate Horton and Jack Horton picking blueberries

2013. Carey Garst on his uncle's land with his two oldest children, Ella and Nathanael

FAMILY

John Edgar Lee (Johnny) Montgomery Jr. b: 07 Jul 1942, Roanoke, Roanoke County, Virginia

Johnny married **Betsy Clarke Whitlow** b: 24 Jan 1942, Rocky Mount, Franklin County, Virginia; m: 25 Jun 1966, Antioch Church of the Brethren, Rocky Mount, Franklin County, Virginia

Johnny and Betsy's children:
John (Edd) Edgar Lee Montgomery III b: 24 Jun 1969, Richmond, Richland County, Virginia
Ann Clarke Montgomery b: 14 Sep 1970, Richmond, Richland County, Virginia
James Whitlow Montgomery b: 29 Jun 1974, Parkersburg, Wood County, West Virginia

CHILDREN AND GRANDCHILDREN
of John (Johnny) Edgar Lee Montgomery Jr. and Betsy Clarke Whitlow

John (Edd) Edgar Lee Montgomery III married **Jill Nannette Handschumacher** b: 10 Dec 1968, Parkersburg, Wood County, West Virginia; m: 20 Aug 1995, Gatlinburg, Sevier County, Tennessee: div.

John Edd and Jill's child:
John (Jed) Edgar Lee Montgomery IV b: 03 Apr 1995, Parkersburg, Wood County, West Virginia

Jed's daughter with **Kathryn Rachel Taylor** b: 26 Jun 1997, Salem, Virginia:
Haisley Paige Montgomery b: 08 Mar 2022, Salem, Roanoke County, Virginia

Katey & Jed   Haisley

John married **Laura Heather McCallum Heaslip** b: 07 Oct 1974, Jacksonville, Duval County, Florida; m: 15 Feb 2012, Rocky Mount, Franklin County, Virginia

Laura's children with William John Heaslip b: 01 May 1970:
Mykah Magnolia Heaslip b: 29 Sep 1999, Fishersville, Augusta County, Virginia
Liam Slade Heaslip b: 08 Feb 2002, Fishersville, Augusta County, Virginia

Mykah & Liam (Laura's kids),
Laura, John Edd

Ann Clarke Montgomery married **Benjamin Lucas Horton** b: 31 Jan 1973, District of Columbia; m: 21 Sep 2002, Rocky Mount, Franklin County, Virginia

Ann and Benjamin's children:
Jack Clarke Horton b: 19 May 2004, Roanoke, Roanoke County, Virginia
Kate Lee Horton b: 07 Mar 2006, Roanoke, Roanoke County, Virginia
Luke Benjamin Horton b: 27 May 2011, Roanoke, Roanoke County, Virginia

Back from left: Kate, Ann, Benjamin
Front from left: Jack and Luke

Jack   Kate   Luke

James Whitlow Montgomery married **Sharon Yvonne Roomsburg** b: 06 Dec 1969, Winchester, Winchester County, Virginia; m: 03 Jun 2000, Strasburg, Shenandoah County, Virginia

Sharon and Mark Randall Wilkins' children:
Nicholas Boswell Wilkins b: 14 Jun 1992, Winchester, Winchester County, Virginia
Sydney Brooke Wilkins b: 25 May 1995, Winchester, Winchester County, Virginia

From left: James, Bryce, Bailey, Sharon

Sharon and James' children:
Bryce Whitlow Montgomery b: 01 Jun 2001, Winchester, Winchester County, Virginia
Bailey James Montgomery b: 21 Jun 2007, Winchester, Winchester County, Virginia

 **Nicholas Boswell Wilkins** married **Sarah Jean Campbell** b: 16 Mar 1998, Jellico, Campbell County, Tennessee; m: 18 Sep 2021, Mount Jackson, Shenandoah County, Virginia

Nicholas and Sarah's child:
Baylor Boswell Wilkins b: 15 Aug 2023, Winchester, Virginia

 **Sydney Brooke Wilkins'** children with **Garrett Kenneth Rowland** b: 17 May 1995, Chambersburg, Franklin County, Pennsylvania:
Eve Harper Rowland b: 02 Nov 2020, Chambersburg, Franklin County, Pennsylvania
Myles Kane Rowland b: 05 Nov 2023, Chambersburg, Franklin County, Pennsylvania

Eve   Myles

 Bryce Whitlow Montgomery

 **Bailey James Montgomery**

The Ella Vevang Montgomery family in 1995

Seated: Johnny Montgomery, Serina Montgomery Garst, Ella Vevang Montgomery, William Montgomery, Kneeling: James Whitlow Montgomery. Standing front row: Betsy Whitlow Montgomery, Frederick Garst Sr., Carey Ferguson Garst, Serina (Monty) Montgomery Garst. Back row: Jill Handschumacher Montgomery, John Edd Montgomery, Ann Clarke Montgomery, Jason Huber and Fred Garst Jr.

WILLIAM LEE MONTGOMERY

Born

July 10, 1953

Rocky Mount, Franklin County, VA

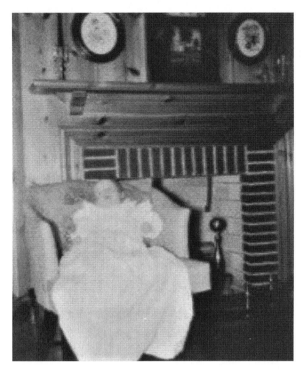

William Lee Montgomery on his baptism day

William and John Ed Montgomery

Ella and Johnny with William

Brothers William and Johnny

Brother and sister, William and Serina

William Montgomery
Wins Oxford Scholarship

William Lee Montgomery, 27, of Rocky Mount has been awarded a graduate fellow scholarship for the 1981-1982 academic year from the Rotary Foundation of Rotary International.

Montgomery who taught English last year at Franklin County High School, is already studying at St. Anne's College at Oxford, and the scholarship will enable him to complete his doctoral program.

The focus of Montgomery's studies at Oxford will be the preparation of a critical old-spelling edition of a Renaissance text. According to his application to the Rotary Foundation, the thesis will combine two areas of special interest to him, bibliography and renaissance literature, as well as establishing a basis for further research in that area.

He wrote that teaching college is his ultimate goal, but that his course of study would also be good preparation for a career in university publishing.

Montgomery graduated from Franklin County High School in 1971 and received his undergraduate degree from Washington and Lee University. He received a master's degree in English Literature from Wake Forest University, Winston-Salem, N.C. and a master's degree in Shakespeare Studies at the Shakespeare Institute of the University of Birmingham, Birmingham, England.

He is one of five winners selected from District 757, which includes the Rocky Mount Rotary Club. The district contains 48 clubs, with 2,855 active members. According to Marshall Flora, of the local Rotary Club, scholarships and exchange programs are a major part of the Rotary work.

The Rotary Foundation is a non-profit organization supported by Rotarians and others throughout the world. It was created in 1917, for the purpose of furthering international understanding through educational and charitable activities. Rotary Foundation Scholarships underwrite the full cost of study abroad, including language instruction where necessary, travel, lodging, food, tuition, books and laboratory fees.

From left: Professor Sir Stanley Wells, William's tutor, research supervisor, and boss at Oxford University Press, where William was working at the time as an editor on a new edition of the complete works for Shakespeare; William's sister, Serina; William; William's brother, Johnny; and his wife, Betsy.

CHAPTER X

ALIDA

Born

December 13, 1910

Vevang Family Farm

Nutley Township, Day County, SD

Died

August 23, 1971

Webster, Day County, SD

Laid to rest in Roslyn Lutheran Cemetery, Roslyn, SD

Alida Vevang was baptized on January 29, 1911

Sponsors: Mr. and Mrs. Ole Hustad, Mr. Nerland and Sina Hustad

U.S. Evangelical Lutheran Church in America Church Records

1911. Front left: Laura, Iver, Selmer, Serina holding Alida, Ella, and Hilda outside their home on the Vevang family farm.

Alida in 1915, age 4

The Fourteenth United States Federal Census taken in 1920
Nutley Township, Day County, South Dakota

Vevang Iver A.	Head	O	m	m	w	54
, Serina	Wife			F	w	47
, Julius S.	Son			m	w	23
, Elmer L.	Son			m	w	18
, Engvald	Son			m	w	17
, Selmer	Son			m	w	15
, Laura M.	Daughter			F	w	11
, Ella H.	Daughter			F	w	10
, Alida	Daughter			F	w	9
, Myrtle H.	Daughter			F	w	5
, Lawrence A.	Son			m	w	4 3/12

396

Alida was confirmed in 1925, at the age of 15

in the Lutheran Christian faith at the Roslyn Lutheran Church

—1925—
Arthur Maurice Farmen
John Walter Hendrickson
Carl Anton Roosevelt Haaseth
Thorvald Hendrick Saga
Axel Allen Granstrom
Adolph Bernard Gilbertson
Alida Vevang
Judith Charlotte Steffenson-Blake
Clara Regina Hanson-Farmen
Belva M. Hallem-Stone
Jensine Marie Hatle-Kesstner
Ella Josephine Rasmussen-Storley
Minnie Lillian Elsie Lensegrav-Denny
Helen Alfhilda Peterson-Paulson
Gertrude Sophie Haaseth-Tchida

The Fifteenth United States Federal Census taken in 1930
Nutley Township, Day County, South Dakota

Vevang	Iver J	Head	O		R	Yes	M	W	64
	Serina	Wife				x	F	W	58
	Ingvald	Son				x	M	W	27
	Laura M	Daughter				x	F	W	22
	Ella	Daughter				x	F	W	20
	Alida	Daughter				x	F	W	19
	Myrtle H	Daughter				x	F	W	15
	Lawrence G	Son				x	M	W	14

The Sixteenth United States Federal Census taken in 1940
Nutley Township, Day County, South Dakota

Vevang	Iver	Head	O	M	W	74
	Serine	Wife	1	F	W	68
	Ingvold	ab	Son	2	M	W	35
	Alida	Daughter	2	F	W	29
	Lawrence	Son	2	M	W	24
Loseth	Seiur	Ingda	6	M	W	33

In the Iver Vevang household were Iver, Serina, Alida, and Lawrence. They also had a lodger, Seiur Loseth. Ingvald was absent in the household as he was in Hayfield Township in Dodge County, Minnesota working on road construction.

Myrtle Vevang and Alida

Alida

Alberta Syverson Vevang and Alida

Sisters Ella, Alida, and Myrtle

Alida was Special to Many

Written by Bonita J. Vevang (Alida's niece)

ALIDA was a strong, hardworking, and independent woman who was the glue that kept the large Vevang family together through her travels and caregiving.

We do not have good records of exact event dates in her life, nor do we know for sure how long she attended school in Roslyn. It is noted in the 1940 census that she attended school through the eighth grade. She is not listed in the school records as graduating from high school, but she was an intelligent woman, and since she was one of the youngest siblings, she no doubt left school early to help her parents on the farm and later cared for them in their retirement years when they moved to Roslyn.

Alida eventually moved to Minneapolis, initially living with her oldest nephew, Spencer Olson, and his wife, Evelyn. She worked for a company that made molds. In about 1957, her sister, Hilda, and her brother-in-law, Ed, moved to Harriet Lake in South Minneapolis. Alida purchased their house in south Minneapolis where she lived until about 1965. She then moved to a newer house on Chicago Avenue, still in south Minneapolis. Her nephew, Henry Hanson, lived with her in both houses. Her niece, Shirley Vevang Gillard, also lived with her for a short time. She might have felt that she could not keep up a house and yard any longer as it was only a short time later when she moved again to an apartment at 7435 Lyndale Avenue, Richfield, MN.

Alida would often be considered the favorite aunt, especially by the nieces. She kept in close contact with her extended family. She often visited sisters, Myrtle in Arlington Heights, Illinois, and Ella Montgomery in Rocky Mount, Virginia, plus families in Webster and Roslyn. Many times, she would take along a niece or nephew.

In about 1970, Alida developed some health problems thought to be caused by environmental issues where she worked. She could no longer work and could not live alone. Her sister, Laura, took care of her in Webster, SD, until her death on August 23, 1971. With her brother, Pastor Selmer Vevang, officiating, the funeral was at the Roslyn Lutheran Church with burial at Roslyn's cemetery close to her parents. It was a very sad day with many tears. Alida was a special person.

At Alida's house while relatives gathered for Shirley Vevang's wedding in June of 1958.
From left: Marilyn Watkins, Alida, James Watkins, Cheryl Watkins, Douglas Hanson, Larry Vevang, Bruce Watkins

Alida's home in Minneapolis, MN

Alida purchased this home at 4848 Third Avenue South
from Hilda Vevang Olson and Edwin Olson

1943
Alida Vevang with her niece, Serina Montgomery

1964
Alida Vevang

At Sonja Danielson's wedding in 1964
From left: Sonja Danielson Cordray, Donald Danielson,
Cheryl Watkins, Alida Vevang and Bonnie Vevang

At Laura Vevang Hanson's home in Webster
From left: Viola Olson Fellows, Alida,
and Pamela Vevang

TO A LADY

To a lady,
      who always made sure
everything was in its place,
      who gave to everyone
in her family,
      who united many people
together through her desire
to travel.

      Who made sure every girl
in the family took their first
trip with her. Many of us
wouldn't have known our aunts,
uncles or cousins, as well as
we do, if it wasn't for her.

      Who did little important
things for others when
they were in a hurry.

      Who tactfully and
righteously laid down her
ideas - the ones she knew.

      She never really had
an immediate family, but
she had a close enough
place in every family.

WE LOVED HER.

      Thank you,

      Alida

Love, Connie   8/23/71

A Tribute to Aunt Alida
Written by Connie Olson (Alida's great niece)

*Alida never really had an immediate
family, but she had a close enough
place in every family.*
WE LOVED HER.

OBITUARY

Alida Vevang

Alida Vevang, daughter of the late Iver and Serina Vevang, was born Dec 13, 1910, in Nutley Township, Day County, South Dakota. She attended the Roslyn schools. In 1942, she moved with her parents to Roslyn where she lived taking care of her parents. After their deaths, she moved to Minneapolis, Minn. She was employed from 1954 to 1969. Due to ill health, she moved to Webster in 1970, where she resided making her home with her sister, Laura (Mrs. Henry M. Hanson) until her death on Aug. 23, 1971, having attained the age of 60 years, 8 months and 10 days.

Alida passed away Monday, August 23, 1971, following an extended illness. Funeral services were held at the Roslyn Lutheran Church August 26, and interment was in the Roslyn Cemetery. Mrs. Marvin Kettering, organist; James Dedrickson, a nephew, was soloist and Rev. Marvin Ketterling was clergy. Pall bearers were her nephews, Spencer Olson, Calvin Olson, Allen Vevang, Henry Hanson Jr., Larry Vevang, Dennis Vevang and Tim Vevang.

She is survived by five brothers, Julius and Ingvald, of Webster, South Dakota, Elmer, of Roslyn, South Dakota, Rev. Selmer E., of Seattle, Washington, Lawrence, of St. Paul, Minnesota, sisters, Hilda Olson, Minneapolis, Minnesota; Laura Hanson, Webster, South Dakota; Ella Montgomery, Rocky Mount, Virginia and Myrtle Watkins, Arlington Heights, Illinois; 27 nieces and nephews and 29 grand-nieces and nephews. Preceding her in death were her parents and two brothers.

Relatives and friends attended the funeral from New Jersey, Minneapolis, Minnesota, Seattle, Washington, St. Paul, Minnesota, Bloomington, Minnesota and other points in Minnesota and Illinois in addition to many from towns in South Dakota.

Those from a distance who attended the funeral of Alida Vevang were Mrs. Harold Hanson, Elizabeth, N.J.; Mr. and Mrs. Ed Olson, Mrs. Allan Fellows and children, Mr. Calvin Olson and boys, Allan Vevang, Mrs. Don Danielson and daughter, Mr. and Mrs. Spencer Olson and family, Mr. and Mrs. Henry M. Hanson Jr., Mrs. F.M. Osellano, Mr. and Mrs. Timothy Vevang, Mrs. Jules Gillard, Minneapolis; Rev. Selmer E. Vevang, Seattle; Mr. and Mrs. Lawrence Vevang and daughter, Bonnie; Mr. and Mrs. Larry Vevang, St. Paul; Mrs. Harold Mussetter, Bloomington, Minn.; Mrs. Clara Olson, Mrs. Melvin Hanson, Elmer Hustad, Harold Tornes, Clifford Stavig, Clinton Hellevang, Mr. and Mrs. Elmer Holm, Sisseton; Oscar Tornes, Milbank, Mrs. Herb Bisgard, Waubay; Mrs. Charles Rathbun, Mrs. Lowell Werdal, Mr. and Mrs. Julius Strand, Webster; Mr. and Mrs. Peter Olson, Britton; Mrs. Pam Schneider, Aberdeen; Dennis Vevang, Springdale, Ohio; Mr. and Mrs. Jerry Forslund, Rosemount, Minn. and Mrs. Charles Watkins, Arlington Heights, Ill. who is spending the week here.

Reporter and Farmer Webster, SD

IN MEMORY OF
Alida Vevang
December 13, 1910 - August 23, 1971

SERVICES
10:00 a.m. Thursday, August 26, 1971
Roslyn Lutheran Church
Roslyn, South Dakota

CLERGY
Rev. Marvin Ketterling
Roslyn, South Dakota

MUSIC
Mr. James Dedrickson, Soloist
Mrs. Marvin Ketterling, Organist

CASKET BEARERS
Spencer Olson   Henry Hanson, Jr.
Calvin Olson   Larry Vevang
Allen Vevang   Gerald Forslund

INTERMENT
Roslyn Lutheran Cemetery
Roslyn, South Dakota

Funeral Arrangements by
MOHR FUNERAL SERVICE
Webster, S. Dak.

**Alida was laid to rest
in Roslyn Lutheran Cemetery
Roslyn, Day County, South Dakota**

*The Lord is my Shepherd
I will dwell in the house of the
Lord forever*

The Lord is my shepherd; I shall not want.

He maketh me to lie down in green pastures: He leadeth me beside the still waters.

He restoreth my soul He leadeth me in the paths of righteousness for his name's sake.

Yea, though I walk through the valley of the shadow of death, I will fear no evil: for thou art with me; thy rod and thy staff they comfort me.

Thou preparest a table before me in the presence of mine enemies: thou anointest my head with oil: my cup runneth over.

Surely goodness and mercy shall follow me all the days of my life: and I will dwell in the house of the Lord for ever.

That the following is a complete list of the receipts
and disbursements made by the petitioner as special administratrix, and as administratrix with the will annexed, in
connection with property of Alida Vevang:

RECEIPTS

1968 Model Chev. Chevel sold to Shirley Gillard	$1700.00
Colored T. V. set sold to Shirley Gillard	150.00
Two table lamps sold to Margaret Vevang	25.00
Dishes, glasses $110.00, camera $10.00 and	
bedspread 10.00 to Evelyn Olson	130.00
Rosalie Danielson, hall chest	65.00
Larry Vevang 2 end tables	40.00
Larence Vevang- chair	10.00
Mrs. Elmer Vevang- table and lamp	50.00
Darlis Dedrickson- desk	100.00
Margaret Vevang - $5.00 gold coin	10.00
Richfield Bank & Trust Co. close out account	1024.23
All State Insurance- refund on car insurance	46.40
Jules Gillard-davenport	25.00
Hilda M. Olson- love seat	200.00
Larry Ingalls- breakfast set	40.00
Robert Wiley-china tray set	7.00
Social Security check	255.00
Deposit-currency	212.00
Money from Great Western Savings and Loan	1226.56
Allen Vevang-respirator $105.00, less $9.87	
for United Parcel service charges for stand	
given to Roslyn Church	95.13
Henry Hanson, Jr. sewing machine	50.00
Total receipts	$5461.32

DISBURSEMENTS

Moha Funeral Home	$1528.88
Gilmer Monument works, grave marker	109.20
J.S.Vevang, repairs for TV	57.36
Northwestern Bell Telephone Co. long distance	
calls	58.20
Charles Watkins, balance on car loan	100.00
Allan Vevang for Portland Lectern $149.00,	
removable letter directory $11.50, black	
ball point pen $2.50 engraving $8.50	171.50
Reporter & Farmer, 2 ads for sale of furniture	3.48
Day County Treasurer, personal property tax	10.96
Clerk fees for special and regular probate	23.00
Printing Notice of Hearing	26.73
Appraisers	9.00
Attorney fees for special and regular probate	
and sales tax	494.00
Fee for petitioner for acting as administratrix	169.01
Total disbursements	$2761.32

Recapitulation

Total amount of receipts $5461.32

Total of disbursements $2761.32

Money on hand $2700.00

Petitioner states that this is the only property
in her hands for distribution ;

Petitioner states that the heirs at law, devisees
and legatees, with their names, relationship and addresses
are as follows:

Julius S. Vevang, brother, Webster,South Dakota
Hilda Olson, sister, 4857 Fremont S. Ave. Minneapolis, Minn.
Elmer Vevang, brother, Roslyn, South Dakota
Ingvald Vevang, brother, Webster, South Dakota
Ella Montgomery, sister, Rocky Mount, Virginia
Rev. Selmer E. Vevang, brother, 9142 N. Mercer Way, Mercer
                                      Island, Wash.
Laura Hanson, sister, Webster, South Dakota
Myrtle Watkins, sister, 105 S. Drury Lane, Arlington Heights, Ill.
Larence Vevang, brother, 1261 Dayton Ave. St Paul, Minn.
Linda Forslund, niece, 512 Fewell Dr. Apple Valley, Rosemount,Minn.
Dennis Vevang, nephew, 346 Bancroft Circle, Springdale, Ohio.
Pamela Schneider, niece, 115 S. Kline, Aberdeen, S. Dak.
Debra Vevang, niece, Box 399, Webster, S. Dak.
Darlis Dedrickson, niece, 1500 South 7th St. Sioux Falls, S. Dak.
Warren Vevang, nephew, 1062 Craig Drive, San Jose, Calif.
Allen Vevang, nephew, 11116 Quinn Ave. S. Bloomington, Minn.
Paul Vevang, nephew, 548 Wilson St. Seattle, Wash.
Timothy Vevang, nephew, 908 9th Ave. South, Apt. 1, Hopkins, Minn.
Beverly Price, niece, 9142 Mercer Way, Mercer Island, Wash.
James Vevang, nephew, 9142 N. Mercer Way, Mercer Island, Wash.
Shirley Gillard, niece, 908 9th Ave. S. Apt. 1, Hopkins, Minn.
                              c/o Timothy Vevang
Bonnie Vevang, niece, 1261 Dayton Ave. St Paul, Minn.
Larry Vevang, nephew, 1261 Dayton Ave. St Paul, Minn.
Spencer Olson, nephew, 604 Minnehaha Parkway, Minneapolis, Minn.
Calvin Olson, nephew, 3843 Huntington Circle, Hopkins, Minn.
Rosalie Danielson, niece, 7045 4th Ave. S. Richfield, Minn.
Viola Fellows, niece, 8245 Wentworth Ave. S. Bloomington, Minn.
Henry M. Hanson, Jr. nephew, 5432 14th Ave. S. Minneapolis, Minn.
Douglas Iver Hanson, nephew, 5230 Malvina Drive, Fairborn, Ohio
Serina Garst,niece, Boones Mill, Virginia
John Ed Montgomery, Jr. nephew, Rocky Mount, Virginia
William Montgomery , nephew, Rocky Mount, Virginia
Bruce Watkins, nephew, 105 S. DruryLane, Arlington Heights, Ill.
Cheryl Watkins, niece, 105 S. Drury Lane, Arlington Heights, Ill.
James Watkins, nephew, 105 S. Drury Lane, Arlington Heights, Ill.
Marilyn Spieth, niece, 9142 N. Mercer Way, Mercer Island, Wash.

(First Feb. 2)
NOTICE OF TIME AND
PLACE FOR PROVING WILL
AND NOTICE TO CREDITORS
STATE OF SOUTH DAKOTA,
COUNTY OF DAY, ss
IN DISTRICT COUNTY COURT
TENTH JUDICIAL DISTRICT
In the matter of the estate
of Alida Vevang, deceased.
THE STATE OF SOUTH
DAKOTA sends greeting to Julius
S. Vevang, Hilda Olson, Elmer
Vevang, Ingvald Vevang, Ella
Montgomery, Rev. Selmer E.
Vevang, Laura Hanson, Myrtle
Watkins, Lawrence Vevang,
Linda Forslund, Dennis Vevang,
Pamela Schneider, Debra
Vevang, Darlis Dedrickson,
Warren Vevang, Allen Vevang,
Paul Vevang, Timothy Vevang,
Beverly Price, James Vevang,
Shirley Gillard, Bonnie Vevang,
Larry Vevang, Spencer Olson,
Calvin Olson, Rosalie Danielson,
Viola Fellows, Henry M. Hanson,
Jr., Douglas Iver Hanson, Serina
Garst, John Edd Montgomery,
Jr., William Montgomery, Bruce
Watkins, Cheryl Watkins, James
Watkins, and Marilyn Spieth,
heirs at law, devisees, and
legatees of Alida Vevang,
deceased, and to all persons
interested in said estate:
NOTICE IS HEREBY GIVEN
that Henry M. Hanson, Jr., has
petitioned this Court to admit to
probate an instrument, pur-
porting to be the Last Will and
Testament of Alida Vevang,
deceased, and to appoint Laura
Hanson as administratrix with
the Will annexed; that the
petition names the above persons
as sole heirs, devisees and
legatees of said deceased, and
said petition which was filed in
this Court on the 26th day of
January, 1972, is hereby referred
to for further particulars.
NOTICE IS FURTHER GIVEN
that said petition has been set for
hearing on the 23rd day of
February, 1972, at the hour of
10:00 o'clock A.M., at the office of
the District County Judge, in the
Court House, in Webster, Day
County, South Dakota, at which
time and place any person interested may appear and be
heard.
All persons having claims
against the said estate are hereby
notified to file the same with the
Clerk of the Above Court, within
four months from the date of the
first publication of this notice, or
be forever barred.
Dated this 26th day of January,
1972.
BY THE COURT
Mildred Ramynke
Judge
ATTEST:
Willard R. Huwe, Clerk
(SEAL)
Holland, Delaney & Vander
Linden
Attorneys for the Petitioner
Webster, South Dakota 57274

Reporter and Farmer
Webster, SD

In the Matter of the Estate of Alida Vevang, deceased
Laura Vevang Hanson appointed as administratrix
of Alida's will

Holland, Delaney & Vanderlinden,
Attorneys for the Petitioner

ALIDA'S FURNITURE - APPRAISAL VALUE AS SET BY JOHN MOSS 9/10/71

Desk	$ 100.00
Davenport	25.00
Sewing Machine	175.00
Breakfast Set with the two chairs	50.00
T. V. Set	150.00 - Sold
Tables (small end)	25.00 a piece
Larger table to match	40.00
Rocker (soft wood)	25.00
Old Chair (dark one)	5.00
Gold Living Room Chair	100.00

Other Living Room Cair was not at the house when appraisal was made as it was out to Elmer's

Love Seat	200.00
Chest that I had in the hall with open front	65.00
China Set Early American that had three plates on it-	15.00
Coffee Grinder	10.00
Three drawer chest that old one from Roslyn	5.00
Mixer	15.00
Electric Pan	5.00
Living Room Lamps	10.00 a piece
Bedroom Lamps	10.00 a piece
Kitchen Lamp	10.00

Other miscellaneous articles were not appraised.

Sirley would like to have the davenport at 25.00

Other living room lamp was not appraised as it was out to Elmer's

All the above articles are for sale including the Love seat.

If any one of you are interested in the above articles, please notify me by mail as soon as you receive this letter.

Please come up the sooner the better to pick-up the things that belong to you as for example Bonnie the bedroom set, Viola the cupboard. Mr. VanderLinden said the all things in her possession at the time of her death were hers regardless where and how she got it

I would like to buy the kitchen lamp at the price quoted.

The car was sold to Shirley Gillard on the 11th of September, 1971 at $1,700.00. Jule took care of this for me.

The dishes are still in the cupboards for any one to buy.

407

At the home of Henry and Laura Hanson after Alida's funeral

In back from left: Selmer Vevang, James Dedrickson and Allen Vevang **Sitting from left:** Evelyn Miller Olson, Laura Vevang Hanson, Henry Hanson Sr., Elna Olson Vevang, Elmer Vevang, Spencer Olson, Alberta Syverson Vevang, Unidentified and Steve Olson **On the floor from left:** Rick Olson, Mark Olson, Darlis Vevang Dedrickson, Keith Dedrickson, Pam Vevang Schneider, Viola Olson Fellows, Ingvald Vevang and Kent Olson

CHAPTER XI

MYRTLE

Born

August 14, 1914

Vevang Family Farm

Nutley Township, Day County, SD

Died

July 22, 2008

Lake Barrington, Lake County, IL

Laid to rest in Good Shepherd Memorial Gardens, Ocala, FL

MYRTLE was the eleventh child born to Iver and Serina Vevang.

1916

Myrtle in 1914   1918   Myrtle and Lawrence

The Fourteenth United States Federal Census taken in 1920
Nutley Township, Day County, South Dakota

Vevang Iver A.	Head	O	M	m	w	54
, Serina	Wife			Fr	w	47
, Julius D.	Son			m	w	23
, Elmer L.	Son			m	w	18
, Engvald	Son			m	w	17
, Selmer	Son			m	w	15
, Laura M.	Daughter			Fr	w	11
, Ella H.	Daughter			Fr	w	10
, Alida	Daughter			Fr	w	9
, Myrtle H.	Daughter			Fr	w	5
, Lawrence A.	Son			m	w	4³⁄₁₂

Myrtle Vevang on the Vevang family farm in about 1924

Myrtle (right) with a classmate

Sisters Myrtle and Ella on the Vevang farm

Myrtle in 1926

Myrtle is the first on the left

Myrtle (second from left) with her school friends

My School Day's Autograph Book

Roslyn, So. Dak.
December 10, 1929

Dear Babe,
When your life on earth is
ended
And on these paths no more
you trod
May your name in gold be
written
In the autograph of God.

Very Sincerely
Gerda Rasmussen
(Peter)

December 10, 1929

When your life on earth is ended
And on these paths no more you trod
May your name in gold be written
In the autograph of God

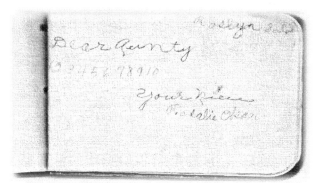

Rosalie Olson, Myrtle's niece, "wrote"
in Myrtle's school autograph book.

No.	Konfirmations Datum.	Konfirmandens fulde Navn.	Alder (Aar.)	Forældrenes fulde Navne.	Hvor døbte.
1	May 19	Esther Bernice Aspen	14	Sylvester + Caroline Aspen	Langford
2	"	Magnus Buchan Gilbertson	14	Gilbert + Mettie Gilbertson	Grenville
3	"	Raymond Morris Hendrickson	15	Ludwig + Betsine Hendrickson	Frou
4	"	Myrtle Agatha Jacobs	14	Laurs + Helen Jacobs	
5	"	Nila Martha Metz	13	Adolph + Martha Metz	Webster
6	"	Hazel Rosina Monshaugen	14	Peter + Inga Monshaugen	Frou
7	"	Grace Mildred Monson	14	Nils + Annie Monson	Grenville
8	"	Bernice Estella Peterson	14	Bennie + Annie Peterson	Skulerices
9	"	Gerda Marie Rasmussen	14	Edw. + Olufa Rasmussen	Frou
10	"	Myrene Elinor Roushaugen	13	Edwin + Millie Roushaugen	Frou
11	"	Lawrence Arthur Vevang	14	Iner + Serine Vevang	Grenville
12	"	Myrtle Kaye Vevang	15	Iner + Serine Vevang	Grenville
13	"	Ernest Johan Nalli	14	Thron + Bertha Nalli	Grenville

U.S. Evangelical Lutheran Church in America Church Records

Myrtle was confirmed in 1929, at the age of 15

Myrtle Vevang and her younger brother, Lawrence Vevang, were confirmed together in the Lutheran Christian faith. They are pictured with their confirmation class on May 19, 1929. Myrtle is the first person standing on the left. Lawrence, age 14 is in the back row, standing second from the right.

The Fifteenth United States Federal Census taken in 1930
Nutley Township, Day County, South Dakota

Vevang	Iver J	Head	O		R	Yes	M	W	64
—	Serina	Wife				x	F	W	58
—	Ingvald	Son				x	M	W	27
—	Laura M	Daughter				x	F	W	22
—	Ella	Daughter				x	F	W	20
—	Alida	Daughter				x	F	W	19
—	Myrtle H	Daughter				x	F	W	15
—	Lawrence G	Son				x	M	W	14

413

Roslyn High School — Class of 1934

ESTHER B. ASPEN

HOWARD J. GULLICKSON

HARRIET A. HANSON

'MYRTLE A. JACOBS

MELVIN L. JENSEN

HERBERT E. JOHNSON

HENRY F. LEHMANN

CLARENCE A. NELSON

EVA M. PEEBLES

MYRTLE H. VEVANG

SIGURD A. WIK

Class Motto
"NOW WE TRY A BOUNDLESS SEA"

Class Flower
YELLOW ROSE

Class Colors
PURPLE AND GOLD

Myrtle H. Vevang

Esther Aspen Nygaard, Howard Gullickson*, Harriet Hanson Coin*, Melvin Jensen, Myrtle Jacobs Larson*, Herbert Johnson, Henry Lehman, Clarence Nelson, Sigurd Wik*, Myrtle Vevang Watkins.

Myrtle Hazel Vevang

After Myrtle graduated from Roslyn High School she went to Fargo, North Dakota to attend Beauty Culture School. She then headed east on a train to live with her Uncle Sam, Aunt Bea, and their family in Elizabeth, New Jersey. She was employed at the Warinanco Beauty Salon.

Myrtle traveled to Washington D.C, New York City, and Coney Island.

Myrtle soon met Charles Watkins, introduced by friends. They courted each other for two years and were married in 1940.

From the photo albums of Myrtle Vevang

The Capitol Building in Washington D.C. and Statue of Liberty in New York Harbor.
The pictures were taken in the late 1930s.

The Sixteenth United States Federal Census taken in 1940
Elizabeth, Union County, New Jersey

Vevang	Selmer ⊕	Head	M	W	34	M	No	C-5	South Dakota
—	Bernice	Wife	F	W	27	M	No	C-2	Minnesota
—	Beverley	Daughter	F	W	5	S	Yes	0	New York
—	Shirley	Daughter	F	W	3	S	No	0	New York
—	Myrtle	Sister	F	W	25	S	No	C-1	South Dakota
Morrison, Ralph		roomer	M	W	34	S	No	C-4	Maine

Myrtle Vevang was considered part of her brother Sam's household. Myrtle was 25 years old.
They also had a boarder named Ralph Morrison.

Bethlehem Norwegian Lutheran Church Group in Elizabeth New Jersey

Myrtle is sledding down the hill.

Bernice Sholl Vevang, Shirley Vevang, Selmer Vevang
and Beverley Vevang

Shirley Vevang and Beverley Vevang

417

One of Myrtle Vevang and Charles Watkins' first dates
was chaperoned by her brother, Selmer Vevang

Myrtle corresponded with Charles while she spent time in Roslyn at her family's home. They wrote to each other almost every day when they were apart for about three weeks. Anne, a friend of Myrtle's from Elizabeth, New Jersey, traveled by train to South Dakota with Myrtle. A gift of cigars was given to Myrtle's father, Iver Vevang, by Charles.

I hope your father likes his cigars

With time on my hands,
Love in my heart,
I am yours, forever.
Charles.

P.S. Write soon and often.

Myrtle wrote —

Anne and I just came back from a nice long walk. The rest of the folks have already gone to bed. Imagine at 9:30. We really do go to bed with the chickens. But it's grand tho. Feel so wide awake in the morning. I woke up just as the sun was rising. The sight of it was so beautiful that I had to wake Anne to admire it.

Thursday Eve
9:30

Charles Dear

Too sleepy to go to bed so here I am spending the leisure time with you.

Anne & I just came back from a nice long walk. Rest of the folks have already gone to bed. Imagine at 9:30. We really do go to bed with the chickens. Huh? But its grand tho. Feel so wide awake in the mornings. One morning I woke up just as the sun was rising. The sight of it was so beautiful that I had to wake Anne to admire it. Of course we both went back to sleep —

Here is one of Myrtle's letters she wrote to Charles, postmarked July 23, 1940. After this writing, Myrtle, Anne and Myrtle's sister, Alida, headed to Webster to pick up their bags as their bags didn't come on the same train.

Yours with love,
Myrt

Myrtle wrote her brother, Ingvald, while he was working in New Brighten, Minnesota. Myrtle tells of how she made it home to Roslyn for a visit. They planned a picnic at Hyde Park, (near Grenville, South Dakota) on the Sunday after this letter was written. From left: Elna Olson Vevang, Calvin Olson, Serina Hustad Vevang, Unidentified, Laura Vevang Hanson, Ingvald Vevang, Myrtle, and Anne. "What's this I hear about you?" Myrtle was referring to Ingvald's engagement to Alberta Syverson.

An excerpt from the July 28, 1940 letter that Myrtle wrote to Charles:

Anne and I brought lunch out to the field this afternoon. We gathered wheat stalks to bring back with us. They're lovely.

Anne behind the horse-drawn sickle hay and grass mower.

[Handwritten letter, page 1]

Wednesday
11:30

My dearest Charles,

Must get a letter off tonite to my love, First. I hope you'll pardon my pencil. No pen around so a pencil it must be.

We're still at Andersen's. Everybody has already gone to bed, — Anne is sitting here fixing her hair. I'm all undressed sitting in bed with my house coat on. I'm not at all sleepy so I wanted to spend perhaps half hour writing to you. Did you get my card? We've had such a lovely day. Mrs. Andersen took us for a ride this afternoon around to the different lakes etc, saw the most beautiful residential homes. Honest they were lovely — Then visited Mrs. Sebel for awhile, Tomorrow we're going shopping and to see Minnesota University, and I'll be back in Elizabeth again & with you. Certainly seems ages since I left. Want it? Or hasn't it seemed that long for you?

[Handwritten letter, page 2]

Found out the train connections last nite. Leaving tomorrow nite at 11 oclock. Get to Chicago in the morning. Spending Friday & Sat in Chicago. We ought to see something of the big city by then. I hope leaving Chicago at 5 P.M. and will be arriving in Newark at 2:52 Sunday afternoon. So dear, don't forget to be there. Will you? Or I'll be awful, awful disappointed. And you wouldn't want to disappoint me then, —

Imagine this will be my last letter and I'm tickled pink as I certainly hate to write letters. I hope I've been kind of good writing. —

This writing is horrid and the pencil I got certainly doesn't help matters any. — So instead trying to write — I'll say goodnite and sweet dreams. Be good until seen at 2:52. I'll be so anxious to see you darling. — Goodnite again, —

Yours — Love Myrtle

[Handwritten letter on Stevens Hotel stationery]

STEVENS HOTEL
CHICAGO
MICHIGAN BOULEVARD
AT BALBO DRIVE
WABASH 4400

OVERLOOKING LAKE MICHIGAN

Friday 12:30

My dearest Charles
Aren't we getting snooty? Wish you were here to enjoy our beautiful room — The Y.M.C.A. is right across from us but — after all I am writing to you. Hah, the other side we can look over Lake Michigan. —

We're going out for dinner now then we may go sight seeing. —

So until Sunday I'll be patiently waiting to see you —

Yours with Love,
Myrtle

[Envelope]

STEVENS HOTEL · CHICAGO, ILL.
MICHIGAN BLVD. AT BALBO DRIVE

LETTERS MAILED
IN HOTEL ENVELOPES
IF NOT DELIVERED ARE SENT
TO DEAD LETTER OFFICE UNLESS
THE WRITER GIVES A RETURN ADDRESS
IF NOT DELIVERED IN ____ DAYS RETURN TO

Myrtle A Vevang
863 Jersey Ave
Elizabeth N.J.

Myrtle and Anne traveled back to New Jersey. The letter above was written on August 7th. They were at the home of Anne's parents in Minneapolis. On August 9th, Myrtle wrote of their being in Chicago. They stayed at the Stevens Hotel. They would be in New Jersey on Sunday. Myrtle wrote: *So until Sunday I'll be patiently waiting to see you. Yours with Love, Myrtle*

Myrtle Vevang's Engagement Told

Miss Myrtle Vevang , sister of the pastor here,
whose betrothal is announced.

MISS MYRTLE VEVANG.
Sister of pastor here, whose betrothal is announced.

MYRTLE VEVANG'S ENGAGEMENT TOLD

Mr. and Mrs. Iver Vevang, of Roslyn, South Dakota, have announced the engagement of their daughter, Miss Myrtle Vevang, to Charles Watkins, son of Mr. and Mrs. W. B. Watkins, of Louisville, Ky. Miss Vevang lives with her brother and sister-in-law, Rev. and Mrs. Selmer E. Vevang, at 863 Jersey avenue. Rev. Mr. Vevang is pastor of Bethlehem Norwegian Lutheran Church. Mr. Watkins resides at 643 Park avenue.

A graduate of Roslyn High School, Miss Vevang studied beauty culture at Fargo, North Dakota, and is employed at the Warinanco Beauty Salon in this city. Mr. Watkins attended the University of Louisville and later Purdue University, where in 1938 he received a degree in engineering. He is employed by the Standard Oil Development Company.

Congregational Records of Bethlehem Lutheran, Elizabeth, New Jersey

Charles Henry Watkins and Myrtle Hazel Vevang
Witnesses: Dr. Leland Beach and Mrs. Ella Montgomery (sister of the bride)
The wedding was officiated by S.E. Vevang Pastor (brother of the bride)

CHARLES HENRY WATKINS

Born

March 21, 1913

Sturgis, Union County, KY

Died

March 11, 2004

Lake Barrington, Lake County, IL

Laid to rest in Good Shepherd Gardens Cemetery, Ocala, FL

CHARLES & MYRTLE WATKINS

Married November 20, 1940
Elizabeth, Union County, New Jersey

Myrtle and Charles' Wedding Party

From left:

Maren Tobiasson (bridal attendant), Myrtle Vevang (bride), Ella Vevang Montgomery (sister of the bride and matron of honor), and Beverley Joan Vevang (niece of the bride and flower girl)

Bryon Dimmock (usher), Rev. Selmer Vevang (brother of the bride & officiated the marriage), Charles Watkins (groom), Ben Geddes (usher), and Dr. Leland K. Beach (best man)

Miss Myrtle Hazel Vevang of 863 Jersey Avenue, daughter of Mr. and Mrs. Iver Vevang, of Roslyn, South Dakota became the bride of Dr. Charles Henry Watkins, of 643 Park Avenue, son of Mr. and Mrs. W. B Watkins, of Louisville, Kentucky at eight o'clock Thanksgiving Eve in Bethlehem Lutheran Church of which the bride's brother, Rev. Selmer E. Vevang, is pastor. He officiated at the marriage, assisted by Rev. J. H. Preus, pastor of Trinity Lutheran Church, Jersey City, New Jersey. A reception was held in the church parlors, which were decorated with palms, fall flowers and candelabras.

The wedding was performed at a candlelight service and white flowers and palms formed the background in the church. Rev. Vevang gave his sister in marriage. Mrs. John Edgar Montgomery, of Rocky Mount, Virginia, sister of the bride was matron of honor and Miss Maren Tobiasson, of Elizabeth, was the other bridal attendant. Dr. Leland K. Beach was best man and Ben Geddes and Byron O. Dimmock were the ushers. Beverley Joan Vevang, niece of the bride, was flower girl. Miss Ann Tobiasson was at the console and played a program of traditional wedding music. Mrs. Hugo Piberg was soloist. The selections included "Lord's Prayer," "O Perfect Love" and "Crown with Thy Benediction."

The bride wore an ivory satin gown with finger-tip length veil flecked with ostrich feathers. She carried a colonial bouquet of gardenias. The matron of honor wore a stitched melody rose faille taffeta gown made along empire lines and the bridesmaid wore a similar gown in delphinium blue. The flower girl wore

Vevang-Watkins Wedding

In the Elizabeth, N. J., Journal appeared an account of the wedding of Myrtle Vevang and Dr. Charles Watkins on Thanksgiving Day an event of much interest to Roslyn friends as Myrtle was one of Roslyn's most popular young ladies. The account follows:

a white frock and carried a small white nosegay. The attendants carried colonial bouquets of yellow chrysanthemums.

A graduate of Roslyn High School, Roslyn, South Dakota, the bride is employed by the Warinanco Beauty Salon. Dr. Watkins attended the University of Louisville and Purdue University where he received his doctor's degree in chemical engineering. He is employed by Standard Oil Development Company.

Out-of-town guests included Miss Dorothy Watkins, sister of the bridegroom, of Louisville, Kentucky, Mrs. Montgomery, of Rocky Mount, Virginia and Mrs. Preus of Jersey City, New Jersey.

After a wedding trip to the New England States, the couple will reside at 533 East Second Avenue, Roselle, New Jersey.

The bride and groom, Myrtle and Charles Watkins, with Beverley Vevang, daughter of Selmer Vevang

The reception table

The bride and groom's table

Dr. Leland K. Beach, gave the best man's speech.

**Myrtle and Charles spent the night of November 21, 1940,
at the Hotel Barnum in Bridgeport, Connecticut.**

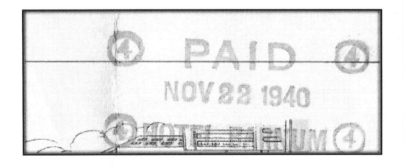

A receipt from the Hotel Barnum upon their departure the next day. The cost for the night was $4.00.

Myrtle Vevang Watkins at Steel Pier in Atlantic City, New Jersey

A picture of Steel Pier in an earlier time

Certificate of Registration for Operator of Beauty Culture
1941-1942

Myrtle and Charles later moved to

29 Roger Avenue in Cranford, New Jersey

1943. Charles Bruce Watkins was born

1945. Cheryl Ann Watkins was born

1946-1949. The family moved to 4222 Arthur Avenue in Brookfield, Illinois.

1948
Twins James Alan Watkins and
Marilyn Louise Watkins were born

James and Marilyn

Marilyn and James

Christmas in 1948. Bruce and Cheryl

1949
Standing from left: Bruce Watkins, James Vevang, Paul Vevang, and Timothy Vevang. Cheryl Watkins is on the horse.

Bruce on the horse

Bruce, James, Marilyn, and Cheryl

Christmas 1949

Cheryl, Marilyn, Bruce, and James

Marilyn and James

The Watkins' family home in Western Springs, Illinois

The Watkins' family in 1956
Charles and Myrtle, Bruce, James, Marilyn, and Cheryl

Mesmerized by the Fire
Bruce, James, Cheryl, Marilyn

Myrtle Vevang Watkins reminiscing of days gone by. She reads letters written from Charles and looks at her high school diploma from Roslyn High School.

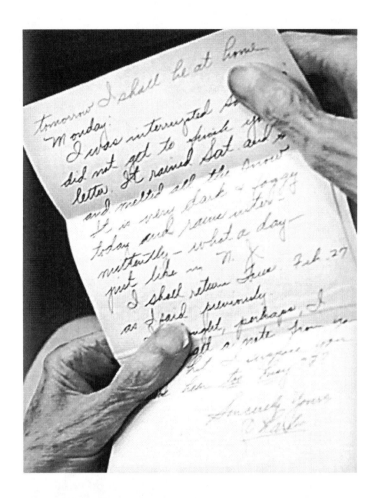

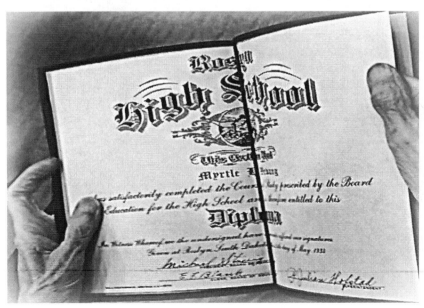

OBITUARY

Charles H. Watkins

Charles H. Watkins Ph.D.

of Lake Barrington

Services for Charles Henry Watkins Ph.D., 90, formerly of Ocala, Fla. and Arlington Heights, will be held at 3 p.m. today, at Davenport Family Funeral Home, 149 W. Main St. (Lake-Cook Road), Barrington. Fr. Fred Licciardi will officiate.

Born March 21, 1913, in Sturgis, Ky., he passed away Thursday, March 11, 2004, at Good Shepherd Hospital in Barrington. Burial will be in Good Shepherd Gardens Cemetery, Ocala.

Charles graduated from Purdue University with his Ph.D. in chemical engineering. He was a 30-year employee of Universal Oil Products, where he worked as a chemical engineer. He held numerous patents in the oil refining and processing industry. In addition, he had articles published in several journals on petroleum products. Dr. Watkins was also the family historian. He was a true southern gentleman. Charles and his wife Myrtle helped finance their four children's and eight grandchildren's college educations.

Survivors include his wife, Myrtle H. (nee Vevang), whom he married on Nov. 20, 1940, in New Jersey; children, Bruce (Kathy) Watkins of Deer Creek, Ill., Cheryl (Stuart) Tanaka of North Barrington, James Allen (Vicky) Watkins of Venice, Fla. and Marilyn (Pete) Speith of Bloomington, Ind.; grandchildren, Pam (Doug) Kraemer, Cecelia, Sonja and Michael Tanaka, Elizabeth and Travis Watkins, and Patti and Missy (Aaron) Ewing; great-grandson, Tyler Kraemer; and sister, Lucille Burnett of Oak Ridge, Ind.

He was preceded in death by his parents, William Bernard and Lillian Gertrude (nee Wynns); sister, Dorothy Handley; and brothers, Harold and W.B. Watkins.

. Visitation will be from 1 p.m. until the time of the services today, at the funeral home.

In lieu of flowers, memorials may be made to the Lou Gehrig's Association of Southwestern Florida, Sarasota, FL 34278.

Friends may visit www.dailyherald.com/obits to express condolences and sign the guest book. For funeral information, (847) 381-3411.

Lake Barrington, Illinois — Services for Charles Henry Watkins Ph.D., 90, formerly of Ocala, Florida and Arlington Heights, will be held at 3 p.m. today, at Davenport Family Funeral Home, 149 W. Main St. (Lake-Cook Road), Barrington. Fr. Fred Licciardi will officiate.

Born March 21, 1913, in Sturgis, Kentucky, he passed away Thursday, March 11, 2004, at Good Shepherd Hospital in Barrington. Burial will be in Good Shepherd Gardens Cemetery in Ocala, Florida.

Charles graduated from Purdue University with his Ph.D. in chemical engineering. He was a 30-year employee of Universal Oil Products, where he worked as a chemical engineer. He held numerous patents in the oil refining and processing industry. In addition, he had articles published in several journals on petroleum products. Dr. Watkins was also the family historian. He was a true Southern gentleman. Charlies and his wife Myrtle helped finance their four children and eight grandchildren's college educations.

Survivors include his wife, Myrtle H. (Vevang) whom he married on November 20, 1940, in New Jersey; children Bruce (Kathy) Watkins of Deer Creek, Illinois, Cheryl (Stuart) Tanaka of North Barrington, Illinois, James Alan (Vicki) Watkins of Venice, Florida and Marilyn (Pete) Spieth of Bloomington, Indiana; grandchildren, Pam (Doug) Kraemer; Cecelia, Sonja and Michael Tanaka, Elizabeth and Travis Watkins, and Patti and Missy (Aaron) Ewing; great-grandson, Tyler Kraemer; and sister, Lucille Burnett of Oak Ridge, Tennessee.

He was preceded in death by his parents, William Bernard and Lillian Gertrude (Wynns); sister, Dorothy Handley; and brothers, Harold and W.B. Watkins.

OBITUARY

Myrtle Vevang Watkins

Lake Barrington, Illinois — Mrs. Myrtle Vevang Watkins, 93, was born August 14, 1914 in Nutley Township, Day County, South Dakota, and passed away July 22, 2008 at home in Lake Barrington. Burial will be at Good Shepherd Memorial Gardens Cemetery in Ocala, Florida.

She is survived by her children, Bruce (Kathy) Watkins of Deer Creek, Illinois, Cheryl (Stuart) Tanaka of North Barrington, Illinois, James (Vicki) Watkins of Venice, Florida, and Marilyn (Pete) Spieth of Bloomington, Indiana; grandchildren, Pam (Steve) Watkins, Cecelia, Sonja and Michael Tanaka, Elizabeth (Dewey) Eardley, Travis Watkins, Patti Spieth and Missy (Aaron) Ewing, great-grandchildren, Tyler Kraemer, Alexia and Zachary Ewing, and brother, Lawrence Vevang of Roslyn, South Dakota.

Myrtle was preceded in death by her husband of 64 years, Charles H. Watkins, Ph.D., her parents, Iver and Serina (Hustad) Vevang and her siblings, Julius, Hilda, Elmer, Ingvald, Selmer, Edwin, Laura, Ella, Alida, and Jacob.

Visitation will be held on Saturday, July 26th, at 11:00 a.m. The memorial service will begin at 12:00 noon. The visitation and the memorial service will be held at the Good Shepherd Memorial Gardens in Ocala, Florida. In lieu of flowers, memorials may be made to Lou Gehrig's Disease Association of Southwest Florida, Inc., (LGDA), Sarasota, Florida 34278 or Hospice of Northeastern, Illinois, 410 S. Hager Ave., Barrington, Illinois 60010. Arrangements by Roberts Funeral Home Downtown Chapel. 352-622-4141. Published in the Ocala Star-Banner from 7/25/2008 - 7/26/2008

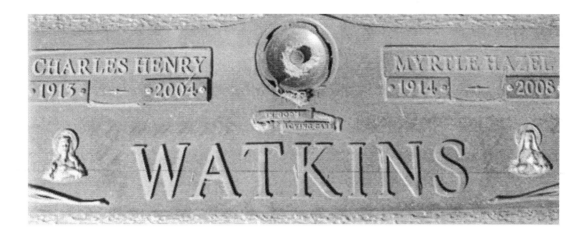

A Personal Reflection

Written by Myrtle's son, James, and delivered at her funeral July 26, 2008

Mom, the Norwegian. She was the eleventh child of Iver and Serina Vevang who emigrated from Norway in the late 1800's and settled on the wind-swept plains of South Dakota. Why a Norwegian of Viking descent would ever stray so far from the open sea is a mystery. Perhaps it was the uncontrollable urge brought on by ancestry to set out from the fjords with wild, pagan energy, driving them to explore and trade in lands beyond the horizon. Or, perhaps not. Nonetheless, it was there on the farm of just a few hundred acres near present-day Roslyn, South Dakota, that our grandparents or great-grandparents carved out a new beginning in a distant land for the Vevang family. Just as the Vikings revered the natural forces of wind, fire and ice, our ancestors instilled in their children the key values of personal strength, hard work, dedication to the family and living a simple but good life. Mom was certainly a good student. Her life is a testament to these values.

Mom enjoyed telling countless stories of life on the farm, living in a small farmhouse with eight or so siblings, walking to school through deep snow in sub-zero temperatures, the horse-drawn buggy that tipped over, and the fire that destroyed the barn are but a few. We can hear Mom saying those were hard times, but we lived through it. Then she would scold us for not appreciating how easy life is today. It was her way of passing along the lessons and values learned from her parents.

There is little doubt Mom held closely to these values throughout her years. Caring for four unruly and easily corruptible children was certainly a test of personal strength that would impress any Norwegian. Sewing clothes, ironing, cooking hot meals every day, making curtains, driving the horde to school, scouts, and countless events. I mean, who does these things today? Yet, Mom was always there. Her deep love for her family was not often expressed in words or tender moments but always by her unquestionable dedication to the family and her quest to provide, protect, and see us prosper.

There was a very special bond between Mom and Dad. To say it was simply love understates their connection. A core belief in mutual respect, honor, and devotion formed the cornerstone of their relationship. They held hands, listened to each other, and always stepped up to the plate when help was needed. They shared the same sense of simplicity, not allowing any modest accumulation of wealth to serve as a distraction to the really important elements of raising a family and living a good life. They were truly happy in their 64 years of marriage, a remarkable achievement that today is not often matched. When Dad passed away four years ago, a large measure of Mom's capacity to be truly happy passed with him.

We would all do well to remember there is a little Norwegian in each of us. Along with the spirit of a Viking, we carry within us the values of strength, hard work, dedication to the family, and living a simple and happy life. There is no finer expression of these cultural values than the way Mom lived her life. Mom, we love you very much and will greatly miss you. You taught us many lessons. Now it is up to us, your children, grandchildren, and great-grandchildren, to live in the way of a Norwegian and make you proud.

FAMILY

Myrtle Hazel Vevang b: 14 Aug 1914, Nutley Township, Day County, South Dakota; d: 22 Jul 2008, Lake Barrington, Lake County, Illinois; buried: Good Shepherd Memorial Gardens, Ocala, Marion County, Florida

Myrtle married Charles Henry Watkins b: 21 Mar 1913, Sturgis, Union County, Kentucky; m: 20 Nov 1940, Elizabeth, Union County, New Jersey; d: 11 Mar 2004, Lake Barrington, Lake County, Illinois; buried: Good Shepherd Memorial Gardens, Ocala, Marion County, Florida

CHILDREN
of Myrtle Hazel Vevang and Charles Henry Watkins

Charles Bruce Watkins b: 25 Jan 1943, Plainfield, Union County, New Jersey

Cheryl Ann Watkins b: 27 Oct 1945, Plainfield, Union County, New Jersey

James Alan Watkins b: 23 Jun 1948, Berwyn, Cook County, Illinois; d: 11 Dec 2020, Venice, Sarasota County, Florida

Marilyn Louise Watkins b: 23 Jun 1948, Berwyn, Cook County, Illinois

CHARLES BRUCE WATKINS

Born

January 25, 1943

Plainfield, Union County, NJ

Charles Bruce Watkins

married

Kathi Marie Glomski

January 25, 1969

Niles,
Cook County,
Illinois

Charles Bruce Watkins

married

Kathy Carlson Hull

September 11, 1993

Fox Lake,
Grant Township,
Lake County,
Illinois

My Life in My Words
Written by Charles Bruce Watkins

1961
Bruce graduated from Arlington Heights
High School, Arlington Heights, Illinois.

Catching the rooster:
Travis with his great-uncle
Lawrence Vevang.

Pamela Rae with her father, Bruce

After what I considered a happy childhood, I graduated from high school in 1961. Many of my happy childhood memories were made while visiting the family in South Dakota. On one vacation there, I think I was about 16, I pleaded with my parents to let me stay there while they went on. They did not let me. Another memory was when my first cousin, Bonnie, and I went to the neighbor's to buy a rooster. The younger kids wanted to try catching it. I think Travis Watkins, my nephew, was the winner.

After high school, I went to Lincoln College in Lincoln, Illinois. In 1964, I joined the Marine Reserves. I got an accountant position where I met my first wife, Kathi. We married in 1969. Our daughter, Pamela Rae, was born in 1971.

I left the accounting business and purchased two taverns in Arlington Heights, Illinois. I was in the business for six years. I got divorced and moved to McHenry, Illinois. I then became a truck driver and owned up to about five trucks. I enjoyed truck driving. I did both over-the-road trucking and locally hauled sand and gravel. I had some great times going over the road. I was even able to take my brother, Jim, with me several times.

I remarried in 1993, to another Kathy. We lived in Johnsburg, Illinois till 2001. We wanted a change, so we sold all the trucks and bought a campground in central Illinois. It was challenging, but a great experience. We sold the campground in 2013. Kathy and I still live in Central Illinois and working at retirement. I have had such a great life, with all my cars, boats, airplanes, motor homes, and motorcycles, but most importantly, I have a great family.

443

FAMILY

Charles Bruce Watkins b: 25 Jan 1943, Plainfield, Union County, New Jersey

Charles married **Kathi Marie Glomski** b: 16 Dec 1948, Oak Park, Cook County, Illinois; m: 25 Jan 1969, Niles, Cook County, Illinois: div.

> Bruce and Kathi's child:
> **Pamela Rae Watkins** b: 23 Sep 1971, Elk Grove Village, Cook/DuPage County, Illinois

Bruce married **Kathy Carlson Hull** b: 19 Oct 1948, Chicago, Cook County, Illinois; m: 11 Sep 1993, Fox Lake, Grant Township, Lake County, Illinois

CHILDREN AND GRANDCHILDREN
of Charles Bruce Watkins and Kathi Marie Glomski

Pamela Rae Watkins married **Douglas Roy Kraemer** b: 27 Aug 1964, Chicago, Cook County, Illinois; m: 07 Nov 1998, Schiller Park, Cook County, Illinois: div.

> Pam and Doug's child:
> **Tyler James Kraemer** b: 22 Jun 2002, Elk Grove Village, Cook/DuPage County, Illinois

Pam married **Steve Allen Stover** b: 23 Feb 1971, Elmhurst, Cook/DuPage County, Illinois; m: 25 Jan 2008, Miami, Miami-Dade County, Florida

> Pam and Steve's child:
> **Owen Michael Stover** b: 09 Sep 2009, Elk Grove Village, Cook/DuPage County, Illinois

Tyler, Owen, Pamela, and Steve

Tyler Kraemer

Owen Stover

CHERYL ANN WATKINS

Born
October 27, 1945
Plainfield, Union County, NJ

Cheryl Ann Watkins

married

John Stuart Tanaka

May 5, 1973

Marcy,
Franklin County,
Ohio

From left: Charles Watkins, Myrtle Vevang Watkins, Marilyn Watkins Spieth, Cheryl Watkins Tanaka,
Stuart Tanaka, Rick Tanaka, Stuart's brother and Emi Saiki, Stuart's aunt

What it Must Have Been Like

Nils Vevang, Cecelia, and Ragnild (Nils' wife)

Cheryl Watkins Tanaka, her husband, Stuart, and their oldest child, Cecelia (left), traveled to Norway in 1981. Cheryl provided audio recordings and pictures of their trip to many of the Vevang relatives for them to get a glimpse of what Vevang, Norway was like.

Spectacular, amazingly beautiful scenery, waterfalls, rugged mountains, fjords, and glacier lakes with fed streams.

Norwegian Legend of the Trolls speaks of a family living under the waterfalls. They come out only at night, and if they were seen, they turned into the rugged mountains, creating the mountainous terrain. They had long noses and one eye. If you would see them, they would become petrified and grow to be mountains, protected under the waterfalls. Trolls had to follow a twisty path down.

Nils and Ragnild Vevang are pictured with Cecelia. Nils was a very warm and caring man, and was honored to show them around Vevang. Nils has the same great-grandfather as Cheryl, myself, and the other 28 Vevang cousins mentioned in this book—Jakob Vevang. Our grandfather, Iver Vevang, was Nil's half-great uncle. *EE-var Vuh-vong* is how they pronounce his name in Norway. Most of the descendants of Jakob stayed in Norway, but Iver went to America as he saw this as an opportunity to prosper. It was said that land waits for those who come. Iver was only 22 when he came to America.

Cheryl and Stuart with their children
From left: Michael Jakob Tanaka, Cecelia Jonn Tanaka, and Sonja Vevang Tanaka

A Family Holiday
Cannon Beach, Oregon — December 2012

From left: Sonja Tanaka, Michael Tanaka, Max Lebessou, Andrew McCartor,
Cecelia McCartor, Stuart Tanaka, and Cheryl Watkins Tanaka
with Grover and Parker in front

Standing: Stuart Tanaka, Andrew McCartor, Michael Tanaka holding Kenzo, and Maxime Lebessou
Seated: Cheryl Watkins Tanaka holding Miles, Cecelia Tanaka McCartor holding Mayfield,
Sonja Tanaka holding Elio, and Tara Reighard.

2021
Back from left: Tara, Michael, Max, Sonja, Drew, Cecelia
Front from left: Kenzo, Elio, Cheryl, Stuart, Miles, and Mayfield

FAMILY

Cheryl Ann Watkins b: 27 Oct 1945, Plainfield, Union County, New Jersey

Cheryl married John Stuart Tanaka b: 08 Dec 1949, Minneapolis, Hennepin County, Minnesota; m: 05 May 1973, Marcy, Franklin County, Ohio

Cheryl and Stuart's children:
Cecelia Jonn Tanaka b: 26 Sep 1978, Tokyo, Japan
Sonja Vevang Tanaka b: 06 Nov 1982, Des Plaines, Cook County, Illinois
Michael Jakob Tanaka b: 27 Dec 1984, Barrington, Cook County, Illinois

CHILDREN AND GRANDCHILDREN
of Cheryl Ann Watkins and John Stuart Tanaka

Cecelia Jonn Tanaka married Andrew (Drew) Robert McCartor b: 11 May 1979, Portland, Multnomah County, Oregon; m: 13 Feb 2010, San Miguel, Mexico

Cecelia and Andrew's children:
Miles Everett Tanaka McCartor
b: 16 Mar 2013, Manhattan, New York County, New York
Mayfield Antoinette Tanaka McCartor
b: 8 Jun 2016, Manhattan, New York County, New York

Sonja Vevang Tanaka partnered with Maxime Jean Andre' Lebessou
b: 12 Aug 1978, Narbonne, France

Sonja and Max's children:
Elio Tanaka Lebessou
b: 07 Jul 2013, Chene-Bougeries,
Canton De Gene've, Switzerland
Kenzo Ruiz Tanaka Lebessou
b: 30 Nov 2017, Paris, France

From left: Elio, Mayfield, Kenzo, and Miles

Michael Jakob Tanaka married Tara Kristin Reighard b: 21 Jan 1987, Brandon, Hillsborough County, Florida; m: 26 Jul 2019, Chicago, Cook County, Illinois

Michael and Tara's children:
Maya McLean Tanaka
b: 13 Feb 2020, Chicago, Cook County, Illinois
Charles Tadashi Tanaka
b: 12 Nov 2023, St. Charles, Kane County, Illinois

JAMES ALAN WATKINS

Born
June 23, 1948
Berwyn, Cook County, IL

Died
December 11, 2020
Venice, Sarasota County, FL

James graduated from Prospect High School, Arlington Heights, Illinois in 1966. He then went on to attend and graduate from the University of Missouri in Columbia, Missouri in 1970, with a Degree in Mechanical Engineering.

Lt. James A. Watkins of the National Oceanic Atmospheric Administration Corps 1971-1974 BOTC 37
Basic Officer Training Class NOAA Ships: Davidson and Pathfinder

Lt. James A. Watkins is in the
front row on the right.

In 1975, Jim wrote a letter to his parents while he worked on-site at the South Pole.

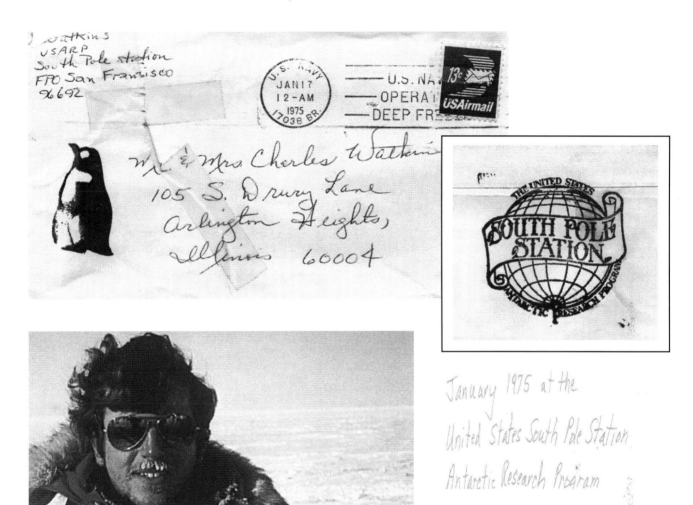

January 1975 at the
United States South Pole Station
Antarctic Research Program

I've been here at the South Pole for about a week now. Things are really pretty comfortable. We were given plenty of warm clothing in Christchurch, New Zealand and our room, similar to a quonset hut, is kept very warm by fuel heaters. Today was one of the colder days at -22°F, but with very lite winds and no clouds made things bearable. No cases of frost-bite yet nor has any of our group suffered from altitude sickness. Ours equivilant altitude is over 11,000 ft (9,000 ft of snow) so you have to take things alittle slower

Christchurch is a real pretty town, very much British, I am told. They have a center square filled with statues, churches and hotels. I took a lot of pictures, next time I'll show them to you. Temperatures there were in the low 80's and I got sunburned in only two hours of walking around town. We were there only one day and we left for McMurdo Bay aboard a C-130, propeller driven cargo plane. The flight took 7½ hours, some 2200 miles. We stayed in McMurdo for one day seeing some of the historical grounds of the early Antarctic explorers. I climbed atop a cinder cone of one of the active volcanoes in the world. From there I could see a magnificent vista of the Ross Sea and the surrounding mountains.

We flew again aboard a C-130 to South Pole Station, some 800 miles onto polar plateau. This place is absolutely flat, no insects, no vegetation, no life what soever except us 40 people. During the Antarctic winter, 13 people will stay here alone in the dark. — I would never want to do that.

Work has been progressing according to schedule. I plan to leave here by the end of the month. Yesterday, a C-130 crashed upon take off at Dome Sea, about 500 miles from here a rescue C-130 was flown in and it too also crashed. It goes to show that no matter how evolved man is, mother nature still holds the cards. The loss of these two airplanes may seriously effect the resupply of this station. We

may have to curtail some of our programs because of the lack of spare parts. Priority is now given to fuel and food.

I have ordered a slide projector so that at the time of the wedding I'll be able to show you some of this beautiful country. I've talked to Vicki via radio ham patch. She is to call you about the rehersal dinner plans. I will try to call you early next week before you leave. Please send me your Florida address so I can drop you a line when I get home.

Please don't worry about me, I'm quite safe and warm and enjoying my little adventure. I sure enjoyed being home at New Year's. I've always looked forward

to returning to the warmth and love you have always shown. I hope you like Vicki and can take her into your hearts as one of your children. She is quite a women, strong, independent and very sincere, a person who is well worth the effort to get to know and understand. We shall be very happy!

There is much more to tell but I'll close for now. Take care and be careful on your way to Florida. Although you may worry about us children, we too worry about you and your little adventures.

Love,

Jim.

454

Mr. and Mrs. Glenn M. Latham
and
Mr. and Mrs. Charles H. Watkins
request the honour of your presence
at the marriage of their children
Vicki Lynn
and
James Alan
on Saturday, the nineteenth of April
nineteen hundred and seventy-five
at two o'clock in the afternoon
U. S. Naval Academy
Main Chapel
Annapolis, Maryland

Wedding Party
From left: Terry Nichols, Bruce Watkins, Steven Young, James Watkins,
Vicki Latham Watkins, Donna Dannels, Vickie Murray, and Iris Taylor

James and Vicki's first child, Elizabeth Anne Watkins, was born in 1978.
Their son, Travis James Watkins, was born in 1980.

Jim, Travis, and Elizabeth sailing

Travis, Vicki, James, and Elizabeth

Jim sent this letter to his siblings, sharing with them the pictures he took of Vevang, Norway. Jim and his wife Vicki traveled to Norway in 2012. Here are parts of that letter and a few of their pictures.

Vevang is very, very small, maybe no more than 30 buildings and a population of less than 100. There are no commercial buildings of any kind except for a convenience store along the highway. Vevang is essentially a one-street town. We saw no cars moving about or any activity. The only person we saw was a man walking down the center of the road. He gave us a polite wave and disappeared into a home. A busy highway separates the town road in two, what I call the waterside and the countryside. The Vevang side is on the waterside. After passing the town sign, and looking down the street, the first building was the Vevang Museum which was a total surprise. No one has mentioned that we have our own museum. Of course, it was closed, and no one was around

to ask to open it. Vicki did get some pictures looking through the windows. It was a drizzly day, so you won't see me posing in any pictures.

During maintenance of the Vevang Museum, there was a red V mark of World War II painted on the wall. The museum was a lodging house during the war. The lodge house, school, and chapel were controlled during the war by the Germans. A propaganda war campaign was started and the sign 'V' for victory was used. Passing the museum, we took a picture of the man walking down the center of the road, most probably a distant relative. Had we known he would be the only person we would see we would have stopped and talked to him. We crossed the highway to the water side of Vevang. The Vevang house is the largest in town. There was no sign or indication that the house was now a bed and breakfast. Maybe the owners tried but gave up? Vicki knocked on the door, no answer, no car. Strange that no one was around and a newspaper in the walkway. A hundred yards or so past the Vevang house the road ends at the wharf. What a happy and simple time it must have been generations ago.

OBITUARY

James (Jim) Alan Watkins

James Watkins passed away peacefully in Venice, Florida, Friday, Dec. 11, 2020, after his long 24-year battle with ALS. Jim was born to Charles and Myrtle Watkins (Vevang) on June 23, 1948. He was the beloved husband for 45 years of Vicki (Latham); loving father of Elizabeth and Travis (Lacy); proud grandfather of Wyatt, Meadow, Odin, and Apollo; and cherished brother of Bruce Watkins (Kathy), twin sister Marilyn (John) and Cheryl (Stuart). A special heartfelt thank-you from our family goes to Laura, Kristen, and Candy for their love and many years of devotion to Jim.

Jim was a licensed professional engineer with a degree in Mechanical Engineering from the University of Missouri. After college, he spent four years as a commissioned officer in the NOAA Corps. Two of those years were spent surveying Alaska's coastline as part of the construction of the Alaska pipeline. Jim always claimed, "the later grounding of the ship, the Exxon Valdez, had nothing what-so-ever to do with the quality of my surveys."

During his 18 years with the Department of Commerce, Jim specialized in directing the design and construction of 21 federal buildings and observatories, most of which he was pleased to point out are still standing today. His job required traveling to such faraway places as the South Pole, Antarctica; American Samoa; Point Barrow, Alaska; and Hawaii. At 39, he became a member of the federal government's prestigious Senior Executive Service.

His last 10 years of service was with the Federal Deposit Insurance Corporation (FDIC) in Washington, D.C., where he completed a $150 million regional office and training center. During the height of the savings and loan crisis in the early '90s, Jim headed an organization of over 400 employees with an annual budget of $100 million, and, surprisingly, Jim said: "I actually knew where all that money was being spent—well, most of it anyway."

Jim was diagnosed with ALS in 1997. Jim and Vicki spent the following year living aboard their sailboat, traveling from Maryland along the East Coast, the Florida Keys, and the Bahamas. They moved to Venice, Florida in August 1999. In May of 2000, Jim was asked to join the board of the Lou Gehrig's Disease Association of Southwest Florida (LGDA) in Sarasota, Florida. Jim became vice president and established the LGDA Patient & Caregiver Support Groups to meet the needs of the local ALS community. Jim was committed to providing help to the ALS community, knowing from experience that by helping others, he could draw upon their strength to help himself.

Jim will always be remembered for his love of family, his legendary spirit, his unstoppable determination, and his passion for sailing. He filled his home with music and the awesome smells of cooking. A sometimes-mischievous comic with a keen and contagious sense of humor, and an ability to touch hearts, Jim was remarkable and courageous in every way. Now, he will make the angels laugh, as he has with us throughout his life.

Contributions: Donations honoring his life may be made to the Robert Packard Center for ALS Research at Johns Hopkins, PackardCenter.org. www.farleyfuneralhome.com/obituary/james-watkins

FAMILY

James Alan Watkins b: 23 Jun 1948, Berwyn, Cook County, Illinois; d: 11 Dec 2020, Venice, Sarasota County, Florida

James married **Vicki Lynn Latham** b: 15 Sep 1953, Wheelus Air Base, Tripoli, Libya, Africa; m: 19 Apr 1975, Annapolis, Anne Arundel County, Maryland, at the U.S. Naval Academy Chapel

James and Vicki's children:
Elizabeth Anne Watkins b: 13 Mar 1978, Kirkland, King County, Washington
Travis James Watkins b: 30 Jan 1980, Kirkland, King County, Washington

CHILDREN AND GRANDCHILDREN
of James Alan Watkins and Vicki Lynn Latham

Elizabeth Anne Watkins married **Dwight Edward Eardley** b: 19 Mar 1978, Sarasota, Sarasota County, Florida; m: 23 Apr 2006, Sarasota, Sarasota County, Florida: div.

Elizabeth and Dwight's child:
Wyatt Arthur Eardley b: 17 Nov 2008, Sarasota, Sarasota County, Florida

Travis James Watkins married **Lacy Michelle Allen** b: 25 Jul 1981, Lewisville, Texas; m: 01 Oct 2011, Melbourne, Brevard County, Florida

Travis and Lacy's children:
Meadow Michelle Watkins b: 16 Jul 2014, Panama City, Bay County, Florida
Odin Allen Watkins b: 21 Jan 2017, Panama City, Bay County, Florida
Apollo Jace Watkins b: 5 May 2020, Panama City, Bay County, Florida

MARILYN LOUISE WATKINS

Born

June 23, 1948

Berwyn, Cook County, IL

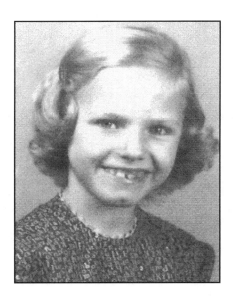

Marilyn Louise Watkins

married

John Griffith Spieth

May 11, 1968

Purdue University,
West Lafayette,
Tippecanoe County,
Indiana

Cheryl Watkins (sister of the bride) and Marilyn Watkins Spieth

Patricia Spieth, Melissa Spieth and Marilyn Watkins Spieth in mid 80s

Marilyn Watkins Spieth

From left: Melissa Spieth Ewing, Alexia Ewing, Patricia Spieth Suttner, and Marilyn Watkins Spieth

Marilyn with her mother, Myrtle, and her daughters, Patricia and Melissa

From left: Cheryl Watkins Tanaka, Kathy Carlson Hull Watkins, Bruce Watkins, James Watkins, Stuart Tanaka, Vicki Latham Watkins, John Spieth and Marilyn Watkins Spieth

Marilyn and John

FAMILY

Marilyn Louise Watkins b: 23 Jun 1948, Berwyn, Cook County, Illinois

Marilyn married **John Griffith Spieth** b: 16 Oct 1947, Alliance, Stark County, Ohio; m: 11 May 1968, at Purdue University, West Lafayette, Tippecanoe County, Indiana

Marilyn and John's children:
Patricia Colleen Spieth b: 28 Aug 1968, Flossmoor, Cook County, Illinois
Melissa Ann Spieth b: 01 Sep 1970, Flossmoor, Cook County, Illinois

Standing from top: Melissa Spieth Ewing, Patricia Spieth Suttner, Marilyn Watkins Spieth, and John Spieth
Sitting from left: Alexia Ewing, Zachary Ewing, and Maxwell Suttner
In front on bottom left: Liam Suttner

CHILDREN AND GRANDCHILDREN
of Marilyn Louise Watkins and John Griffith Spieth

Patricia Colleen Spieth married **James Allen Suttner** b: 13 Jun 1967, Bloomington, Monroe County, Indiana; m: 22 May 2010, Bloomington, Monroe County, Indiana

Patricia and James' children:
Maxwell John Suttner b: 30 May 2009, Bloomington, Monroe County, Indiana
Liam Wynn Suttner b: 22 Nov 2011, Bloomington, Monroe County, Indiana

Patricia and James

Maxwell and Liam

Melissa Ann Spieth married **Aaron Shawn Ewing** b: 23 Aug 1970, Ypsilanti, Washtenaw County, Michigan; m: 23 Nov 2002, Scottsdale, Maricopa County, Arizona

Melissa and Aaron's children:
Alexia Jaden Ewing b: 06 Apr 2004, Phoenix, Maricopa County, Arizona
Zachary Richard Ewing b: 23 Dec 2005, Phoenix, Maricopa County, Arizona

Alexia, Melissa, Aaron, and Zachary

CHAPTER XII

LAWRENCE

Born

October 14, 1915

Vevang Family Farm

Nutley Township, Day County, SD

Died

October 3, 2016

Hudson, St. Croix County, WI

Laid to rest in Roselawn Cemetery, Roseville, MN

LAWRENCE

was the last of twelve children born to
Iver and Serina Vevang.

Left: Lawrence in 1916 as a baby

Right: Lawrence with his sister,
Myrtle, at the front door of
the Vevang family home.

The Fourteenth United States Federal Census taken in 1920
Nutley Township, Day County, South Dakota

Vevang	Iver A.	Head		O	m	m	w	54
	Serina	Wife				F	w	47
	Julius S.	Son				m	w	23
	Elmer L.	Son				m	w	18
	Engvald	Son				m	w	17
	Selmer	Son				m	w	15
	Laura M.	Daughter				F	w	11
	Ella A.	Daughter				F	w	10
	Alida	Daughter				F	w	9
	Myrtle A.	Daughter				F	w	5
	Lawrence A.	Son				m	w	4 3/13

Lawrence with
his niece, Rosalie
Olson, daughter
of Hilda Vevang
Olson, in 1927.
Seven years and
seven months
separate their
ages.

Lawrence was confirmed on May 19, 1929, at the age of 14

Myrtle and Lawrence were both confirmed in the Lutheran Christian faith.
Myrtle, 15, is the first person standing on the left.
Lawrence, 14, is in the back row, standing second from the right.

U.S. Evangelical Lutheran Church in America Church Records

The Fifteenth United States Federal Census taken in 1930
Nutley Township, Day County, South Dakota

Still in the Iver Vevang household: Iver and Serina, Ingvald, Laura, Ella, Alida, Myrtle, and Lawrence.

The Fifteenth United States Federal Census taken in 1930
Eden Township, Marshall County, South Dakota

In the nearby Eden Township, located in Marshall County, Margaret Rose Pitzl lived with her family. She would become Lawrence's wife in a little over a decade. Margaret was born on a farm between Webster and Roslyn. In the Pitzl home with Mathias Pitzl, his wife Rosalia, and their children — Mathias Jr., Justina, John, Henry, Bernard, and Margaret. Margaret was eleven years old. Mathias and Rosalia were of Austrian descent.

465

Lawrence (center) and Myrtle with school friends

Lawrence on the Vevang farm

"During a summer storm, Lawrence ran to get the horses from the barn. The door swung off the barn and knocked Lawrence to the ground. He was unconscious and was taken to the doctor."

Written by Myrtle Vevang Watkins
Lawrence was age 18 at the time.

cyclone on farm   1932-1933

Lawrence ran to get horses from barn
door swung off & collapsed near
Lawrence & knocked unconscious
taken to 'dr.
age 18

Lawrence goofing around with his brothers
From left: Elmer, Lawrence, Ingvald, and Julius

Lawrence on US 85 Alternate in the Black Hills
between Deadwood and Edgemont, South Dakota

Harley-Davidson World War II
45 cubic inch V-twin military
motorcycle model

When Lawrence went to the Draft Board to register for enlistment, Lawrence's father, Iver, who was now 76 years old, went with Lawrence to explain that Lawrence was needed to farm their land. The country needed the farming operation to continue full steam through the war, so Lawrence was excused from the military.

**Lawrence Vevang
Draft Registration Card
October 16, 1940**

In the 1940 United States Federal Census, Lawrence was considered part of the Iver and Serina Vevang household, along with his brother, Ingvald, and his sister, Alida. Sieur Loseth was a lodger in the household.

MARGARET ROSE PITZL

Born

February 18, 1919

On a farm between

Webster and Roslyn, Day County, SD

Died

August 15, 2020

St. Paul, Ramsey County, MN

Laid to rest in Roselawn Cemetery, Roseville, MN

Wedding Party
Bernard Pitzl, Lawrence Vevang, Margaret Pitzl Vevang, and Rosalie Olson

LAWRENCE & MARGARET VEVANG

Married December 4, 1941
Eden, Marshall County, South Dakota

RECORD OF MARRIAGE

South Dakota State Board of Health

HUSBAND	WIFE
LAWRENCE VEVANG	MARGARET PITZL
ROSLYN, DAY COUNTY, SD	EDEN, MARSHAL COUNTY, SD
AGE 26	AGE 22
NORWEGIAN	GERMAN
BACHELOR	MAIDEN

Lawrence Vevang Weds Eden Lady

Reporter and Farmer
Webster, SD

Miss Margaret Pitzl, daughter of Mr. and Mrs. Math Pitzl Sr., of Eden became the bride of Lawrence Vevang, son of Mr. and Mrs. Iver Vevang of Roslyn, at a ceremony in the Sacred Heart Rectory at Eden, South Dakota, on Thursday afternoon, December 4, 1941. The Rev. M. J. Lennon officiated.

The bride was lovely in a gown of white satin made with shirred fitted bodice and full sweeping skirt. Seed pearls trimmed the halo which held her illusion veil. She carried a bouquet of American Beauty roses and white pompoms. Miss Rosalie Olson, the bride's only attendant and niece of the groom, wore a gown of coral taffeta and a corsage of white pompoms and roses. The groom and Bernard Pitzl, who acted as best man, wore dark suits. Each wore a white carnation boutonniere.

After the ceremony a reception was held at the Math Pitzl home for close friends and relatives of the bride and groom. Buffet lunch was served to the guests. The table was centered with a three-tier wedding cake topped with a miniature bride and groom.

Guests present at the reception were: Mr. and Mrs. Iver Vevang, Mr. and Mrs. Elmer Vevang and Miss Alida Vevang of Roslyn, Mr. and Mrs. Ed Olson of Waubay, Mr. and Mrs. Henry Hanson of Webster, Miss Phyllis Opitz, Miss Marjorie Schlekewy, Mr. and Mrs. Math Pitzl Jr., Mr. and Mrs. John Pitzl, and Mr. and Mrs. George Pitzl, all of Eden. The newlyweds left on a honeymoon trip to Fargo and upon their return will make their home on a farm near Roslyn.

Lawrence Arthur and Margaret Rose Vevang Family History

Written by Bonita J. Vevang

Lawrence Arthur Vevang was the youngest child born to Iver and Serina Vevang on October 14, 1915, on the Vevang farm in Nutley Township, Day County, South Dakota. He attended school in Roslyn, SD, until the age of approximately 15. It was common in those days for a son to leave school before graduating so that he could work on the family farm full-time. From his father, he learned how to plant grain and take care of the farm animals.

On December 4, 1941, Lawrence married Margaret Rose Pitzl, daughter of Mathias and Rosalia Pitzl, who farmed west of Eden, South Dakota. Margaret was born February 18, 1919, on a farm north of Webster, SD, and south of Roslyn, SD. Margaret went to country schools both in the Webster and Eden areas. She attended her freshman year at a high school in Eden, SD, and her sophomore year at Lake City, SD. Her junior and senior years were spent at Webster graduating in 1937.

Lawrence was 26 years old, and Margaret was 22 years old when they married. They honeymooned in Fargo, North Dakota, where on December 7 while they were in a bowling alley, they heard the news that Pearl Harbor, Honolulu, Hawaii, had been bombed by the Japanese. President Roosevelt and Congress immediately approved war against Japan and Germany and the nation began preparation. Shortly after his return to the farm, Lawrence went to the Draft Board to register for enlistment. Lawrence's father, Iver, who was now 76 years old, went with

Lawrence to explain that Lawrence was needed to farm their land. The country needed the farming operation to continue full steam through the war, so Lawrence was excused from the military. Iver and Serina continued to live on the farm until the spring of 1942 when they moved to a house on the southeast corner of Main and Carlton Streets in Roslyn. Lawrence and Margaret had their first child on August 2, 1943, born in Webster, South Dakota, named Bonita (Bonnie) Justyne Vevang. Larry Mathias Vevang was born on February 19, 1945, in Webster, South Dakota.

Life on the Farm Remembered

Life on the farm was hard work for the adults but fun for the youngsters. Before the early 1950s when Lawrence was farming, horses were still being used for fall threshing. Eight or nine farmers would pool their resources and take turns going around to their farms to harvest the crops. One farmer owned the threshing machine, and the other farmers would contribute a dollar amount for their share in using the machine. Lawrence owned the threshing machine.

The farmers would start threshing early in the morning and work until late afternoon or early evening. When the crew worked at the Vevang farm, Margaret oversaw preparing food for morning break, noon lunch, afternoon break, and dinner. Eventually, because of the enormous work, it was decided that the men would have their dinners at their own homes. A neighbor or her sister-in-law, Elna Vevang, would come for the day to help. The noon

Margaret & Lawrence Vevang

meal was large and filling; often consisting of fried chicken, dumplings, mashed potatoes, vegetables, pie, and cake. Homemade cinnamon rolls and tea or lemonade would be brought out to the field mid-morning and mid-afternoon. Watching all the activity, both in the kitchen and out in the field, was exciting for Bonnie and Larry, especially in the evening when the farmers would bring their teams of horses into the water tank. Since Bonnie and Larry were still quite young, they did not have to do a lot of work, just help a little with the easy tasks and stay out of the way of the adults.

A Hired Hand

As farming was labor intensive in those days, it was quite common for a farmer to have what they would call a hired hand, who was usually a bachelor who had no farm of his own. Lawrence's hired hand was Elmer Amundson. He was a nice, mild-mannered man, who liked his drinks. The children were fond of him. In the summertime, he either stayed in the milk house that had a cot at the far end or he would stay in the extra upstairs bedroom. He generally stayed only during the busy times of spring, summer, and fall.

One or two summers, Lawrence also hired a Swedish man named Sorn. Sorn was a little unkempt, and one warm summer day Margaret noticed his clothes were very soiled and she told him she was going to wash his clothes. Sorn did not like the idea and called her an "Austrian Gypsy" but he reluctantly gave her his clothes to wash. Margaret had a good laugh about her new nickname.

Farm Pets

The farm still had an assortment of animals: cows, a few workhorses, chickens, pigs, cats, and dogs. The big dog's name was Curly because he had curly hair. A few years later a smaller dog named "Tippy" arrived. Tippy had a litter of puppies in 1955 much to the delight of Bonnie and Larry. Homes had to be found for the puppies as it was not possible to keep that many dogs around the farm place. Margaret's brother, Henry, and wife, Doris, took one of the puppies home with them to South St. Paul, Minnesota, and named him "Punky." But Punky never forgot Bonnie and Larry. A year later when the youngsters visited Henry and Doris, Punky jumped all over them barking in glee.

Two small chickens became Bonnie's pets when they were abandoned by their mother hen. The other chickens ignored these two chicks, and Bonnie decided they needed their own place to stay so Elmer Amundson was asked to build a small "chicken coop" about the size of a doghouse where the chicks made their permanent home. Bonnie fed them in their coop, and they stayed there every night. They became "pets" to the family and were very friendly to anyone who would visit the farm.

Larry and Bonnie on the Vevang farm in 1955

Relatives Visit the Farm

The farm was a fun place for the city relatives to spend their vacations, and the visits were always a highlight of the summer. Margaret's sister, Tina Friedrick (who was Bonnie's godmother), her husband, George, along with their children, Marlene, George (Junior), and Bobbie would come for a week-long visit. The cousins would have a delightful time running around the farm. On one occasion, Lawrence was moving his flatbed trailer and all the kids jumped on for a ride. Larry was sitting in the front with his legs dangling over the side and when Lawrence made a turn, somehow Larry's foot was caught. He was immediately driven to the hospital in Webster but there was little or no damage to his foot.

In the Vevang Woods
Back: Hazel Gilbertson Vevang, Alida Vevang,
Margaret Pitzl Vevang, and Myrtle Vevang Watkins
Front: Larry Vevang, Charles (Bruce) Watkins,
James Watkins, Sonja Danielson, Bonnie Vevang,
Cheryl Watkins, and Marilyn Watkins

Lawrence's sister, Myrtle Watkins, her husband, Charles, and their children, Bruce, Cheryl, Marilyn, and Jim from Arlington Heights, Illinois, also came to visit numerous times. This provided a great opportunity for the cousins, including Linda, Dennis, Pamela Vevang, and Douglas Hanson from Webster, along with the Chicago cousins, to get together with Bonnie and Larry for some carefree summer fun. Some of the visitors would stay on the farm and some would stay with Grandpa and Grandma in Roslyn. One summer when cabins were rented on the south side of Pickerel Lake, four-year-old Bruce walked out to the end of the dock and fell into deep water. Uncle Lawrence jumped in to save him. Lawrence was a hero after that incident.

473

Education

Bonnie and Larry went to school in Roslyn. The classes were small with approximately twelve students in each grade and two grades in a room. The two-story school building had four classrooms on the first floor for the elementary students and on the second floor was one large room, a few smaller rooms for the high school and the principal's office. The basement was used as an auditorium until it was divided between a lunchroom and a classroom. In second grade Bonnie and her friend, Linda Stavig,

were chosen by their teacher to be the flower girls in the fall carnival. Two years later, Larry was chosen for a role in the carnival. School was fun, and lots of nice friends were made.

Margaret was always interested in the religious education of her children and in the fall of 1954, she decided to send Bonnie and Larry to the Sacred Heart Catholic grade school in Eden. The bus driver who was going to Eden to pick up the high school students and bring them back to Roslyn stopped at the end of our driveway where Bonnie and Larry would be waiting; they then took the same bus home again in the evening. It was a fine example of public and private schools working together to transport the students. The following year Bonnie and Larry returned to the public school in Roslyn.

Margaret's Family

In 1953 Margaret's mother, Rosalia Pitzl, had a stroke and could not speak nor care for herself. Margaret made the nine-mile trip to Eden almost every day to take care of her, but eventually, it was decided to move Rosalia to the Vevang farm. She stayed in the downstairs bedroom and was completely bedridden except when she was carried to the rocking chair in the living room for special occasions. She had problems speaking. In those days the medical profession had no treatment or rehabilitation for stroke victims. In the fall of 1955, Rosalia's condition worsened, and she was taken to the Webster hospital where she died. The visitation was held in her small house in Eden with services at Sacred Heart Catholic Church in Eden and burial was at St. Michael's Catholic Cemetery. Margaret's father, Mathias, continued to live in Eden until he died in 1960.

Lawrence and His Family Leave the Vevang Family Farm and the Vevang Farm was Rented

The Vevang farm was rented out to James Hendrickson and his wife, a young couple from Roslyn, South Dakota. Living on the farm was enjoyable for the family. However, because the economic conditions in the rural areas were less than favorable in the 1950s, many people were leaving the farm, heading west or to large population areas for better opportunities. In the fall of 1955 Lawrence and Margaret decided to leave the farm also and the Vevang farm was rented. Lawrence had heard that there was hiring to build an Air Force Academy at Colorado Springs, Colorado, so in early November, Lawrence set off on his own heading west in his black 1950 Ford pick-up. They planned that Margaret and the children would join Lawrence when he was settled. Lawrence was hired to operate a bulldozer to get the land ready for a new Air Force Academy a few miles north of Colorado Springs, Colorado, the job lasting only a few weeks. He then stopped at a tire shop to inquire if any jobs were available in the area. They hired him, and he was retreading tires for the remainder of his stay in Colorado Springs.

1424 North Nevada Blvd.

Margaret, Bonnie, and Larry traveled by Greyhound bus in early December 1955 to join Lawrence. Lawrence had found a couple of rooms for rent from Mrs. Warrenberg at 1424 North Nevada Boulevard, a beautiful tree-lined street with large older homes. The large two-story house had been turned into a rooming house. Lawrence and Margaret had one bedroom on the first floor with a shared bathroom and kitchen. Bonnie and Larry shared two rooms on the second floor: a small room with a desk, wardrobe, and closet, and a closed-in porch at the front of the house, furnished with twin beds.

Living in Colorado Springs was exciting because of the beautiful mountains and the lovely climate. Pike's Peak could be seen from the kitchen window, and the weather was so nice on New Year's Day that the neighbors were having a picnic in the backyard. There were also a lot of opportunities to get in the pick-up truck for a spin around town and towards the mountains. Pike's Peak was 14,110 feet above sea level, so the pick-up was never driven to the top, but the family did visit the Garden of the Gods frequently and drove in the canyons up to the Cave of the Winds. Bonnie and Larry were small enough so that all four could fit in the front seat of the pick-up.

Bonnie was enrolled in the seventh grade at North Junior High, approximately four blocks south and four blocks east of home. The home and neighborhood life were enjoyable for Bonnie. She became acquainted with a girl on the other side of the block, and they would hang out together, sometimes going for bicycle rides. (The bike might have been borrowed because her bike was still on the farm.) Bonnie always liked adventure so exploring the city with her family made the Colorado Springs experience special. Larry was enrolled in the fifth grade at a nearby elementary school and had the opportunity to join the Cub Scouts.

Back to South Dakota, Lived in Veblen, South Dakota

While the stay in Colorado was pleasant, a decision was made to return to the Midwest so in late March 1956, all four family members squeezed into the pickup and returned to South Dakota nonstop. The farm had been rented out to James Hendrickson, so Lawrence got a job with Lien Road Construction of Veblen, South Dakota. A two-bedroom apartment was rented, one-half block from Main Street in Veblen and about two blocks from the school. The apartment was attached to the north side of a commercial garage, so a small, high window in Bonnie and Larry's bedroom looked right into the garage where vehicles were being repaired. The walls of knotty pine gave the apartment a cozy look. Bonnie and Larry finished off the seventh and fifth grades at the Veblen grade school.

From left: Margaret Pitzl Vevang, Bonnie Vevang, Larry Vevang and Lawrence Vevang

Bonnie celebrated her 13th birthday in Veblen on August 2 in bed with "walking" pneumonia. The five-year-old neighbor girl whom Bonnie had befriended along with her mother came over with a much-welcomed birthday card. Bonnie had spent two or three weeks confined to bed. Margaret had taken her to Webster, a 30-mile drive on a gravel road, to see Dr. Duncan who prescribed penicillin pills. Larry went along for the ride. Since Lawrence was working, he did not go. Driving that many miles on gravel roads in those days was quite a feat but the weather was nice and a stop at Roslyn on the return trip was fun, as there was a household of relatives at Elmer and Elna's house. Myrtle, Charles, and the cousins from Arlington Heights, Illinois, were visiting.

Move to South St. Paul Minnesota

The stay in Veblen was delightful but it lasted only until August 1956 when another move was made, this time to South St. Paul, Minnesota. Henry, Margaret's

509 North Concord Street

brother, and Doris Pitzl had just moved to their home in a new development in Inver Grove Heights, Minnesota, and their small one-bedroom house was available for rent at 509 North Concord Street. There were three houses on the lot: A large house in front overlooking Concord with steps to the street level, a small two-room house in middle, and a one-bedroom house in the rear. A hill led up to nice homes two blocks west. The family crowded into the one-bedroom house in the rear. Approximately a year later the landlord indicated they were interested in selling the property. Lawrence and Margaret jumped at the chance and purchased the property which included all three houses for $8,500. They moved into the larger front house and had tenants in the two smaller houses in the back.

Lawrence started a job working in the hog kill area at Swift and Company, four blocks away. Margaret enrolled Bonnie in the eighth grade and Larry in the sixth grade at St. Augustine Catholic School. After graduating from St. Augustine both Bonnie and Larry attended South St. Paul Junior High for one year and then attended South St. Paul High School where they graduated in 1961 and 1963.

Margaret worked at various jobs: waitress and dishwasher at the café across the street and a clerk at Sears in downtown South St. Paul. Margaret was always looking for better opportunities and one day while she was at a bank in St. Paul, she started a conversation with a bank employee who told her about some free training for keypunch operators (today called data entry employees). Margaret took the training and landed a job with the State of Minnesota, where she worked for almost 25 years with a short interruption for a job at a plastics plant in downtown St. Paul. Margaret retired in about 1983. Lawrence continued working for Swift, and later worked for the St. Paul Union Depot Company and Univac for a short time.

Lawrence Yearned Life on the Farm

But Lawrence always had the desire to return to the farm. In the late 1960s, Lawrence began spending only the winters working in St. Paul and spent springs, summers, and early autumns on the farm, planting crops and raising cattle. Eventually, he stayed on the farm the full year and only came to St. Paul to visit the family.

In the early 1980s, the decision was made to remodel the farmhouse. By that time, it was rather "dated" and needed a lot of work. Larry was the chief restorer, with the help of Lawrence, Margaret, Bonnie, and James J. Sirian Jr., Bonnie's close friend. The downstairs bedroom was converted into a bathroom. The steep staircase was moved to one side of the living room, new windows were installed in the entire house, the two small bedrooms upstairs were made into one large bedroom, new water well was put in, and new cabinets and a sink went into the kitchen, etc., etc. A new "pole" building was erected in the early 1990s for the storage of farm machinery. The blacksmith shop that Iver had erected saw its last days at about the same time.

Farm Life and City Life

In 1968, Lawrence and Margaret purchased a duplex at 1261 Dayton Avenue, St. Paul, pictured. Eventually, the house in South St. Paul was sold. Lawrence continued living on the farm until 2006 when he fell and broke his femur bone. After an operation, he went to his son's house near Hudson, Wisconsin, during rehabilitation and remained there until

his death on October 3, 2016, when his heart stopped. He died peacefully at his son's house surrounded by his wife, Margaret; his children, Bonnie, and Larry; and his daughter-in-law, Sandra. Funeral services were held in Roseville, Minnesota, with burial at the Roselawn Cemetery in Roseville. Margaret Pitzl Vevang retired in about 1983. Margaret passed away on August 15, 2020, at her residence, at 1261 Dayton Avenue, St. Paul, Minnesota. She was 101½ years old.

Lawrence & Bonnie   Margaret, Larry & Bonnie   Bonnie & Larry

477

Auction sale!

Reporter and Farmer
Webster, SD. 1988

Family reunion

Sixty members of the family of Iver and Serina Vevang from Minnesota, New Mexico, Illinois, Florida, California, Wisconsin, Virginia and many other communities in South Dakota gathered for a reunion recently.

Attending were Hilda Olson, oldest member, at age 89; Jim and Evelyn Miller and Viola Fellows, all of Minneapolis; Margaret and Bonnie Vevang, James J. Sivan Jr., St. Paul; Linda, Jerry and Amy Forslund, Apple Valley, Minn.; Larry, Sandy, Brent, Julie and Marc Vevang, Hudson, Wis.; Charles and Myrtle Watkins, Ocala, Fla.; Ella Montgomery, Rocky Mount, Va.; Serina Garst, Bones Mill, Va.; Stewart, Cheryl, Cecilia, Sonja and Michael Tanaka, Barrington, Ill.; Marilyn Watkins Spieth, Bloomington, Ind.; Don and Rosalie Danielson, Richfield, Minn.; Douglas Iver Hanson, Santa Fe, N.M.; Bruce Watkins, McHenry, Ill.; Kalli Cordray, St. Augustine, Fla.; Warren and Jan Vevang, Scotts Valley, Calif.; Jim and Travis Watkins, Silver Springs, Md.; Valarie, Danielle and Heather Downs, Santa Cruz, Calif.; Myrtle Brown, Freemont, Calif.; Jim, Darlis, Kim and Keith Dedrickson, Sioux Falls; William and Debra Menzel and children, Aberdeen; Lawrence, Elmer and Elna Vevang, Roslyn and Hazel Vevang and Laura Hanson, both of Webster.

The day was spent with a tour of the Vevang farm northeast of Roslyn and a dinner served at the senior citizens building, Roslyn. An impromptu program, conducted by Warren Vevang, was held. Greetings from Bea Vevang were read. Prizes went to Stewart Tanaka, Ella Montgomery and Valarie Downs. Later they all met at Jim and Darlis Dedrickson's cottage at Pickerel Lake.

The farm auction is an institution in rural communities like Day County.

Every year from early spring to late fall the auction bill can be seen, advertising the close of another farm, the sale of another group of old equipment, the demise of a way of life for another family or husband-and-wife team.

People sell out for many reasons—death, retirement, health, financial breakdown. Each auction seems to symbolize the increasing number of empty farmsteads appearing in South Dakota, and proves once more that the rural population grows smaller while the farms get larger.

People flock to auctions for many reasons, too. Some come to buy, hoping to find a bargain. Many come out of curiosity—they want to see who and what are at the sale. Some come to offer support to the friends who are selling out, others come because they know they can find their neighbors there—taking the day off too—and can get in a good visit.

Marvin, Edmund, and Clarence Holden have retired and rented their farms. These photos were taken at their auction northwest of Webster.

HIS EYE on the auctioneer, but apparently not too interested in bidding at the moment, Lawrence Vevang of rural Roslyn relaxes with a cup of 25-cent Bergen ALCW coffee. For some reason . . . maybe it's curiosity, maybe the chance to watch people or chat with fellow farmers . . . far more people seem to come to auction sales to watch than to buy.

The farm auction is an institution in rural communities like Day County. Every year from early spring to late fall the auction bill can be seen, advertising the close of another farm, the sale of another group of old equipment, the demise of a way of life for another family or husband-and-wife team.

People sell out for many reasons: death, retirement, health, financial breakdown. Each auction seems to symbolize the increasing number of empty farmsteads appearing in South Dakota and proves once more that the rural population grows smaller while the farms get larger.

People flock to auctions for many reasons, too. Some come to buy, hoping to find a bargain. Many come out of curiosity, they want to see who and what are at the sale. Some come to offer support to friends who are selling out; others come because they know they can find their neighbors there, taking the day off too and can get in a good visit.

His eye on the auctioneer, but apparently not too interested in bidding at the moment, Lawrence Vevang, of rural Roslyn relaxes with a cup of 25-cent Bergen ALCW (American Lutheran Church Women) coffee. For some reason, maybe it's curiosity, maybe the chance to watch people or chat with fellow farmers... far more people seem to come to auction sales to watch than to buy.

Reporter and Farmer, Webster, SD

5 of the 12 Vevang siblings

From left: Elmer Vevang, Ella Vevang Montgomery, Myrtle Vevang Watkins, Hilda Vevang Olson and Lawrence Vevang

13 of the 30 Vevang cousins

From left: Larry Vevang, Serina Montgomery Garst, Jim Watkins, Marilyn Watkins Spieth, Linda Vevang Forslund, Rosalie Olson Danielson, Cheryl Watkins Tanaka, Viola Olson Fellows, Bonnie Vevang, Bruce Watkins, Doug Hanson, Debbie Vevang Menzel and Warren Vevang

A painting by a friend of Margaret Vevang of the farm as it would have looked in the early 1940s

State of South Dakota
2011
Century Farm Award

Presented To

Lawrence and Margaret Vevang

*In recognition of your farm
Having been in the same family
For over 100 years*

Dennis Daugaard
Governor

Walt Bones
Secretary of Agriculture

"Agriculture is the first and most precious of all the arts" — Thomas Jefferson

Century Farm

Vevang Farm, Roslyn, South Dakota
Established 1902

south dakota
farm bureau

Finding the Farm

Drive east from Roslyn, SD, on Highway 25 for about one mile to 437th Avenue. Turn left onto the gravel road and drive north for a little less than a mile, then turn right onto the Vevang property.

479

A Glimpse into the Past

Iver Vevang carved his initials on the wooden boards of the granary and hash-marked bushels of grain yields through the years.

The
Land
Today

OBITUARY

Lawrence A. Vevang

A LIFE REMEMBERED

With Lawrence's passing it seemed like the end of an era. He was the youngest of Iver and Serina's children, and he was the last of his siblings to pass on. He was also the closest to the farm that his parents had built from scratch. He loved that piece of land and lived on it the majority of his life, managing to get back to it after spending a few years in the city. Since he could not stay there alone in old age, he spent his last years living with his son, Larry, and daughter-in-law, Sandy. But he still visited the farm often with Larry.

Lawrence spent two months on the farm in his last summer, leaving his beloved land the end of August 2016. In his last days he said he saw his brothers, Ingvald and Julius, sitting with him in the living room, perhaps to let him know that they would be there to welcome him into the next life. Lawrence passed away peacefully the morning of October 3, 2016, having lived for 100 years, 11 months, and 20 days. It truly was the end of an era.

A Life Remembered

PALLBEARERS

Todd Vevang	Brian Vevang
Brent Vevang	Julie Hager
Marc Vevang	Nicholas Vevang

HONORARY PALLBEARERS
Chantelle Vevang
Justin Vevang
Patrick Vevang

In Loving Memory Of

Lawrence A. Vevang

October 14, 1915 – October 3, 2016
One Hundred Years, Eleven Months, Twenty Days

FUNERAL SERVICE
Mueller-Bies Funeral Home
2130 North Dale Street
Roseville, Minnesota

Monday, October 10, 2016 at 12:00 PM

OFFICIATING
Dan Schuster

INTERMENT
Roselawn Cemetery
Roseville, Minnesota

VEVANG
Lawrence A.
Age 100
Passed away October 3, 2016
Survived by wife, Margaret; daughter, Bonita Vevang; son, Larry (Sandra); 5 grandchildren; 9 great-grandchildren; and 3 great-great grandchildren. Preceded in death by 4 brothers and 5 sisters. Funeral service 12:00 PM Monday, October 10 at MUELLER-BIES FUNERAL HOME-ROSEVILE, 2130 N. Dale St. @ County Rd B. Interment Roselawn Cemetery. Visitation Monday at the funeral home from 11:00 AM-12:00 PM.
MUELLER-BIES 651-487-2550
www.muellerbies.com

VEVANG

Father
Lawrence A.
1915 - 2016

Mother
Margaret R.
1919 - 2020

Daughter
Bonita J.
1943 -

Parents of Bonita J. & Larry M.

OBITUARY

Margaret R. Vevang

In Loving Memory Of

Margaret R. Vevang

February 18, 1919 – August 15, 2020
One Hundred One Years

Funeral Service
Mueller-Bies Funeral Home
2130 N. Dale Street
Roseville, Minnesota
Wednesday, August 19, 2020 at 11:00 AM

Officiating
Fr. Robert Fitzpatrick

Interment
Roselawn Cemetery
Roseville, Minnesota

Pallbearers

Todd Vevang	*Brian Vevang*
Brent Vevang	*Julie Hager*
Marc Vevang	*Nicholas Vevang*

IN LOVING MEMORY

Margaret was born February 18, 1919 to Mathias and Rosalia Pitzl on a farm north of Webster, SD. She was the youngest of 10 children. She moved west of Eden, SD with her family when she was about 10 years old. She attended country grade schools near Webster and Eden and went to high school in Eden, Lake City, and Webster, graduating from Webster High School in 1937.

On December 4, 1941, she married Lawrence Vevang of Roslyn, SD, and lived on the Vevang farm until 1955. The winter of 1955-1956 was spent in Colorado Springs, CO, and they spent the summer of 1956 in Veblen, SD before moving to South St. Paul, MN. In 1968, they moved to a Victorian house in the historic section of St. Paul. MN where she lived the rest of her life. She worked for the State of MN for 24 years as a data entry clerk.

Margaret loved to entertain her family with lavish dinners. She also loved to travel, especially to Europe many times, including twice visiting her relatives in Apetion, Austria, where her parents had immigrated from in the early 1900s. She was always a very busy lady who loved to tend to her yard, cook, visit friends and relatives and transport people to doctor appointments.

She is survived by her daughter, Bonita J. Vevang; son, Larry (Sandra) Vevang: 5 grandchildren, Todd (Beth) Vevang, Brian Vevang, Brent Vevang, Julie (Chad) Hager, and Marc Vevang; 9 great-grandchildren; and 4 great-great-grandchildren. She is preceded in death by her husband, Lawrence; 4 sisters, 5 brothers, all of her sisters and brothers-in-laws, and numerous nephews and nieces.

FAMILY

Lawrence Arthur Vevang b: 14 Oct 1915, Nutley Township, Day County, South Dakota; d: 3 Oct 2016, Hudson, St. Croix County, Wisconsin; buried: Roselawn Cemetery, Roseville, Minnesota

Lawrence married Margaret Rose Pitzl b: 18 Feb 1919, Rural Webster, Day County, South Dakota; m: 04 Dec 1941, Eden, Marshall County, South Dakota; d: 15 Aug 2020, St. Paul, Ramsey County, Minnesota; buried: Roselawn Cemetery, Roseville, Minnesota

CHILDREN
of Lawrence Arthur Vevang and Margaret Rose Pitzl

Bonita (Bonnie) Justyne Vevang b: 02 Aug 1943, Peabody Hospital, Webster, Day County, South Dakota

Larry Mathias Vevang b: 19 Feb 1945, Peabody Hospital, Webster, Day County, South Dakota

BONITA JUSTYNE VEVANG
"BONNIE"

Born
August 2, 1943
Webster, Day County, SD

Bonnie on her birthday with cousin Linda Vevang

Bonnie Vevang

Bonnie, Lawrence, Margaret, and Larry

Bonnie as bridesmaid at Larry's wedding in 1965

Bonnie with her friend, James J. Sirian Jr.

James J. Sirian Jr. and Bonnie Vevang

A Little About Bonnie's Life

Bonnie accepted her first job at Farmers Union Central Exchange (later Cenex, and now CHS). In 1962 she decided to take a few business courses at Globe Business College. Throughout her early career, she worked for various companies as either an administrative assistant or executive secretary. She also attended school at the University of Minnesota in the evenings to receive her bachelor's degree in business. Starting in 1989, she worked at the Internal Revenue Service as a tax consultant and later at the U.S. Department of Agriculture as a workers' compensation administrator and later as a debt management specialist.

Bonnie has a keen interest in traveling and has visited various countries and states: England, Scotland, Ireland, Iceland, France, Germany, Austria, Switzerland, Italy, Luxemburg, USSR, Hong Kong, China, Canary Islands, Morocco, Mexico, and Canada, along with many of the states, including Alaska and Hawaii. The first trip to Europe was taken in 1969 with her mother, Margaret, and cousin, Mary Ellen Pitzl. On that trip, arrangements were made to visit relatives in Vienna and Apetlon, Austria. Margaret and Bonnie again visited these same relatives in 1983 when touring Europe with Margaret's sister, Rose.

Bonnie retired in December 2009 and spent a few years just relaxing a bit, traveling as much as possible, and catching up on projects. At the end of 2013, she noticed that her mother, Margaret, should not be living by herself any longer and Bonnie moved in with her and stayed with her until Margaret passed away in her sleep on August 15, 2020, at the age of 101½. Bonnie misses her mother a lot and is glad that she could make Margaret's last years as comfortable and happy as possible.

Over the years Bonnie's favorite companion has been James J. Sirian Jr. Jim was a very caring person. He especially loved youngsters and could always relate to senior citizens. When Margaret Vevang got older and had dementia, Jim would sit patiently with her and carry on long conversations about her early years that she could remember. Jim was always at Bonnie's side when she had serious medical problems, and he would drive her to and from her medical appointments and wherever she wanted to go. He once told Bonnie that if she needed long-term care when she was older, he would provide the care for her. But that was not to be as Jim passed away on April 9, 2021, very suddenly at the age of 88. He is sadly missed by many people, especially Bonnie. Bonnie now contemplates how to rebuild her life without her favorite person. She has volunteered at the Christian Life Ministries which is a family resource center and looks forward to traveling again.

LARRY MATHIAS VEVANG

Born

February 19, 1945

Webster, Day County, SD

Larry Mathias Vevang

married

Sandra Alice Wakefield

January 30, 1965

St. Mark's Church,
St. Paul,
Ramsey County,
Minnesota

Wedding party. Front: Dennis Wakefield and Debra Kannel.
Middle: Dorothy Wakefield Hofacker, Bonnie Vevang, Sandra Wakefield Vevang, Larry M.
Vevang, Michael A. Wakefield. Back: Muriel Lentsch, Walter Hofacker, James Hintz.

At Larry and Sandy's wedding reception
From left: Hilda Vevang Olson, Alida Vevang, Gerald Forslund, Margaret Pitzl Vevang, Linda Vevang Forslund,
Lawrence Vevang, Dennis Vevang, Alberta Syverson Vevang, Henry Hanson Jr., Ing Vevang,
Rosalie Olson Danielson, Sonja Danielson Cordray and Don Danielson

After graduating from South St. Paul High School in 1963, Larry worked for the railroad for about two years as a Machinist Apprentice before accepting a job at Northern States Power (now Xcel) as a Relay Specialist. He worked there for about 35 years before retiring in 2001. Larry married Sandra Wakefield in 1965 and had five children: Todd, Brian, Brent, Julie, and Marc. They lived in a couple of apartments in St. Paul before buying a triplex at 175 North Fairview Avenue, St. Paul. They built a house at 594 Gilbert Road, Hudson, Wisconsin, where they still live.

1972. Sandra, Brian, Todd, and Larry. Brent is in front.

The Lawrence Vevang family pictured in 1986

Seated in front row from left: Julie Vevang, Lawrence Vevang, Marc Vevang, Margaret Pitzl Vevang

Back row: Larry Vevang, Brian Vevang, Brent Vevang, Todd Vevang, Sandra Wakefield Vevang, Bonnie Vevang

The Larry Vevang family in 1999. Front row from left: Marc Vevang, Julie Vevang, Larry Vevang, Sandra Wakefield Vevang, Elizabeth (Beth) Bakker Vevang, and Chantelle Vevang. Back row: Brian Vevang, Brent Vevang, Patrick Bakker Vevang, Justin Paukune Vevang, Todd Vevang, and Nicholas Vevang

Caretakers of the Vevang Farm

Larry Vevang
and his sons
and grandsons

FAMILY

Larry Mathias Vevang b: 19 Feb 1945, Peabody Hospital, Webster, Day County, South Dakota

Larry married **Sandra Alice Wakefield** b: 28 Jan 1944, Durand, Pepin County, Wisconsin; m: 30 Jan 1965, St. Mark's Church, St. Paul, Ramsey County, Minnesota

Larry and Sandra's children:
Todd Larry Vevang b: 24 Jul 1965, St. Paul, Ramsey County, Minnesota
Brian Allen Vevang b: 20 Jan 1968, St. Paul, Ramsey County, Minnesota
Brent Aaron Vevang b: 13 May 1971, St. Paul, Ramsey County, Minnesota
Julie Denice Vevang b: 11 May 1974, St. Paul, Ramsey County, Minnesota
Marc Jon Vevang b: 20 May 1979, River Falls, St. Croix County, Wisconsin

CHILDREN AND GRANDCHILDREN
of Larry Mathias Vevang and Sandra Alice Wakefield

Todd Larry Vevang married **Elizabeth Louise Bakker** b: 28 Aug 1965, White Plains, Westchester County, New York; m: 11 Jun 1988, Vail, Eagle County, Colorado

Todd and Elizabeth's children:
Justin Lee Paukune Vevang b: 30 Sep 1982, Leadville, Lake County, Colorado
Patrick Jonathon Bakker Vevang b: 26 Oct 1984, Glenwood Springs, Garfield County, Colorado
Chantelle Michelle Cherie Vevang b: 09 Aug 1989, Vail, Eagle County, Colorado
Nicholas Todd Vevang b: 29 Jun 1991, Red Wing, Goodhue County, Minnesota

Justin Lee Paukune Vevang married
Michelle Elizabeth Marie Ulm b: 14 Jan 1985: div.

Justin and Michelle's children:
Chyanne Keile Vevang b: 01 Oct 2004,
Hudson, St. Croix County, Wisconsin
Mavarik Charles Wayne Vevang b: 25 Feb 2010
Loveland, Larimer County, Colorado

Justin married **Tiffany Marie Olson** b:17 Aug 1977,
St. Paul, Ramsey County, Minnesota; m: 28 Sep 2015,
Greeley, Weld County, Colorado

From left: Mavarik, Tiffany, Justin, and Chyanne

Patrick Jonathon Bakker Vevang married **Keri Lynn Johnson** b: 09 Feb 1989, Maplewood, Ramsey County, Minnesota; m: 20 May 2017, Maplewood, Ramsey County, Minnesota

Patrick and Keri's children:
Jaxson Patrick Vevang b: 28 Nov 2012,
New Richmond, St. Croix County, Wisconsin
Kendra Marie Vevang b: 30 Nov 2018,
New Richmond, St. Croix County, Wisconsin

**Chantelle Michelle
Cherie Vevang**
b: 09 Aug 1989,
Vail, Eagle County,
Colorado

Nicholas Todd Vevang
b: 29 Jun 1991,
Red Wing,
Goodhue County,
Minnesota

Brian Allen Vevang b: 20 Jan 1968,
St. Paul, Ramsey County, Minnesota

Brian's child:
Zacharia Allan (Johnson) Becker
b: 24 Dec 1992, St. Paul,
Ramsey County, Minnesota

Brent Aaron Vevang b: 13 May 1971,
St. Paul, Ramsey County, Minnesota

Brent's child:
Cole Michael Vevang b: 17 Dec 2004,
Maplewood, Ramsey County, Minnesota
(Cole's mother: **Roxann Lynn Bruner**)

Julie Denice Vevang b: 11 May 1974,
St. Paul, Ramsey County, Minnesota

Julie married **Chad Jerod Hager** b: 28 Mar 1975,
Denver, Denver County, Colorado; m: 06 Jul 2002,
Hudson, St. Croix County, Wisconsin

Julie and Chad's children:
Trennen Maximus Hager b: 22 Jun 2006,
Hudson, St. Croix County, Wisconsin
Zander Hendrix Hager b: 17 Sep 2008,
Hudson, St. Croix County, Wisconsin

Marc Jon Vevang b: 20 May 1979,
River Falls, St. Croix County, Wisconsin

Marc's children with **Missy Kessler**:
Savanna Alice Vevang b: 31 Mar 2006,
River Falls, St. Croix County, Wisconsin
Vincent Marc Vevang b: 09 Aug 2007,
River Falls, St. Croix County, Wisconsin

July 6, 2002
Front from left: Chantelle Vevang, Nicholas Vevang, Lawrence Vevang and Patrick Vevang
Standing from left: Brent Vevang, Sandra Vevang, Marc Vevang, Julie Vevang Hager,
Chad Hager, Larry Vevang, Brian Vevang, Margaret Vevang, Elizabeth Vevang,
Bonita (Bonnie) Vevang, Justin Vevang and Todd Vevang

The Vevang farm continues to be in the Vevang family, owned now by Larry Vevang and Bonnie Vevang.

CHAPTER XIII

ROSLYN

Day County
South Dakota

Incorporated
August 17, 1914

Rocks and fire and Myron Floren, these are some things that have made Roslyn sing.

Aberdeen American News, Aberdeen, South Dakota. September 15, 1986.

They are the songs of pain and hope and strength and ultimately the quiet joy that comes when a people have the ability and resilience to take life's bad turns and make something better. They are the traits for which Norwegians sometimes see themselves as very special.

Roslyn is set among the eye-pleasing, but hard to farm hills of northern Day County. In 1986 a good dinner of ribs and kraut is three bucks. A haircut runs the same at 85-year-old Elmer Vevang's one-stool barber shop. Two bucks, his handwritten sign says, for children under twelve. It seems they like to do business in small, round numbers here.

The big fire of 1964 missed Elmer Vevang's shop. It took out the meat market and the hardware store and the pool hall next door. A vivid series of color snapshots from that fateful November 28, a day of sub-freezing temperatures and a high wind and no chance for firefighters to win, is almost lost among the Jack and Bobby Kennedy pictures and the plaque honoring Elmer for 50 years of business (that was eleven years ago) and the other memorabilia on the walls of his tiny shop.

"Thought the barber shop was going to go, too," recalls Elmer, a man of few words and even less interest in seeing them in print. "Then the wind changed from the southwest. It didn't get so hot." From the ashes, the burned-out block of the business district rose again.

Today's Roslyn was not always Roslyn. Originally, Roslyn was over a ways on H.H. Russell's homestead. He named the tiny settlement after his native Roslyn, England, and he was the first postmaster in 1882. Roslyn sprang to life in 1914 when the town's buildings were hauled by crude means to the current site. A $60,000 bonus was raised by assessing rural property owners so the Fairmont & Veblen Railroad Company would build a rail link. The lots were sold at public auction on August 20, 1914, and the new Roslyn was born amid a flurry of cash and high hopes.

There is only one church in Roslyn but what a church it is. Construction began in 1942, after the congregation walked out of its old white wooden church for the last time to the hymn "Built on the Rock the Church Doth Stand." Today the new church is an inspiring testament to the workmanship that love of faith inspires. Built of rock, it is also an insight into the subtler channels of the Norwegian mind. Much of the surrounding farmland was so stony it was difficult to work. So, the Roslyn people made their new church out of the very stuff that had frustrated them.

There is something earthy about it. There is something very symbolic, Christ as the Rock of the Church. Roslyn was born in 1914 with a musical flourish, and music has been a part of its legacy. Records of the Roslyn Lutheran Church show Myron Floren was baptized and confirmed there, and the world-renowned accordionist is still listed today as a member. Roslyn is proud of its most famous former citizen.

Side Note: Myron Floren shares the same direct line ancestor Tron Oysteinson Hustad with our direct line ancestor Serina Hustad Vevang.

The Roslyn Lutheran Church was first named Grenville Lutheran Church

Original church

New church built in 1942

Rev. K.O. Storlie was the first Lutheran minister to come to the Roslyn area in 1882, when settlers gathered in the various homes for church services. On August 6, 1883, a meeting was held at the Nels Dahl home and plans were made to organize a church. Rev. Storlie and another minister, Rev. O. Lokensgaard, held services when they could make a trip to the area. Plans to build a church in Grenville Township were made in 1888 — the name Grenville Lutheran Church was adopted, and the church was completed and dedicated in 1889.

Grenville Lutheran Church was eventually moved to Roslyn in 1916, and several years later it was renamed to Roslyn Lutheran Church. After being damaged by a windstorm in 1941, the congregation realized the need for a new building. On August 2, 1942, Jake Dedrickson Construction and church volunteers initiated construction, completing the building for it's first use by April 22, 1943.

Sources:
History of Day County, Day County Historical Research Committee, pg. 777;
75th Anniversary of the Roslyn Lutheran Church, published in 1958, pg. 5;
100th Anniversary of the Roslyn Lutheran Church 1883-1983

Hilda (15) with her teacher,
Helen Song (20), in 1914.

In Serina Vevang's busy near-pioneer life she always found time to do what she could for her church realizing the importance of the teaching of God in helping her and her family. Roslyn was a small thriving town with a population of approximately 200 people mostly of Norwegian descent. At one time the town simultaneously had three grocery stores, two liquor stores, two bars, two dance halls, two service stations, a meat market, a barber shop, a blacksmith shop, an implement dealer, a hardware store, a restaurant, a hotel with café, bank, public school, and the Lutheran Church. The town was crowded every Saturday night as families would come into town for socializing and entertainment.

However, over the years the town changed. Businesses ceased operations for economic reasons; there were fewer farms in the area to patronize the businesses; it was easier to travel to the larger towns in the area and the advent of television provided entertainment at home. The Saturday night get-togethers, while still practiced on a small scale, was not the big event it had been in the past. By the end of the twentieth century, only a few businesses were remaining: the bank, one bar, and one service station. A nursing home was established in the 1960s and is still in operation as of this writing.

Roslyn Consolidated School

Iver and Serina had twelve children, two of whom died in infancy. In the early years, the children went to a one-room schoolhouse close to Hazelden Lake, slightly northeast of the Vevang farm. In 1914 and beyond, they attended school in Roslyn. Some of the children furthered their education.

1914 School Photo. Selmer Vevang is the first boy standing on the left. Elmer Vevang is the first fellow in the front. Ingvald Vevang is the fifth from the left in the front (as indicated on the photo). Possibly, Laura and Ella are also in this photo. They would be about eight and seven years old, respectively. They may be in the second row of the four short girls. The first might be Laura, and the fourth Ella.

Silver Jubilee

25 years in Roslyn

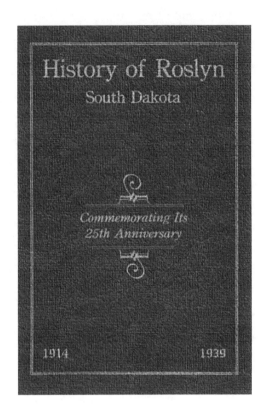

History of Roslyn, South Dakota

1914 to 1939

Commemorating Its 25th Anniversary

Dedication

Respectfully to the pioneers, whose faith and courage in this community made the founding of our town possible.

To Friends Far and Near

This year, 1939 brings to a close our first 25 years of existence but opens the door for many years of progress and prosperity. Drought, depression and adverse conditions shall not dim our faith, but Roslyn shall go forward, serving the needs of its citizens and the country surrounding it.

Dedication

Respectfully to the pioneers, whose faith and courage in this community made the founding of our town possible, and lovingly to the youth, who so gayly and eagerly tread our streets now, but later will take up responsibilities and carry on—we dedicate this history of the town of Roslyn.

Mrs. Elmer Nerland
Mrs. E. P. Ronshaugen

To Friends Far and Near

Roslyn greets you on this our Silver Jubilee! This year, 1939, brings to a close our first 25 years of existence, but opens the door for many years of progress and prosperity. Drouth, depression, and adverse conditions shall not dim our faith, but Roslyn shall go forward, serving the needs of its citizens and the country surrounding it.

Ed Kampen, Creamery	John Hanson, Hanson Produce
J. Schad, Farmers & Merchants Bk.	F. M. Gottschalk, Cash Store
H. Gullickson, Roslyn Elevator	Ted Gilbertson, Fairway Store
Walt Waldowski, Roslyn Hotel	Emil Stavig, Stavig Service
Ben Hong, Roslyn Lumber Yard	John Peterson, Meat Market
C Kjorsvig, Roslyn Garage	Elmer Vevang, Barber
C. Krause, Roslyn Liquor Store	Ed Blank, Blank's Hardware
A. Swanson, Roslyn Hardware	H. J. Baukol, Baukol's Store

Reporter and Farmer Webster, SD

Diamond Jubilee

75 years in Roslyn

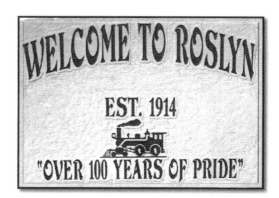

Reporter and Farmer Webster, SD

Excerpts from the Roslyn Diamond Jubilee book

Building the railroad to Roslyn in the fall of 1915

Snowstorm in 1922

Crowd watching the Soo Line train going through Roslyn, South Dakota

Memories of Growing up in Roslyn in the '20s

By Calvin Schad

"Roslyn South Dakota Diamond Jubilee," pg. 57
Published by the *Reporter and Farmer* in 1989

Summer days were crammed with activities of our own invention, organization, and imagination. When warm weather came, the shoes and socks went. It was barefoot time for the rest of the summer with its hazards of broken glass, nails, and even bumble bees, but we healed quickly and kept going. By fall we could even run barefoot through a stubble field full of thistles. On hot days we made gum from the strings of tar dripping off the back of Monson's Store. I recall free movies being shown on the south wall of Monson's Store. We had crank telephones and kerosene lamps, and some homes even

had ice boxes. By the end of the '20s, most of the homes had some kind of squawky radio and we could listen to such fabulous characters as Lil' Orphan Annie, the Baron Munchausen, and Amos-n-Andy. All the merchants had wonderful stores filled with marvelous items and mysteries. I recall the shop in the back of Swanson's Hardware where one could fix anything. In Pete Johnson's Blacksmith Shop, he heated iron to rosy-red hot in the forge and pounded it into different shapes. The lumber yards were great places for climbing. The stores always had a barrel of vinegar in the back room and a barrel of lutefisk in front. The big butter churn in the creamery was another fascination. Sometimes the butter-maker would let us dig fresh butter out of the little cracks with our fingers before he washed the churn.

Some summer days were spent rolling a tire for miles or climbing up and sliding down the school fire escape. Sometimes we watched the Soo-line engine flatten pennies on the tracks, or we played hopscotch or shot marbles. We trapped gophers. Tails were kept in a tobacco can and the county treasurer paid a 2-cent bounty each for them. The schoolyard was our playground for kid games and the swings, and the merry-go-round were popular rides. The big bell on the fire-hall would ring at 9:00 p.m. signaling the end of the day for all town kids who then headed for their homes. How we would envy the country kids who would stay and play until their folks were done shopping and visiting and were ready for their trip back to the farm. I used to sleep over with friends once in a while and some of them lived on farms. What a great experience to get to stay on a farm with Francis Waddle, Lawrence Vevang, Gordon Stavig, and Henry Lardy. Gypsies would come to town on occasion, and this created great excitement because we seemed to think there was always the risk of being kidnapped! Fall would finally come and with it came shoes and socks, school, and maybe a new pair of pants or a new dress to wear or new shoes to buy. It would soon be time for the cozy comfort of flannel sheets for those chilly nights ahead. In the winter it was a great Saturday sport to hitch a ride with your sled behind a farmer's bobsled as he headed out of town with his groceries. Monson's had a real Olympic-class hill and we used to slide on it by the hour. Mrs. Monson had to be a real saint to put up with all our chatter and noise day after day, winter after winter. That hill doesn't look nearly as big today as it did back then.

Remember Saturday night baths? Carrying drinking water from the town well? Outdoor privies? Frozen Milky Ways from Lauri's Pool Hall? Hot bologna from the Butcher Shop? Flying homemade kites? Making slingshots and our own May baskets? Remember family games on winter nights, jigsaw puzzles, dominoes, checkers, cards, singing, conversing, and reading? The list is endless and different for each of us and wonderful for all.

Deprived? Not if you grew up in Roslyn in the 1920s.

Death may end a life,
but not a relationship.

Let us remind ourselves, that those who have
died are still a part of us, guiding us in ways
we are learning and growing from.